GURDJIEFF

GURDJIEFF

by

LOUIS PAUWELS

with paintings
by
FELIX LABISSE
GEORGES ROHNER
FERRO

SAMUEL WEISER, INC.
New York, N. Y. 10003
1972

First Published in France 1954
under the title
"Monsieur Gurdjieff"

First American Edition Published 1972
Published by Arrangement with Times Press Ltd.
© 1964 by Times Press Ltd.

SAMUEL WEISER, INC.
734 Broadway
New York, N. Y. 10003

All rights reserved. Printed in the United States of America.
No part of this book may be used or reproduced in any manner
without written permission except in the case of brief
quotations embodied in critical articles and reviews.

ISBN 0-87728-178-5

Library of Congress Catalogue Card Number 71-188373

Printed in U.S.A. by
NOBLE OFFSET PRINTERS, INC.
New York, N.Y. 10003

BY THE SAME AUTHOR

Saint Quelqu'un,
   roman Editions du Seuil.

Les Voies de Petite Communication.
   Illustrations de Robert Lapoujade
   Préface de Francois Mauriac.
   Editions du Seuil.

Le Château du Dessous,
   roman Gallimard.

Le Matin des Magiciens.
   Louis Pauwels and Jacques Bergier.
   Gallimard.

Dawn of Magic.
   Louis Pauwels and Jacques Bergier.
   Anthony Gibbs & Phillips.

To
LISE DEHARME
*and to the friends
round her table
who reconciled me
each week
with this world.*

*René Alleau
Elisa et André Breton
Max Pol Fouchet
Julien Gracq.*

CONTENTS

	Page
Foreword by H. L. Dor	xiii
Preface	1

Part I

THE MAN WHO IS NOT ASLEEP

Chapter	1	A Strange Traveller	20
	2	Rom Landau's Story	37
		Postcript to Chapter 2	62

Idiots' Pasture

Chapter	3	Have You Known A Man?	66
	4	Which You Would You Change?	71
	5	Are You Ever Awake?	80
	6	Provisional Conclusion	95

Notes on a Secret Book

	7	Music and Writing	100
	8	Mr. Kenneth Walker's story	104
	9	A study by M. Denis Saurat	113
	10	An article by Mr. Gorham Munson	123

Part II

THE FOREST PHILOSOPHERS

		Page
Chapter 1	Gurdjieff Leaves Russia	128
2	Paris, New York, Fontainebleau	135

What was seen by Outsiders

Chapter 3	Mr. G. E. Bechhofer's article	142
4	An Account by Denis Saurat of his visit to Gurdjieff in 1923	168
5	Knowing and Being	181

The Way the Disciples Lived

Chapter 6	An Article by Dr. Young	192
7	Dr. Young's Experiences at the Priory	200
8	Georgette Leblanc and Maeterlinck	214
9	First extract from *La Machine à Courage* by Georgette Leblanc	218
10	The Little Review	228
11	Margaret Anderson's Article	230

Katherine Mansfield's Last Hope

Chapter 12	D. H. Lawrence, Middleton Murry, Ouspensky	239
13	Orage	249
14	Katherine Mansfield's letters to her husband written from the Priory	268
15	She Dies	305

Part III

MR. GURDJIEFF AND US

		Page
Chapter 1	After 1934	318

Witness for the Prosecution

Chapter 2	Paul Sérant	325
3	Aldous Huxley on Drugs	343
4	Pierre Minet's Testimony	348
5	Luc Dietrich and Irène Reweliotty	351
6	Extracts from Irène-Carole Reweliotty's Private Journal	356
7	René Dazeville	362

Witness for the Defence

Chapter 8	Extracts from *A Personal History* by Dorothy Caruso	371
9	Second extract from *La Machine à Courage* by Georgette Leblanc	381
10	By Rene Barjavel	395

The Old Man and the Children of the Age

Chapter 11	A Non-Conformist Catholic	397
12	By Pierre Schaeffer	400

Postscript	453
Acknowledgements	457

FOREWORD

by H. L. Dor

THE WORLD moves towards unity. Convened ostensibly to promote reunion of Christian Churches, the Council in Rome takes a first step towards assembling all men of faith. More especially, the great human reservoir of Asia — whether Hindu, Moslem or Buddhist—must be helped to withstand a new upsurge of materialism as dangerous as any suffered by the West during the Industrial Revolution.

Understanding is a two-way trend. Many Catholics, for instance, hope that the Orthodox Church, being closer to Eastern concepts and practice, may provide a channel. The Council in Rome is less the inception of a new movement than the gathering of strands which already exist into one solid bridge.

For years, single men and small groups have been reaching across to one another from East to West, and vice versa. Two of the books chosen by Times Press for publication in January deal with such attempts.

A Benedictine Ashram, by the Abbé J. Monchanin, S.A.M. and Dom Henri Le Saux, O.S.B., shows how Catholic monks can lead the life of Indian gurus and translate Christian faith into the terms of perennial Eastern mysticism. *Gurdjieff,* by Louis Pauwels, outlines an adaption of Eastern methods to the needs of a Western society.

Many will say the books have nothing in common. On one hand, two saintly priests work in humility, poverty and charity. On the other, an extraordinary figure, part magician, part charlatan, whom some look upon as a satanist, others as superman, springs onto the stage out of a weird past of Tibetan monasteries, Sufi exercises and Tsarist Intelligence Service, to gather around himself a heteroclite crowd of eccentrics and advance through a maze of catastrophic scandals towards some unknowable end.

Nevertheless, the comparison is being worked out by events. Before dying, Gurdjieff indicated to his representative in England, John Bennett, that his successor would come from the Dutch Indies. Bapak Subuh arrived from Indonesia, and the Gurdjieff centre of Coombe Springs was placed at his disposal. There he transmitted the force granted to him by "opening" those who came, and showing them how to exercise with the Latihan. The English branch of Subud had been formed.

French monks, colleagues of Dom Henri Le Saux, investigated this new development. They invited Bennett to see them. Their Abbott granted permission for them to be "opened." Some time later, Bennett joined them in the Catholic faith.

Bapak himself is a Moslem. Most of his disciples are Christian. The strands run together.

Obstacles of all kinds stand in the way. One of the first to be encountered is the lack of a common vocabulary and automatic understanding. For instance "opening" suggests some form of activity. Many are bewildered when they find that it is the passive transmission of a force from one to another. Later they are alarmed to see what violent reactions can be obtained through mere acceptance. Phenomena known for centuries to all and sundry in the East suggest possession by evil forces to those unaccustomed.

Louis Pauwels was brought to the edge of death by the Gurdjieff exercises. On leaving hospital he decided to see what happened to others. He found that many had been less fortunate and had in fact died.

His book is a record of madness, suicide and waste. It is also a revelation of how ordinary and extraordinary people all over the world found themselves, thanks to the Gurdjieff disciplines and insight. Pauwels has compiled an anthology of the extreme results produced by Eastern methods in the West.

Exactly the same book could now be written about Subud. The monthly magazine *Fate*, which has been publishing extracts from "Gurdjieff" in every issue since May, prefaced most with quotations from authors on Subud. They reveal a pattern of startling similarity.

The July number for instance reproduced John Bennett's own description of the death after being "opened" of a helper in the early days. During twenty-one days his symptoms suggested violent insanity. He smashed down doors, broke one of Bennett's ribs and had to be kept under permanent guard. Then he recovered, became very gentle and, after three days of peace, died.

As the effects of Gurdjieff and Subud are often similar, so their cause would appear to be the same. The root of all these teething troubles of reunion between East and West lies in the very divergence of evolution which made it necessary.

Pauwels chooses Paul Sérant as his first witness for the prosecution to state the case against Gurdjieff. This young French author points out that certain Indians strictly forbid the practise of Tantric exercises by Westerners on the grounds that they can only lead to insanity. He concludes that Gurdjieff's teaching would not cause the same disequilibrium in the East as it does in the West.

If we turn to Hussein Rofé's "Reflections on Subud", we find an almost identical passage. He observes that, in the West, a much higher percentage of those who are "opened" go temporarily off their heads.

When the first of the young helpers at Coombe Springs died after being "opened", Pak Subuh said that he had never seen anything like it in twenty-five years. It would not have happened in Indonesia.

Such accidents are not inherent to any geographical distinction. Rational Greece saw no difficulty in accepting occult teachings from the East. Sixteenth century missionaries, who first penetrated Japan and China, represented Christ with the face of Buddha. Only recently have scientific and industrial revolutions brought about a cleavage between civilisations, which continued to develop along divergent lines, and too much can be made of the differences.

Though often painful and dangerous, the casualties of Gurdjieff and Subud may prove superficial. The tiny cut, which makes an haemophiliac bleed to death, is none the less slight because the injured man dies. Only the most disturbed Westerners, whom an artificial civilisation has weakened beyond the norm, fail to withstand these contacts. Underneath the traumas produced by rapidly changing modes of life and thought, the collective unconscious still unites all races as it has done since the beginning of time.

The thought that creeds, symbols and rituals are found to be the same all over the world, less because remote ancestors emigrated on Kon-Tiki rafts or moved across now submerged Atlantean continents, than because these figures have all been drawn from the same archetypes in a collective unconscious which still links us all together, is a friendly one. Unfortunately for most of us the idea remains theoretical. As Gurdjieff would say, such words are only " pouring from the empty into the void." Unless they see and feel, men cannot understand.

The writers working to produce *Fate* have long since found that theories and facts by themselves make no impact. If *Fate* publishes an article on the Egyptian dog-headed god Anubis, everyone agrees that it is a suitably "occult" subject. If *Fate* shows that these monstrous crossings between man and beast run as a permanent thread through every century and every form of art, readers accept that they reveal a deep common trend in the religions of mankind. If *Fate* illustrates the thesis with photographs of these figures taken equally from the walls of Cathedrals, Indian temples, Aztec pyramids and Hellene groves (where goat-footed Pan created panic), readers will flick through them and concede the point.

If, however, *Fate* reproduces contemporary examples of this universal and timeless art, such as the paintings of monstrous women with the heads of insects, felines or bursting figs, that Felix Labisse draws straight from his subconscious, then a howl goes up at the horror. For once the reader has been made to see. Words theories, arguments no longer occult the subject. It stands revealed.

The operative word is "contemporary". In February, to illustrate the theory of Fulcanelli that sculptures on the cathedrals held the key to nuclear fission as the pyramids did to astronomy, *Fate* reproduced a section of the porch at Notre-Dame. Not till weeks after publication were the editors themselves startled into realizing what the figures in the frieze were actually doing. Cathedrals are apt to be taken for granted.

The rest of the world may by now have accepted Labisse as a great artist and have stopped noticing his paintings in their museums. In England, however, there is no doubt that he still jerks into attention those who are not expecting him. Faces grow alert. Discussions flare. He too is an "arch-disturber."

Is the immediate response due to the connection between the myths he uses and the collective unconscious within ourselves? A woman with the head of a lioness. Another whose arms grow into the head of a predatory bird. Hands are nearly always gloved. Eyes are veiled under a curtain of hair. The psychiatrist can interpret for ever.

Birds represent the creative spirit, the anima. In the

pictures they are either flying away, or screened from the figures, or intruding with long, cruel beaks. With a painter, creation lies through the hand. It turns into a bird and reaches for the breast from which nourishment comes, but it looks destructive, and the blind face behind its surgical bandages cannot see to prevent.

Often the hand grasps the breast, but a glove is interposed and stops contact. Does the creator wish to be protected from his own creation ? Yet the force will out, as in the famous painting of a young girl with the bursting head of an overripe fig on top of a pregnant body, though even there a protective pun is embedded in the title: *Jeune Figue posant pour Leonard de Vinci une Annonciation.*

Nevertheless, the symbols could hardly be less literary. They spring straight from a dream world which has its own realities. As the years progress, the human shapes tend to fuse into the landscape. Then the landscapes themselves become starker. Finally you are left with the *Libidoscaphes,* where black crags surround desolate seas, from the depths of which rise great pink blobs of matter.

Labisse is an early master of surrealism. He renews himself constantly, but always along the lines of delving deeper into his own natural and historical subconscious. Ferro, on the other hand, brings the concept into our own times.

Primitive man was afraid of wild beasts. Modern man fears machines.

The monsters of today are no longer centaurs in the hills, mermen in the sea, or a bull-headed predator sitting in his palace at Knossos. They are the hybrids of men and machines, looming up out of our own cities.

The very form of Ferro's complex designs turns each creature into a cog of his mechanics. It is impossible to grasp at one and the same moment any single part and the whole. Yet it is not until all the details are memorised that the meaning of the totality becomes apparent.

This is the new complexity. While the world of the Cathedrals and of Hieronimus Bosch showed a teeming mass of angels, saints, sinners, demons and fabulous beasts, proliferating wildly on all sides with the randomness of nature, that of our century shows the same multiplicity, but linked inside one functional engine. Both are concepts of continuity, but the emphasis has changed from the individuality of the participants to their integration in a common purpose.

Because Gurdjieff attached so much importance to making men see and because the greatest hope for religious unity lies in the collective unconscious, from which our beliefs spring and which we all share, it was agreed to illustrate this book with paintings from contemporary surrealists who draw their subjects from this common fund. Labisse and Ferro are active examples of the method.

So as not to limit vistas too exclusively, Georges Rohner was also asked for permission to include some of his work. He is not a surrealist, but his immense, sombre "Radeau de la Meduse" was hung immediately adjacent to them at the Salon de Mai this year.

His line could not be more definite, but the very precision makes his objects, sheets, curtains and clothes, come alive in a menacing way, as if to wrestle with his figures. His workers are as drowned in empty landscapes as the corpses floating on the surface of a windless sea after the wreck of the Meduse. His objects hold a still mineral threat and recumbent figures stretch arms aloft in despair. Even when they are tossing an apple, it turns out to be the one which made Eve fall.

Here is another dimension of sight. If we really look at any object, we see the whole contained therein. How many viewers on looking at " Le Lit " (1952) noticed at first glance the form of the girl sleeping under the sheet ? Beyond such obvious discoveries, the exact line in every case leads straight into a mutation of our understanding. Click ! The shutter rises and there is a discovery.

One end product of Gurdjieff's training was mastery of the senses. What Thomas de Hartmann did for his music can unfortunately not be transmitted through the medium of print. It may be, however, that Rohner will convey something of the same effect through his vision. Greater acuity allows both to distinguish more clearly and to penetrate deeper. The first is an improvement. The second can lead to revelation.

The object of this foreword is only to explain the aim of the publishers in translating and producing the book. It is part of a design to provide material for the study of those movements which are bridging the gap between East and West. It is hoped that it may be followed by a sister volume on Subud. An effort will also be made, whenever possible to make the impact visual. There are too many merchants of theory. The time has come to see, to do and to understand.

ISLE OF MAN — NOVEMBER 1963

PREFACE

A few months ago, two men as different from each other as they could be, asked me to undertake this work: Pierre Lazareff and Jean Paulhan.

Pierre Lazareff, who started *Paris Soir* and is now editor of *France Soir, Elle* and *France Dimanche*, is an intensely active man with many-sided interests. Jean Paulhan on the other hand, editor of the *N.R.F.*, and a lover of rare things, is mysterious and reserved.

Pierre Lazareff broached the subject one evening as we were dining in a restaurant in the Bois de Boulogne. There was an orchestra which seemed to prolong the noise of the telephones, the teleprinters and the printing presses. We ate quickly; between mouthfuls he took long puffs of his cigarette, darting his eyes from one object to another as he fidgeted in his chair, talking very fast in a grating voice.

Jean Paulhan spoke of it one morning in spring, after a game of " Boules " in the deserted gardens of the Arènes de Lutèce. We were in his bedroom. He walked about on tip-toe so as not to disturb the courtship of two goldfish who were entwining their fins at the foot of his bed. He let the words fall from his half-opened lips in a sing-song voice, without moving his eyes, one arm folded across his chest, stepping round the furniture with extreme caution, as though he were surrounded by china that a breath might shatter.

I could go on indefinitely describing these two men, and every characteristic in one would find its opposite in the other. I am convinced, however, that fundamentally they are alike. Race, family, education, profession, points of view, tastes, ways of thinking and expressing themselves, the quality of their will-power, their emotions, their sensitivity, their physique, everything that distinguishes one human being from another — none of this can convey the special essence of a man. I find it impossible to say what can convey it, but it seems to me that, whatever differences there may be in the psychology and temperament of these two men, in their heart of hearts, they are identical.

Paulhan, seated at his table surrounded by a screen, in his silent room, amuses himself by translating a little Madagascan poem, and gets up every now and then to wind up a minute musical box; while Lazareff rings up Tangier, receives calls from London, with twenty colleagues banging on the door of his office; rushes to the printing press, jumps into his car to go to the Elysée, has an idea for an article, while pocketing an air ticket to Rome.

Now, I can easily imagine that these two men are secretly asking the same question, feeling the weight and flavour of this question in the same way and cherishing exactly the same ambition. They live very different lives but feel the same need to be aware of something that cannot be reduced to terms of their work — for the one his complete absorption in experiments in language that he carries almost to absurdity, in word-games with ridiculously strict rules; for the other, the absorption of a moulder of public opinion in hectic action, in the wild excitement of being a clearing-house for current events and ideas.

Now, this irreducible something is, for both of them, the uncertainty of being real, and the same dazzling conviction that there are keys to the door of real existence. And it follows that the inner and outer actions of both — different as they are — tend to form the same kind of magnetic centre, functioning in the same way, drawing towards them the same hidden forces and turning them in the same direction. This, at any rate, is as clear as day to my eyes which, as the result of an experience that endangered their normal functioning, are particularly sensitive to these invisible sights.

When one realizes that the way to Paulhan is the same as the way to Lazareff one has a conception of human relationships that has nothing in common with the conception that governs our ordinary society. One is conscious of entering a kind of secret society, a society whose approaches have not yet been explored. I have only spoken of these two men, as they are in a way bound up with this work, but I could certainly say the same of a hundred people I know — people who are members of this society which is the only truly united family. This kind of secret society is the only one worth belonging to if one wants to live in a state of wonder on earth.

Of course the know-alls will say that Paulhan persuaded me to undertake this book because all strange forms of thought and expression amuse him, and Lazareff, because he knows the public appetite for "magic" and picturesque characters. These know-alls cannot bear the kind of secret society that I mentioned just now. They must have a simple interpretation of human relationships. If people do not fit into psychological and other generally accepted categories and have hidden means of communication between themselves, these know-alls begin to doubt the value of their own ways and feel done out of their wretched little schemes for using others for their own purposes. I've only allowed myself to mention Paulhan and Lazareff, and to disclose the existence of this hidden family in order to incite these know-alls to sarcasm, and thus persuade them to close this book at once. Having said this, I must add that I might not have come to the point of collecting these documents, testimonies and studies at all if I had not received, last February, the following letter:

Dear Sir,

I am a young writer who has been doing the same " work " as yourself for nearly two years, in one of the G. groups directed by Madame de S. and another. I want to see you urgently. If you will be kind enough to see me, I won't come alone, I will bring my friend who is in the same position as I am. I am well aware that you have no reason to see two strangers with no introduction. However, I ask you to do so as soon as possible.

Yours sincerely,
Frances Rudolph

I asked them at once to come and see me at home. Two young American girls came in, on the verge of death. One had come from Virginia and the other from New York State to follow Gurdjieff's teaching in Paris. They were extremely thin, and one felt that their nerves were vibrating, tying themselves in knots in their necks and around their hearts. Their blood seemed to circulate unwillingly; their faces were grey and their eyes hypnotized. They were at their last gasp, ready to take the plunge into death, in fact already bending over it — fascinated. I knew this. I recognized in them, in every detail, my own past agonies, and I could have gone on describing to them all night their fears, their physical torments and the feelings they had when the threads that held them to life first became frayed and then snapped altogether. After two years of " work " as this word is understood by Gurdjieff, I found myself in hospital, as weak as a kitten, one eye nearly gone, on the verge of suicide and calling desperately for help at 3 o'clock in the morning. The young women told me that they realized that *" they were destroying them."* They begged me to encourage them to break away at once from the " teaching." They were not yet sure if they should go on to the end of this ordeal or if they should fly from the " teaching," the " work " and the influence of their " masters " before it was too late. But they came all the same to beg me to drag them off the road to perdition; I believe it was their last effort before the final slide. They risked it without even knowing who I was, as one risks one's last card. I really believe that they gambled their lives when they wrote to me. I tried to save them, or rather I tried to push them with all my strength towards sanity. They are now in

America, at a seaside resort. They sleep, eat, bathe and learn again to abandon themselves to physical pleasures, to feel themselves connected with the elements, with things and people and with their own bodies. One by one they are taking up again the threads of life. You will read their testimony later.

Frances Rudolph and Patricia X, with their dull hair, blue wrists and horror-stricken eyes, proved to me again that " spiritual war is quite as brutal as physical war," as Rimbaud says, and that after a certain stage of metaphysical anxiety has been reached the least disturbance of the mind provokes an oscillation of the body between life and death. These are terrifying truths, and when one has oneself felt the depths of fear, one hesitates to go back to situations where their evil influence is at work. But with these two girls begging for my help I could not hesitate. I was forced to re-live my old torments in order to find the strength and the words with which to persuade them to escape at once from this " teaching " — from " masters " who seemed to be preparing for them a complete spiritual collapse, and to be pushing them, body and soul to the most terrible death. I was forced to remember men and women I had known who underwent the same dangers for the same reasons; and finally, I was forced to think of others who followed this " teaching " and who, of all the " pupils " had the richest of inner lives, I mean Luc Dietrich, René Daumal, Katherine Mansfield and Irène Reweliotty, who all died young.

It seemed to me urgent and necessary to gather as many clear documents and testimonies as possible, on the person, the doctrine and the influence of George Gurdjieff and on the activities of the groups that he founded in France and elsewhere; to try to put into perspective the experiences of thousands of his pupils, to give accurate information on an enterprise unprecedented in this century, so as to bring home to a wide public both its dangers and its unusual importance.

When I say " a wide public " I am referring to the secret family of minds I spoke of before, in connection with Pierre Lazareff and Jean Paulhan. I think there is today, in the so-called civilized world, or at least in the parts of the civilized world where a State religion — Fascism or Communism — has not plunged all minds into an absolute void, a large number of men and women who are seeking the answer to a question that neither science, philosophy, the Churches, nor present-day politics can answer completely. They seek in most cases in spite of themselves, in spite of all the efforts they make to forget its urgency in the distractions of love, action, alcohol, and the pursuit of social power, of money, æstheticism, etc.

I find it hard to formulate this question in all its aspects, but it seems to me that it bears on the following points: — Am I Real ? Is man, perhaps, nothing but a continuous stream of feelings, moods, desires, ideas and memories, all mixed up and shifting more or less mechanically ? Is there not, perhaps, behind this very illusory " me," a " me " outside this stream, a really free " me " ? Everything that I think I do, in reality just *happens* to me. It happens in exactly the same way as " it rains " or " it freezes." I think, I read, I write, I love, I hate, I belong to such and such a party, to such and such a philosophy, to such and such a Church, I throw myself into such and such an action, battle, research, but in actual fact, all this *happens* to me. I am pulled by a thousand strings. Can there be, in the depths of man, some place where *I* decide, *I* rule, where *I* contemplate in complete independence and freedom? It seems, however, that many signs are made to me. I feel that my destiny, my adventures, my actions, my dreams, light up these signs in the darkness, signs that I cannot understand, but that are evidently meant for me. I would understand them if I had other eyes behind my ordinary eyes — if I had a big Me behind my blind and slavish little me. These signs would tell me clearly how I am attuned to the great currents of Universal energy, and precisely what rôle I am meant to play in life. Is there no way of understanding these signs? Is there not somewhere in me a point from which all that *happens* would be immediately clear, whether it had to do with the material or the moral world, a point from which all that I see, know or feel would at once be comprehensible, whether the movements of stars, the arrangement of the petals of a flower, the dramas of the civilization to which I belong, or the spontaneous stirrings of my own heart?

"The whole Universe," says the writer Robert Kanters, "is like an immense coded telegram which, down to its smallest detail, speaks to man of his nature and destiny, and requires to be deciphered if he wants to gain knowledge, wisdom and salvation." Could not this intense need to know, that I carry with me in spite of myself through all the adventures of my life, one day be satisfied? Is there not somewhere in man, in myself, a road that leads to knowledge of all the laws of the world and to a place where my own life is mingled with the energy that keeps the whole Universe alive ? Is there not in the depths of myself, hidden by centuries of neglect, the key of knowledge and of eternity ? All the signs that I can see dimly, though unable to interpret them, lead me to think that a great key-board of relationships plays in and around me. Sometimes in a flash I can feel it play, an almost imperceptible sign makes me aware of it. These relationships could perhaps give us the key of the world. Is it not possible that all that happens around me is the flow of a series of symbolic images of what is really happening ? Is there not behind my little " me " a big " Me " who possesses the key of these symbols, the understanding and explanation of all these relationships ? I could almost believe that these signs are made in order that I should feel from time to time a blinding certainty in the depths of my inner darkness. To-day these signs shower upon us and make us more and more aware that man has other feelers, other powers than those known to our s c i e n c e, language, religion, philosophy, morals and politics, upon which we base the actions of our daily lives.

It may be that in some distant age, it was found possible to manipulate this key-board ; to develop these powers consciously, and to make the transition to another state of being in which life and death are no longer held to be contradictory and from which all acts, from the humblest to the most noble, are perfectly in tune with the laws of Universal energy ? Moreover, it may be that the memory of the possession of these things still lingers in us—in the longing for Revelation, for a primeval Tradition, whose traces are confused but which still exist here and there, in the customs and beliefs of "primitive" people, in Tibetan monasteries, in ancient habits and in books of spells that have been handed down to us, in our living poetry and in our extraordinary sensitivity to signs.

Here, then, are some of the aspects of the QUESTION that so many p e o p l e are asking themselves to-day. There is a kind of mentality and an attitude to life that is common to them all, but which escapes the tests of our phsychology. I could not possibly describe them here. I should have to write an enormous novel, like "The Possessed". This novel would have the curious merit of being ten thousand times more true to our present reality than any other account of contemporary life. A description of this family of minds and the way it has been rapidly growing during the last few decades might, in fact, bear witness to this "phenomenon-key" of our age. This accelerated growth has many causes that I cannot enumerate here but it is sufficient to become conscious, on a global scale, of the upheavals that have overthrown the beliefs advocated by the Churches, faith in History, love of progress, faith in the unlimited powers of Rationalism, etc., to see clearly that more and more people are coming to ask themselves this QUESTION about the ultimate meaning of our destiny and of the world; that in all the different forms of contemporary thought this QUESTION remains unanswered, and that it has to be faced from the extreme freedom of the natural state and in complete loneliness. "A mystic in the savage State" as they said of Arthur Rimbaud. The phrase fits these people, adventurers in the noblest meaning of the word, who incorporate in their modern ways, the ancient, hidden way. The same fore-knowledge, the same fundamental questioning gives to all their activities a sort of likeness and creates between them secret and very rapid means of communication. They are, in fact, giving a new direction to our minds, our knowledge and our language and causing spiritual and temporal powers to change hands. One day this will become apparent.

Coinciding with the sudden growth of this " family " George Gurdjieff arrived in the West. The doctrine and methods he brought with him were calculated to seduce some of the best minds of the day. That is why his influence has developed so rapidly during the last thirty years or so, amongst the intellectuals of France, England and America. I think it would be true to say that to-day tens of thousands of men and women of the Western " élite " have been influenced by his " teaching," and influenced in a much more profound way than would be possible by any contemporary philosopher.

George Gurdjieff had, in fact, a direct answer to the QUESTION; or rather he promised an answer. He promised it through a doctrine that combined a system of human psychology and physiology handed down from the most ancient traditions, with certain little-known facts of contemporary science. Besides this, he taught PRACTICAL exercises that had remained secret until his day — dispersed amongst ancient traditions, or mixed and confused in symbolical, emotional or dogmatic sources. He directed these exercises with an amazing authority; he developed his Cosmological system with incomparable intelligence; and finally, over all who approached him, he undoubtedly exercised super-human powers. I am sure that I am not exaggerating when I declare that in the bosom of this " family of minds " that I have been describing, George

Gurdjieff collected around him the most important and the most profoundly active " secret society " that could have been found anywhere in the modern world. This society counted amongst its members: Orage, the famous English literary critic, Ouspensky, Rowland Kenny, editor of the "*Daily Herald*", Frank Lloyd Wright, the best-known American architect, Dr. Walkey, one of the most famous surgeons of New York, Sharp, the founder of the "*New Statesman*", the physicist J. G. Bennett, a disciple of Einstein, Margaret Anderson, editor of "*Joyce*", Arnold Keyserling, Dr. Young, Aldous Huxley, Arthur Koestler, Madame Tchekov, Georgette Leblanc, the first wife of Maeterlinck, Katherine Mansfield, Luc Dietrich, René Daumal, Louis Jouvet, Pierre Schaeffer, René Barjavel, etc. I am only giving a few names as an indication at the beginning of this book. In the course of it one will find many others associated in one way or another with Gurdjieff. I have no wish to awaken the wrong sort of interest by a list of famous personalities; I only want to point out that here we are a very long way away from those " esoteric groups ", occultists, spiritualists and the like, that, since the middle of last century have proliferated in America and Europe. We are not amongst the self-taught " enlightened," the neurotics and the repressed spinsters that make the fortunes of the " Seers". We are, I think, at the heart of all the dramas and adventures, inner and outer, that are lived through to-day by a considerable number of people aware of signs of a mystical nature, that seem to multiply in our times. In this connection the " Gurdjieff business " is most enlightening.

George Gurdjieff died in November 1949. Since his death the groups that he founded and the teachers that he instructed are growing in importance. There are more and more "pupils", oddly enough mostly in America. It is even more than likely that someone else will turn up soon, from some Eastern country, to take his place at the head of the movement. It is quite probable, too, that we shall see sister movements arise and develop during the next few years. Perhaps Gurdjieff has only paved the way.

It therefore seems to me important at this moment to give the public as much material as possible for knowledge and judgement. But this book is only addressed to the "family of minds" that I have been speaking of ; it is for this family alone that I have undertaken it. It is quite possible that readers for whom it is not intended will find opportunities for raising small scandals, and more for congratulating themselves on ignoring, forgetting and despising the fundamental anxiety that binds this family together and that has impelled many of its members towards Gurdjieff. No matter; it is not to be expected that a report on the "Gurdjieff Case" would make sense to outsiders.

The documents, testimonies and other writings gathered here throw light, as far as possible, on the following aspects of the GURDJIEFF CASE:
1. The man, his origins, life, adventures, work and many facets of his extraordinary personality.
2. His basic doctrine, his methods of teaching, the various reasons for his influence and the different ways in which he exercised this influence.
3. The "clientèle" of the "groups" directly or indirectly controlled by him, and the different forms of their activities.
4. The effects of Gurdjieff's personal influence.

5. The kind of "work" imposed on members of these groups.
6. The effects of this work on the physical, sexual, psychological, intellectual and moral behaviour of his disciples.
7. The existence of a certain state of mind brought about by this teaching in most intellectual circles.
8. The existence of a living literature sprung from this "secret society".

Nevertheless, my chief concern has been to weigh up the effects of this teaching on the disciples. For I can think of nothing more helpful to all who have taken part in "groups" and don't yet know if they were right or wrong to give up the "work"; to those who are still "working"; to those who might be tempted to-day to risk themselves in this adventure; to those who have embarked on some "way" similar to the "way" proposed by Gurdjieff and finally, to those who cannot and never will cease to ask themselves if there is a possible answer in this life to the QUESTION. Nothing seems to me more useful than to be of service to this large family.

To produce this book I have had to act as compiler, journalist and detective all in one. The compilation alone required the methods of a police enquiry, as a clever conspiracy of silence has been organized around most of these writings, which moreover were widely scattered. I could count neither on Gurdjieff's assistants nor on his present pupils, none of whom had knowledge of more than three or four books and articles that were "acceptable". Nor could I count on the old adepts who knew more, but whose waning devotion has left its mark in the form of a curious fear ; nor even on the few who had carried out researches, because unfortunately the reasons for their researches prevented them from making the results available. On the other hand, I could be certain of meeting with much resistance and many obstacles and have had to use guile to overcome them.

As for the journalism, it has been of two kinds:
1. To find people able to bear witness; to seize on whatever might be useful in their experience, and to present these statements in as sincere, simple and precise a form as possible.
2. By a series of conversations, sometimes indiscreet, to add to my own recollections as much information as possible about the people, the events and the atmosphere of this society.

Finally there was my detective work on certain aspects of Gurdjieff's activities that may seem irreconcilable with his character as a spiritual leader. On this last point, and on certain other results of my researches, I shall keep silent or only speak indirectly when necessary. I must add a few more words of warning. I think most of Gurdjieff's ideas on the double nature of man, on the possibility of his evolution and on his position in the cosmos, are extremely seductive. I am not sure of being able to convey them properly, partly because I lack the scientific and philosophical training that would enable me to translate them into simple language without losing any of their breadth, and partly because I have not yet passed the first stage in my studies of these ideas. I have not, therefore, wished to push myself forward in any way; besides, I have two good reasons for modesty. Firstly, that Ouspensky, the scholar gifted with all the necessary knowledge, has given us the essential Gurdjieff doctrine in his two books — " *In Search of the Miraculous* " and " *The*

Psychology of Man's Possible Evolution". Secondly, that my intention has been to convey, not what we should feel had we already attained higher consciousness, but what goes on in the head, heart and body of those who go in search of this consciousness, step by step with Gurdjieff. The joys and dramas of beginners are what seemed to me worth describing. I have not, therefore, had to make a complete résumé of Gurdjieff's ideas as many of these are not suited to beginners.

Now, as far as I know, no-one in the West has passed the first stages of the teaching. He himself affirmed this with great scorn. So that many of Ouspensky's brilliant displays seem to me to derive solely from intellectual curiosity, and have no connection with the living experience of the Westerners who belonged to this Society. Intellectual curiosity is, of course, legitimate, but I am not trying to satisfy it here. This book will only present aspects of the doctrine that have some connection with the experiences of the " elementary " students.

You will be asking yourself if it is possible to get beyond this first stage — I wonder, too. Is there really a Way to become a TRUE MAN, an AWAKENED MAN, as Gurdjieff says ; is there any hope of reaching this state, in the interests of which these great efforts and sacrifices are made ? This is the ultimate QUESTION, and I don't know the answer. All that I can know about, are the dramas of those who have attempted to reach it, under Gurdjieff's guidance, or rather of those who have prepared themselves seriously for the attempt. In the course of this work I shall relate my own experiences and thoughts during my time with the group. I shall also tell how and why I turned away from it ;

but don't think that I have collected these witnesses in order to justify my own withdrawal. I don't feel I have any profound need to justify myself in this way, and my real object is quite other. It is possible, however, that the writings collected here will produce the same conclusions as those that I have reached myself. Should that be so, I hope with all my heart that these conclusions will not be considered final, and that, having closed the book, the reader will go on asking himself if there can possibly be a way of arriving at absolute Freedom and Knowledge. Those who go on asking themselves this question are the salt of the earth. They have to resist both their unbridled arrogance, that says " yes " and their laziness of Spirit that says " no ". The ceaseless resistance to these two all-pervading human weaknesses is what makes of them noble scape-goats. It also makes them the only witnesses worth having. I like to imagine that at the end of this battle of resistance, if there is an end, and of these arduous and exhausting trials, they will find the thread that will lead them to the answer and will realize that all that is needed to keep hold of it is a lightness of touch and the spontaneity of childhood.

Part One

THE MAN WHO IS NOT ASLEEP

1

A Strange Traveller

One afternoon in November, 1916, a celebrated Russian journalist was preparing to leave from the Nicholaevski Station in St. Petersburgh, for a journey across the Empire. He was going, on the eve of the Revolution, to " sound public opinion ". His compartment was full of Orientals whose business interests caused them to travel all over the country. They were shouting and waving to each other and calling out addresses, names and figures. At the last moment, as the bell sounded, a man got in and sat down opposite the reporter. His appearance and movements seemed exceptionally important and dignified ; one might have imagined him a monarch returning to his kingdom. He excited such a lively curiosity in the journalist that a few days later he devoted the first of his articles to him.

" My travelling companion," he wrote, " remained silent and apart. He was a Persian or a Tartar ; he wore a good astrakhan cap and had a French novel under his arm. He drank tea from a glass which he put carefully to cool on the table by the window. Every now and then he glanced with the greatest scorn at his noisy neighbours, who in turn watched him closely, with respect mixed with fear. What struck me most about him was that he seemed to belong to the same Southern oriental type as his companions, a band of vultures in search of a carcass. His skin was bronzed, his eyes jet black and his moustache like that of Gengis Khan. Why then, did he so despise his own flesh and blood? A little later I had a chance of hearing him speak:

"They're in a great state" he said. In his dark, imperturbable face his polite oriental eyes seemed to smile faintly. After a short pause he went on: "Yes, in Russia to-day there are plenty of opportunities for an intelligent man to make a great deal of money." And, after another short pause, he explained: "After all, this is war. Everyone wants to become a millionaire." In his quiet, cold tone I thought I could detect a kind of inhuman and fatalistic bragging that verged on cynicism, and I asked him rather abruptly: "What about you?"

"What?" he asked.

"Don't you want to become a millionaire, too?" His only answer was a vague and rather ironical gesture. I thought perhaps he had not heard or had not understood, so I repeated:

"Are you not anxious, too, for profit?"

He smiled in a particularly calm way and answered gravely:

"We profit from everything. Nothing can stop it. War or no war it's always the same for us. We always profit."

"What do you deal in, then?"

" In solar energy."

I would have liked to prolong the conversation and to have found out more about the psychology of a man whose capital depended entirely on the arrangement of the solar system, which never seems to be disturbed, and whose interest, therefore, was well beyond the business of war and peace . . ."

The strange man was George Ivanovitch Gurdjieff. Two years ago, in 1914, he had come back to Russia after more than twenty-five years of mysterious wanderings. He was then nearing fifty, but one felt in him an ageless strength, a courage and calmness turned towards eternal things. He advertized his presence in Moscow by inserting a few lines in the newspapers announcing that a " Hindu " would shortly present a fantastic ballet called " The Battle of the Magi " which would reveal, for the first time, oriental magical techniques and would revive the most important and most ancient of sacred dances. Attracted by these notices, several people in search of the miraculous, had attempted to get in touch with the " Hindu ". He, meanwhile, sat outside a café dressed in a fur-lined coat and bowler hat, squeezing lemon juice into cups of black coffee, replying to all comers that their questions were premature and turning the conversation to other things. If his questioner was merely showing idle curiosity, he would turn away abruptly ; if on the other hand, he turned out to be one of the many professional " occultists ", he would reply coldly that there must be some mistake, that he was just a carpet merchant, and would then unfold his Bokhara rug, extol its quality and try to sell it. But occasionally he would start talking seriously ; then one heard no more about ballets or fakirs, but about methods of acquiring a certain consciousness of oneself, a certain inner unity and freedom. In a few weeks about thirty intellectuals from Moscow and St. Petersburgh, struck by what he told them on these occasions, formed a group around him, and soon, so great was their interest, that they lived for these talks alone and allowed him complete control of their destinies.

Ouspensky, the philosopher and writer, on his return from a long journey through India, being himself in search of the " miraculous ", had seen the notices in the papers. But his researches were serious, with no leaning towards the picturesque and no taste for aesthetic or sentimental exaltations. He wanted "facts", techniques and doctrines that would be acceptable to a scientific mind. He greatly mistrusted " occultists ", " Hindus " and fakirs, but so as to leave no stone unturned and in spite of his scepticism, he was persuaded by friends in the end to meet Gurdjieff.

" My first meeting with him entirely changed my opinion of him and of what I might expect from him.

" I remember this meeting very well. We arrived at a small café in a noisy though not central street. I saw a man of an oriental type, no longer young, with a black moustache and piercing eyes, who astonished me first of all because he seemed to be disguised and completely out of keeping with the place and its atmosphere. I was still full of impressions of the East. And this man with the face of an Indian rajah or an Arab sheik whom I at once seemed to see in a white burnous or a gilded turban, seated here in this little café, where small dealers and commission agents met together, in a black overcoat with a velvet collar and a black bowler hat, produced the strange, unexpected, and almost alarming impression of a man poorly disguised, the sight of whom embarrasses you because you see he is not what he pretends to be and yet you have to speak and behave as though you did not see it. He spoke Russian incorrectly with a strong Caucasian accent; and his accent, with which we are not accustomed to associated philosophical ideas, strengthened still further the strangeness and the unexpectedness of this impression.

" I do not remember how our talk began ; I think we spoke of India, of esotericism, and of yogi schools. I gathered that G. had travelled widely and had been in places of which I had only heard and which I very much wished to visit. Not only did my questions not embarrass him but it seemed to me that he put much more into each answer than I had asked for. I liked his manner of speaking, which was careful and precise."

What did he say, this Arab sheik in black coat and bowler, when he wasn't playing the rôle of carpet-merchant, fakir or petrol king of Baku ? He spoke, in his atrocious accent, about apparently very simple things; but one soon realized that the angle from which he examined these things was new. Ouspensky has written at length about this and it would be pointless to do it again here ; nevertheless, some of the sentences quoted by the author in " *In Search of the Miraculous*" are the very same that all who knew him have often heard, whether in Moscow in 1914, in Tiflis in 1919, at Fontainebleau in 1923, later in London, Berlin and New York, or during 1930 to 1949 in his flat in Paris in the Rue du Colonel Renard, or outside the Café de la Paix.

" 'Before speaking of psychology we must be clear to whom it refers and to whom it does not refer,' he

[Gurdjieff] said. '*Psychology* refers to people, to men, to human beings. What *psychology*' (he emphasized the word) ' can there be in relation to machines ? Mechanics, not psychology, is necessary for the study of machines. That is why we begin with mechanics. It is a very long way yet to psychology'."

He used to say, too:

" 'It is possible to stop being a machine, but for that it is necessary first of all *to know the machine.* A machine, a real machine, does not know itself and cannot know itself. When a machine knows itself it is then no longer a machine, at least, not such a machine as it was before. It already begins to be *responsible* for its actions'."

Or again:

" '... man's chief delusion is his conviction that he can *do.* All people think that they can do, all people want to do, and the first question all people ask is what they are to do. But actually nobody does anything and nobody can do anything. This is the first thing that must be understood. *Everything happens.* All that befalls a man, all that is done by him, all that comes from him — *all this happens.* And it happens in exactly the same way as rain falls as a result of a change in the temperature in the higher regions of the atmosphere or the surrounding clouds, as snow melts under the rays of the sun, as dust rises with the wind.

" 'Man is a machine. All his deeds, actions, words, thoughts, feelings, convictions, opinions, and habits are the results of external influences, external impressions. Out of himself a man cannot produce a single thought, a single action. Everything he says, does, thinks, feels — all this happens. Man cannot discover anything, invent anything. It all happens'."

"In order *to do* it is necessary *to be*. And it is necessary first to understand what *to be* means," says Gurdjieff. "One must learn to speak the truth. This also appears strange to you. You do not realize that one has to learn to speak the truth. It seems to you that it is enough to wish or to decide to do so. And I tell you that people comparatively rarely tell a deliberate lie. In most cases they think they speak the truth. And yet they lie all the time, both when they wish to lie and when they wish to speak the truth. They lie all the time, both to themselves and to others. Therefore nobody ever understands either himself or anyone else.... To speak the truth is the most difficult thing in the world; and one must study a great deal and for a long time in order to be able to speak the truth. The wish alone is not enough. *To speak the truth one must know what the truth is and what a lie is, and first of all in oneself.*"

While this strange man was speaking thus, it became evident that his words "besides their ordinary meaning, contained another completely different meaning." To decipher the hidden meaning one had to begin by grasping the ordinary, simple meaning. Gurdjieff's words, in the most simple meaning, were always full of sense, but they also had other meanings and one suspected, like Ouspensky, that "the deepest meaning lay hidden for a long time." Probably for as long as this man, with his piercing gaze and ironic smile, refrained from showing his serious disciples the road to follow and the tasks to perform, though he well knew the direction of the work and the details of tasks.

Thus, a really important group was formed round Gurdjieff. Ouspensky and other Russian intellectuals were soon to experience the most important adventure of their lives. Later, hundreds of writers, psychologists, journalists, philosophers, scientists, actors, musicians and painters of different nationalities, French, English, American and Austrian, as well as thousands of men and women from what is known as the " élite " of Europe and America, were to feel the impact of this strange traveller who, one afternoon in November 1916, as the train was pulling out of St. Petersburgh, declared calmly to a stranger, between sips of tepid tea :

" I deal in Solar energy."

For the time being this traveller is on his way back to his native town in the Caucasus, Alexandropol. His work of recruiting disciples had barely started when the miseries of war made travelling about the Empire impossible, and he disappeared. If the disciples were really serious in their desire to work with him, if they were really intended to " progress ", then they would find him, however difficult this might be.

At this period Alexandropol was not a town, but a conglomeration of villages and a place of various cultures. The Armenian quarter reminded one of Egypt, with its flat-roofed houses sprouting grass. From the hill beyond the cemetery, with its coloured onion-shaped domes, one could see the snowy heights of Mount Ararat where Noah's Ark came to rest. The centre of the town was Russian, with a typical oriental market, draughty stalls, coppersmiths crouched on mats, sooth-sayers, story-tellers and jugglers. Gurdjieff's parents' house was in the Greek quarter, and the ravines on the outskirts were inhabited by the wild Tartars. Many worlds met in the town, the dreamers', the actors', the speculators', the merchants', and the warriors'. Above the tents and roofs, rose the mountain where life began to flower again for the Just, after the wrath of the Deluge.

Gurdjieff was then forty-eight. His parents were Greeks from Asia Minor. His father seemed to belong to a very ancient culture; he knew innumerable legends and recited thousands of verses in many different idioms. When three of the disciples, one of whom was Ouspensky, managed to rejoin Gurdjieff in June 1917, they found him to be a gentle and considerate son.

"His relationship with his father was full of extraordinary consideration. G's father was still a robust old man, of medium height, with an inevitable pipe in his mouth and wearing an astrakhan cap. It was difficult to believe that he was over eighty. He spoke very little Russian. But with G. he used to speak for hours on end and I always liked to watch how G. listened to him, occasionally laughing a little, but evidently never for a second losing the line of the conversation and the whole time sustaining the conversation with questions and comments. The old man evidently enjoyed these conversations and G. devoted to him all his spare time, and not only did not evince the least impatience, but on the contrary the whole time showed a very great deal of interest in what the old man was saying."

Ouspensky tells us: "He had passed his young years in an atmosphere of fairy tales, legends, and traditions. The 'miraculous' around him was an actual fact. predictions of the future which he heard, and which those around him fully believed, were fulfilled and made him believe in many other things.

"All these things taken together had created in him at a very early age a leaning towards the mysterious, the incomprehensible, and the magical."

He had studied medicine and had also studied for the priesthood. No doubt he had practised for a year or two before leaving the Caucasus on his travels. In the course of these journeys, which he undertook for mystical reasons, "he came across many phenomena telling him of the existence of a certain knowledge, of certain powers and of possibilities exceeding the ordinary possibilities of man, and of people possessing clairvoyance and other miraculous powers." He let it be understood that he had, during his twenty or twenty-five years of roaming, met *remarkable* men, and he emphasized the word *remarkable*. He used to say, too, sometimes, that he had been one of a group of priests, scientists, doctors and scholars who had set themselves the task of scouring the world in search of a knowledge hidden away in more or less inaccessible monasteries, in secret schools, in songs and dances, and on monuments neglected by the modern world; a knowledge whose key could only be obtained through various initiatory trials. When one asked him what had happened to other members of this group he replied that they had remained in various parts of the East, but that he had been called on to finish his life in the West and to teach what could be taught. This Ouspensky affirms, having heard it from Gurdjieff himself. "After great difficulties, he found the sources of this knowledge. About schools and where he had found this knowledge that he undoubtedly possessed he spoke very little and always superficially. He mentioned Tibetan monasteries, the Chitral, Mount Athos; Sufi Schools in Persia, in Bokhara and Eastern Turkestan; he mentioned dervishes of various orders, but all of them in a very indefinite way."

And so he came back to Russia, in about 1914 at forty-six years of age, with knowledge and powers of which our civilization knows nothing. Perhaps he had been sent by some high authority on a special mission to the West ? He had in any case a remarkable gift for presenting in language acceptable to modern intellectuals the fundamentals of traditional teaching. In Moscow and St. Petersburgh he began successfully trying out with certain interesting people, a system of philosophy and exercises of the body and mind in which the most ancient human knowledge mingled with an amazing precision and as though by some blinding inner necessity, with modern Western psychological methods. Whatever he said, no matter what the subject or the occasion, his words took on an exceptional importance. This did not strike the mind only, but impressed itself on the whole of one's nature. As for the man himself it was evident in a few seconds to anyone to whom he was willing to show himself in his true colours (which he was able to conceal at will) that he was the possessor of special powers and of superhuman energy, and that he enjoyed almost absolute inner freedom and unity.

As regards his journeys, we have information to-day that Ouspensky either did not possess or did not think suitable to divulge. Some information I have promised to keep secret, but I can say that if one follows Gurdjieff from 1890 to 1914, using only well-authenticated documents, it will be seen that his roaming led him to the very place where a traveller in search of mystic knowledge would find the most ancient schools of wisdom, and be welcomed, should he possess the necessary luck and Gurdjieff's extraordinary gifts. Moreover, I think I can confirm what Mr Rom Landau says further on: Gurdjieff was the principal Russian secret agent in Tibet for ten years. (Kipling knew this.) He was given important financial posts by the Tibetan authorities and control over the equipment of the army. He was able to play a political rôle, as they knew him to possess spiritual powers and in this country that is all-important, especially amongst the high-ranking priesthood. He was tutor to the Dalai Lama, and escaped with him when the English invaded Tibet. (This explains the difficulties he had later in London with Lloyd George, in spite of all his friends could do. Let us add that for services rendered to France during the War, in India and in Asia Minor, he enjoyed the protection of Poincaré who personally authorized his establishment in France.) It is more than likely that Gurdjieff was not really interested in his political games at all, but lent himself to them with secret amusement just as he did to his carpet-selling in St. Petersburgh and to his other "affairs" at the Café de la Paix in Paris. His real work was elsewhere.

At the end of 1916 he came back to his house in Alexandropol at the foot of Mount Ararat, to listen to his old story-telling father. In June of the following year he rented a house at Essentuki for a few disciples who had managed to reach him in spite of the civil war. It was there, in this old house covered with roses, on the edge of the Black Sea, that he expounded the better part of his teaching during long conversations with about a dozen men and women, soon to be dispersed by the Revolution. We shall never know more about this than what Ouspensky tell us, but everything leads one to believe that Gurdjieff was hastily unburdening himself before plunging into "modern" Europe, under a rather different guise. When the Bolshevik trouble reached the South he left his group and disappeared.

We next hear of him in Tiflis, where from a little

shop, he is issuing pamphlets and posters about his newly founded "Institute for the Harmonious Development of Man." It was a matter of perfecting the *subversive* teaching techniques that he hoped to apply in the Europe of this " Age of Light," without troubling too much about the first highly exaggerated attempts. After several trials, in Constantinople, Berlin and London, he finally established himself, in 1922 in France, in the Chateau of Avon, near Fontainebleau. Here the " Institute for the Harmonious Development of Man " takes on its final shape.

From this time on Ouspensky is silent about him, and it is the Gurdjieff of the years 1922 to 1949 that we shall speak of in this book. It is the Gurdjieff of these years who troubled so deeply many contemporary artists and intellectuals.

In 1924, while many people were anxiously wondering what was going on in the Chateau of Avon where Katherine Mansfield had just died, Gurdjieff went off to America to organize a sister " Institute " there. He also presented publicly in New York, his "Movements," that is to say, exercises resembling those of certain dervishes, which formed an important part of his teaching.

On his way back, while driving himself in a powerful car as he loved to do, he had a terrible accident. The doctors said he would die, but he recovered rapidly from several fractures of the skull. However, he felt that he must now give up his work at the Institute and close the Chateau. Until 1930 he wrote a great deal and saw people in his flat near the Etoile. One could see him any morning sitting outside the Café de la Paix, an elderly gentleman with a white moustache and fur cap, drinking coffee and eating little cheeses that he took out of his pocket, and much beloved by the waiters for his handsome tips.

From 1930 onwards, he taught many small groups in France and the United States. We will explain more about the importance and the form of this teaching later on; we shall recall the meetings that took place, either in his flat or elsewhere; the extraordinary dinners over which he presided; the sessions of " Movements " and the " readings " of his manuscripts.

" How can one, in a few words, describe this extraordinary man ?" asks Mr. Gorham Munson in an article published in 1950 in the American magazine *"Tomorrow."* "A twentieth-century Cagliostro ? But all the information we have about Cagliostro is contradictory, and the stories we shall hear about Gurdjieff even more so. I, personally can vouch for his amazing capacity for work. He only slept three or four hours a night, and yet always seemed to have enough energy in the daytime for his many different activities. Those who had to work with him were often ready to drop with fatigue, whereas he, having worked for twenty hours on end, would reappear fresh and well after a short sleep. Last winter, in the Wellington Hotel, he used to go to bed at three or four in the morning and by seven the lift-boys saw him again. (He was eighty-three at this time.) He then went to his " office "— a restaurant in Fifth Avenue, where he received visitors all the morning.

I sometimes ask myself what our civilization of specialists would do, if certain figures of the Renaissance were to come back amongst us — such men as Roger Bacon, a forerunner, or Francis Bacon, or Paracelsus. I think we should find them baffling and their many-sidedness puzzling. Historians and biographers have never been able to understand their shocking lack of conformity. Gurdjieff to me was an enigma. I saw in him not so much the great religious teacher as one of these strange Renaissance figures. He never claimed that his ideas were original, on the contrary he said they came from an ancient science and were transmitted by esoteric schools. His humour was Rabelaisian, the rôles he played were dramatic and the impact he made on all who came near him was staggering. Sentimentalists expected to find in him the pale figure of Christ as portrayed in literature; they went away swearing that he was nothing but a practitioner of black magic. Some among the unbelievers are asking themselves still if he didn't know more about Relativity than Einstein.

Orage, one of Gurdjieff's chief assistants, called him the "Pythagorian". This emphasizes very well Gurdjieff's strangeness in the heart of our civilization, which could hardly be compared to the great period in classical Greece. How can one explain the interest of all these Western people in Gurdjieff's oriental ideas? There is a simple explanation — they appeal to all who seek relief from personal unhappiness in psychoanalysis, pseudo-religious cults and mass movements such as fascism and communism. The ideas have a therapeutic interest which attracted many people to the groups. But leaving that aspect aside for the moment, let us ask what it is appeals to a sophisticated thinker such as Aldous Huxley, so typical in this respect. The answer is that Western culture is going through a crisis; our epoch has known two World Wars and an economic slump. All thinking men must have been profoundly disillusioned by the hope placed in "progress". The First World War did not create a "world fit for Democracy". The prosperity of the 1920's led to a general scarcity. The Second World War turned into the Cold War. The socialists' dream was wrecked in the Totalitarian nightmare. The idea of "progress" has had to give way to the tragic feeling that Western man has come to a dead end. All efforts for good have produced nothing but evil. Gurdjieff, and with him Ouspensky and Orage, while confirming the general despair, and destroying the little faith we have left in the resources of our Western Culture, have given us hope. Aldous Huxley, that most modern of moderns, attended, they say, a few of Ouspensky's lectures and then finally turned to Gerald Heard, himself heavily indebted to the East. In Huxley one finds this tendency of the modern mind to turn, in the midst of our crisis, towards ideas and doctrines that remain outside the current of Western culture. Of the crisis itself, Orage, Ouspensky and their master Gurdjieff have painted a picture as black as any coming from the Western pessimists, but at the same time, as luminous as the beginnings of Christianity. It is in this contrast of light and shade that one must seek the principal reason for the attraction that these three men exert on modern man."

Having lost the wish to live George Ivanovitch Gurdjieff died very quickly in the American Hospital at Neuilly in October 1949, at the end of his eighty-third year.

He had not said everything; he had not had time, or rather, amongst the thousands of men he knew, he had not been able to find the one capable of extracting his real secrets. His groups were very numerous and very active, but for some time past he had seemed indifferent to the " work " they carried out. There had been several misunderstandings and divergencies; he merely shrugged his shoulders and seemed much amused. More than one drama developed around him, there were deaths, sufferings, moral, physical and spiritual, many illnesses of the mind, excess of pride in some and of despair in others, destructions, monstrosities, extreme naiveté, plenty of prime fools, squared fools and cubed fools, as he used to say — lifting his glass of vodka to drink to one or other of these categories. There were great flashes of genius, signs of saintliness, triumphs of evil. There were scandals, too. There was something of everything. He would pick over this " garbage " — growling insults. Sometimes, on the other hand, he distributed sweets: he always had plenty in his pockets.

From his bed, without moving, he looked at his intimates, those who, after his death, would continue to spread the doctrine in France, America and elsewhere. They would probably have more and more " pupils " and more and more material means. On the money side, thank you, it had always been alright and was getting better and better ; the publicity, too.

He looked at them all quietly. " I am leaving you in a fine mess " he said. Then he sank back and turned his gaze inward.

2

Rom Landau's Story

Mr. Rom Landau published a book that had quite a success. It contained interviews with some men who were considered spiritual leaders—Kayserling, Bo Yin Râ, Stefan George, Rudolf Steiner, Krishnamurti, George Jeffreys, Frank Buckman, Ouspensky and Gurdjieff. I like the words that end the the very modest preface to this book, which bears witness to a life devoted entirely to the search for words able to give back a meaning to life in this world, where we all feel lost:—
" The core of the adventure is a search for God. It is for the reader to decide whether such a search can be sacrilegious."

"I had for long been anxious to meet Gurdjieff, and at last, when I was in New York, it was arranged that I should see him. I asked Mr. Orage to give me an introduction, but, as at the time the two men were barely on speaking terms, Orage considered that his introduction would only shut Gurdjieff's door against me.

Eventually, however, I was given a letter of introduction to a very old friend of Gurdjieff's in New York, who was only too willing to arrange the interview, and who asked me to ring him up three days later to find out the exact date of the meeting. When I rang him up on the appointed morning he advised me to get into touch with Mr Gurdjieff's secretary.

I asked him whether I should mention his name. "Oh no," came the answer, "that would not be a recommendation. But you might say that a Mr. L. advised you."

"But I don't know Mr. L.", I replied.

"Then just say that you had been told that Mr. L. was going to talk to Mr. Gurdjieff about you, and to arrange for your interview."

I rang up the secretary. She knew nothing at all about a conversation between Mr. L. and Mr Gurdjieff; but she said that if I wrote a letter, giving all the reasons for my proposed visit and stating in detail who I was, she would take it to Mr. Gurdjieff. I wrote the letter and two days later the secretary rang me up: Mr. Gurdjieff would see me at 2.30 p.m. in his rooms, numbers 217 and 218 at his hotel.

Before my interview I had lunch with a distinguished American writer who was supposed to have known Gurdjieff for many years, and I asked him about Gurdjieff. "I have never actually spoken to him," he said, "but I often went to his classes and to his dances. I must confess that he is an enigma to me."

"Do you think it is true that he sometimes uses his strange faculties for other than spiritual purposes?"

"It would be unfair to affirm this. All the unorthodox things we hear about him may be parts of a system of deep spiritual significance. You must not forget that

Mme. Blavatsky, too, often tried to obtain genuine reactions from her pupils by shocking and antagonizing them. Gurdjieff may perhaps be doing something of the sort. There was a time when Orage and others of Gurdjieff's followers tried to induce me to join them and to become one of Gurdjieff's assistants. I refused persistently for a number of years, and I must say I am glad that I was never intimately associated with them."

"Is it true that Gurdjieff has changed thoroughly since his motor accident?"

"He certainly seems to have done so. He was almost dead for a very long time, and it may be that such a deep experience has transformed him. As you may have heard, his first book came out quite recently. It surprised me, for it showed me a new, more altruistic, less materially minded Gurdjieff."

"Where can one get this book?"

"I fear nowhere. It has been printed privately, and Gurdjieff sends it only to those he considers worthy of being instructed by him. He happened to send me a copy, but its style is so atrocious that I had the greatest difficulty in getting through it."

"Have you seen him recently?"

"Yes, at a reception last spring. I must tell you of an interesting incident which occurred that day. A friend of mine, who is one of our great novelists, was sitting at my table. I pointed to a table at which Gurdjieff was sitting, and asked her whether she knew him. "No, who is he?" she replied, looking across. Gurdjieff caught her eye, and we saw distinctly that he suddenly began to inhale and to exhale in a particular way. I am too old a hand at such tricks not to have known that Gurdjieff was employing one of the methods he must have learned in the East. A few moments later I noticed that my friend was turning pale; she seemed to be on the verge of fainting. And yet she is anything but highly strung. I was very much surprised to see her in that strange condition, but she recovered after a few moments. I asked her what the matter was. "That man is uncanny," she whispered. "Something awful happened," she continued, but began after a moment to laugh in her broad natural way. "I ought to be ashamed, nevertheless I'll tell you what happened. I looked at your 'friend' a moment ago, and he caught my eye. He looked at me in such a peculiar way that within a second or so I suddenly felt as though I had been struck right through my sexual centre. It was beastly!" My host stopped for a second, and added smilingly: "You had better be careful. The man you are going to see can certainly make use of strange powers: he had not learned them in Tibet for nothing."

"I so often hear about his experiences in Tibet," I replied: "but I am somewhat suspicious of those Tibetan tales. Every other messiah, from Mme. Blavatsky onwards, claims to have gathered knowledge in the mountains of Tibet. How do you know that Gurdjieff has actually ever been there?"

"I happen to possess first-hand proofs. Some years ago there was a luncheon in New York, given, if I remember aright, for Gurdjieff. A number of distinguished men had been invited, among others the writer, Achmed Abdullah, who told me that he had never seen Gurdjieff before, but that he was very much looking forward to meeting this unusual Armenian. When Gurdjieff entered the room Achmed Abdullah turned to me and whispered: 'I have met that man before. Do you know who he really is? Before the war he was in Lhasa as an agent of the Russian Secret

Service. I was in Lhasa at the same time, and in a way we worked against each other'. So, you see, it is quite true that Gurdjieff had been at the very fountain of esoteric knowledge. Some people said he was in Lhasa as a Secret Service agent, in order to disguise the real purpose of his visit, which was to learn the supernatural methods of the Lamas. Other people maintain that his esoteric studies were only a pretext behind which he could hide his political activities. But who can tell?"

Gurdjieff lived in one of the smaller hotels in 57th Street. When the reception clerk at the hotel desk telephoned up to announce my visit, I was told to go " right up " to number 217. I knocked at the door, and entered a small darkish room. A tall young man with a cigarette in his mouth was standing at the door to receive me. "How do you do," he said; "he will be with you in a moment; please sit down." He looked presentable and cultured; but I have hardly ever seen a pair of more frightened eyes. I admit that it was not difficult to allow one's imagination to detect features that may not have existed in reality. Yet I had come to this meeting determined not to dramatize it, but to observe as keenly as possible and to gather first-hand knowledge. The story of Gurdjieff was dramatic enough as it stood. There could be no doubt about the expression on the young man's face. He was very pale, his eyes glowed feverishly, and he gave me the impression of someone who had just seen a ghost. He smoked his cigarette nervously, with his eyes focussed all the time on the adjoining room. There was no door between the two rooms, and I could discern in the far one a bed and some luggage. The reception room in which we were sitting was, in comparison with those of most hotels of the district, shabbily furnished. Several cheap black suitcases were lying on the floor in front of an empty fireplace. I heard someone opening the door from the passage to the bedroom, and a moment later Gurdjieff joined us.

"How do you do," he said in very bad English and with a strong oriental accent. I was particularly struck by the way he pronounced the 'h'. It was not the light English 'h', but the deep, gutteral 'ch' of some German words, or rather the 'chr' of Eastern languages. Gurdjieff was wearing a waistcoat half unbuttoned, no coat, dark trousers and bedroom slippers. You could see the braces under his waistcoat.

"Excuse this costume," he said; "I have only just finished lunch." He then pointed at me and said to the young man: "This Englishman very precise." he obviously meant punctual. "He really English," he went on, without allowing me to contradict; "not like you all, half-Turks, half-Turks." He turned towards me: "Americans are not English, for me they are only half English and half, half"—he was trying to remember the word—'half Turkish.' He laughed and continued instantly, "You excuse my English. It awfully bad. I speaking my own English, you know—not modern, but pre-Shakespearian English. It awfully bad, but my friends understand. And I understand everything in real modern English, so you go and speak. This man" — he pointed to his pupil — "will translate my pre-Shakespearian English for you. He knows."

"Oh, it is perfectly clear to me, Mr Gurdjieff," I tried to contradict; "I understand everything you say."

"Then have a cigarette."

"Thanks, I am afraid I don't smoke."

Painting by Felix Labisse from " Planete "

Felix Labisse: Le bonne conduite, 1950

Felix Labisse: *Les malheurs de la guerre,* 1942

Felix Labisse: Histoire naturelle, 1943

Felix Labisse: L'aventure permanente, 1944

Felix Labisse: *Les matins d'Iphnema,* 1950

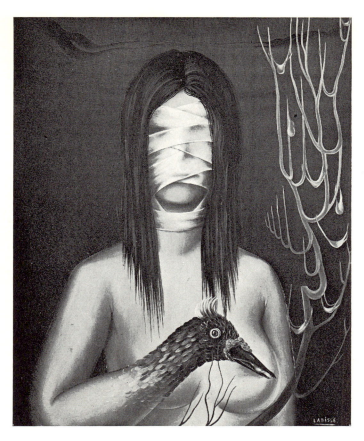

Felix Labisse: La Léda étrangère, 1950

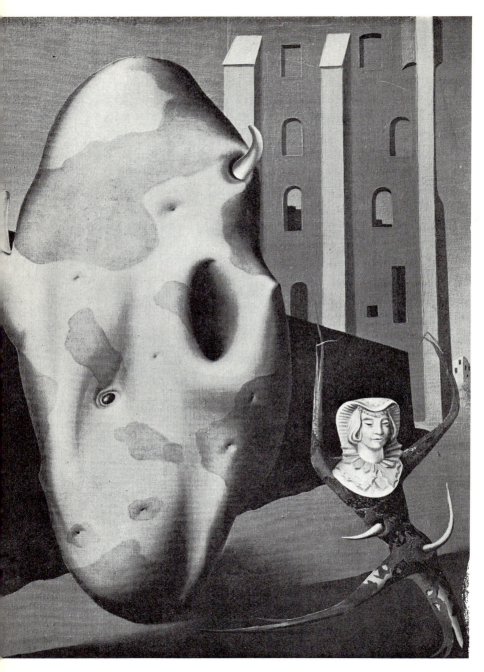

Felix Labisse: *La conjuration d'Amboise*, 1955

"Oh, not smoke one of those Americans ! No I give you wonderful cigarettes, real cigarettes, Turkish and Russian. Say what ?" He placed a large box of Russian cigarettes in front of me.

"Thanks all the same," I said: "but I really do not smoke."

"Come, come, they good, *prima, prima*. If not smoke these, I can give you . . . what calls itself non-smoking cigarettes. What call you ?" he turned to the young man who explained: " Mr. Gurdjieff keeps special cigarettes for non-smokers, perhaps you would care to take one."

I was beginning to feel slightly uncomfortable, but I tried to treat the whole matter as a kind of joke, and I said light-heartedly: "Thanks awfully, I am sure I should be sick straight away if I smoked any of your cigarettes; and no-one here would enjoy that. I have never smoked in my life," I lied.

I sat down on a little sofa not far from Gurdjieff, who was reclining comfortably in a big chair. The young man had remained all through our conversation on his chair near the fireplace. He kept on glancing nervously towards Gurdjieff, and it was impossible to imagine that he could ever laugh or smile. Terror seemed the only expression of which his face was capable—or was it some hysterical form of expectation?

Gurdjieff's face was manifestly Levantine. The skin was darkish; the twisted moustache was black, though distinctly greying; the eyes were very black and vivid. But the most Levantine feature of his face was the mouth: it never remained quite shut and it exposed the teeth, one or two of which had been darkened as though by constant smoking. He was quite bald and slightly stout; yet you could see that he had been goodlooking in his earlier days, and it was obvious that women must have been very susceptible to this virile Levantine type of man.

He was very obliging and smiled constantly, as though trying to show me his most attractive side. Nevertheless I began to feel very queer. I am not easily influenced by 'telepathic' enticement, and am not at all what is called a 'good medium'; no doctor or hypnotist has ever succeeded in hynotizing me. On this particular occasion I was very much on my guard and prepared to counteract any possible psychic influence. And yet I was beginning to feel a distinct weakness in the lower parts of my body, from the navel downwards, and mainly in the legs. This feeling grew steadily every second. After about twenty or thirty seconds it became so strong that I knew I should hardly be able to get up and walk out of the room.

I had been specially careful not to look at Gurdjieff and not to allow him to look into my eyes. I had avoided his eyes for at least two minutes. I had turned all the time towards the young man, to whom I had said: "I shall talk to you, and perhaps you will be so kind as to translate my words to Mr. Gurdjieff in case he does not understand me." The young man had agreed, and I remained facing him, with Gurdjieff on my right. And yet the feeling of physical weakness pervaded me more and more.

I was intensely awake and conscious of what was going on within me, and I was observing this fascinating new experience with the keenest awareness. The feeling inside my stomach was one of acute nervousness, amounting almost to physical pain and fear. This weakness did not upset me above the navel: it was limited to the stomach and legs. My legs were suffering from the sensation similar to that which people experience before a trial at court, an examination, or a visit to the dentist. I was sure that if I tried to get up, my legs would sag under me and I should fall to the floor.

Though I had not the slightest doubt that my queer state had been produced by Gurdjieff's influence, I was perfectly composed and determined to get out of it. I concentrated more and more on my conversation with the young man, and slowly the feeling inside seemed to melt away, and I began to feel normal again. After a couple of minutes I had definitely left Gurdjieff's 'magic circle'.

There are several explanations of my queer experience. It might have been a form of hypnosis or even auto-hypnosis which, for certain reasons, could affect only the lower half of my body without touching the brain and the emotional centre. But I doubt if it was either. It may have been a form of electric emanation such as Rasputin is said to have possessed in a high degree. This form of radiation seems to act even if its owner is hardly conscious of it, and it belongs to him almost in the way that certain odours belong to certain coloured races.

There may have been another reason for my strange experience. According to clairvoyant people, who have disciplined their gift to such an extent as to be able to use it with the fullest consciousness, a clairvoyant examination may produce effects similar to that which I had just experienced. Rudolf Steiner examined people occasionally in that way, the object of such an examination being to see the person's spiritual instead of his merely physical picture. But Steiner was always fully conscious of what such an examination entails. " The thought that a human being could be merely an object of observation," he said in one of his books, "must never for a moment be entertained. Self-education must see to it that this insight into human nature goes hand in hand with an unlimited respect for the personal privilege of each individual, and with the recognition of the sacred and inviolable nature of that which dwells in each human being."

Of course I could have protected myself against a 'clairvoyant examination'. Had I come to meet Gurdjieff in an open instead of a defensive state of mind he would probably not have succeeded in achieving whatever he was aiming at. No 'psychic' power is strong enough to affect a loving, human attitude, and there are other methods by which it is possible to protect oneself against an unwanted clairvoyant scrutiny.

When the feeling of nervousness and weakness in my legs had disappeared, I turned towards Gurdjieff. "I was told," I said, "that you had lately published a book. As to my knowledge you have never published anything before, everything I know about your ideas is secondhand. I should be grateful if you would tell me where I can buy your book."

My host got up, went to one of the black suitcases on the floor, took out of it a thin book, and came up to me. "Here it is, and, you know, no money can buy it. It is only for a few. But I present it to you. You find all in it you want."

I thanked him and went on: "I was told you were

preparing a large book that will contain all your teaching and your experience of many years."

He waved his hand as though the big book I mentioned meant nothing to him. "I writing nine books always, they thick so—so." He showed with his fingers that each one of these books was at least three or four inches thick.

"There seems to be a manuscript of one of your books in the possession of one of your former pupils in London. Is it one of the proposed nine volumes?"

Gurdjieff made a contemptuous gesture: "That nothing, just nothing. They all have my visions."

I looked enquiringly at the young man. "He means versions," he whispered.

"I always write three visions. Only last is for publication. No-one knows last one only myself. Others are here and there and here. They all have them, and then begin their own teaching on them. But that mean nothing. I have pupils all across the world, in all countries, groups are everywhere. In England alone fifteen, in fifteen cities. And all try to do new teaching on my teaching. Ach, but means nothing, just nothing." He snapped his fingers in a gesture of contempt.

"Is it true that you are preparing a group of disciples who will eventually become a sort of esoteric school, out of which your knowledge will radiate into the world?"

"You find everything in this book, everything." He pointed to the little volume in my hand. "Everything is there. No good you now speak to me. You not know me. You first read this book and then come to me.

Then we speak together. But now you not know what ask. First read this book, everything in it."

I understood that Gurdjieff had no wish to answer my question and that he considered the conversation finished. But I was determined to stay on for another few minutes and to see more of him. "Is Ouspensky's teaching in your opinion original or based on yours; and do you consider him the most important of all your former followers?" I continued as though I had not noticed his impatience.

"He just been one of my pupils, one of thousand, ten thousand." He again made one of his deprecatory movements with one hand. Whenever he made one of these gestures he looked the perfect Levantine: evasive in his answers, hyperbolical and anxious as to what effect he was producing. It may be that all the mannerisms and inconsistencies of his behaviour were parts of a method and that by employing such a system of "tricks" he was able to discern my "reactions" more clearly than he would otherwise have discerned them. Nevertheless I could not make myself believe that the pursuit of truth need ever require such a bewildering method of approach. Why should a man with great knowledge and experience require a technique of rudeness, of antagonizing his pupils, of constant evasiveness? Did not his knowledge suffice to "look" into me and to examine my "natural reactions" on a basis of ordinary human relationship? And yet some serious-minded people had been under his spell. He had treated some of them like slaves, and yet they had forsaken all their former beliefs and blindly followed him. His hypnotic powers, the physical attraction he must once have possessed, the fire in his eyes could not alone have produced such effects. Ouspensky had undoubtedly been right when he had told me that one had to separate the system represented by Gurdjieff from Gurdjieff the man.

Now that I had seen and apprehended Gurdjieff the man, I felt I could leave him. For once the original had been true to the accounts of him.

I got up, and Gurdjieff said: "You first read this book. It has everything, and then you come to me again. We then talk."

"When and where can I see you again?" I enquired.

"My office, Childs."

I looked up without understanding. The young man near the fireplace helped: "He means the Restaurant Childs in Fifth Avenue and 56th Street."

"I have three Childs, they all my office. Here I work in the morning. But evening my office Childs. You come and we then drink coffee together and speak more. I there every evening six to eight."

"Thank you, Mr. Gurdjieff. I shall certainly visit you there after I have read your book."

I went straight to my hotel, which was no distance away, and when I reached my room I became conscious of a strong desire to wash my hands. I washed them in very hot water for about five minutes, and then felt better, and sat down to record my strange experience.

* * *

The book that Gurdjieff had presented me with was bound in a most curious sort of paper: it resembled suede leather and yet gave a harshness to the touch that almost set one's teeth on edge. I felt that this binding was not chosen without a purpose. On its cover were the words:

G. GURDJIEFF
THE HERALD OF COMING GOOD

*First Appeal to
Contemporary Humanity*

Price from 8 to 108 French francs

Paris 1933

Inside the book there was a green registration blank with the number of my copy and a space for supplying such details as to whether it was "acquired accidentally or on advice," the sum paid, and name and address of the adviser. As I had been presented with my copy I escaped this procedure.

The book was an announcement of what Gurdjieff called, without undue modesty, "Coming Good." By this he meant the books that he was promising to place before the world in the near future. The little book was an amazing publication. It gave you in many instances the impression of the work of a man who was no longer sane. And yet it was impossible to sweep aside Gurdjieff's statements as the self-adulation of an insane mind. (Some of the statements quoted in the earlier pages of this chapter have been taken from *The Herald of Coming Good*.)

Gurdjieff here promises to disseminate the whole of his knowledge, which seems to include many esoteric secrets. He announces the publication of three series of books, comprising ten volumes, the title of the whole series to be "All and Everything." The first series will be called "An Objective Impartial Criticism of the Life of Man," and will contain such subjects as "The Cause of the Genesis of the Moon," "The Relativity of Time Conception," and "Hypnotism"; the second series will be called "Meetings with Remarkable Men"; the third will be "Life is real only when 'I am'." We are told that the original manuscript is written in "Russian and Armenian," and that "the first book of the first series is already being printed in the Russian, French, English and German colloquial languages," and that "translations are already being finished in the Armenian, Spanish, Turkish and Swedish languages." Only the three books of the first series will be universally accessible. The contents of the second series will be made known "by means of readings, open to those who have already a thorough knowledge of the contents of the first series." "Acquaintance with the contents of the third series is permitted only to those people who . . . have already begun to manifest themselves . . . in strict accordance with my indications," Gurdjieff explains, "set forth in the previous series of my writings."

The style itself exhibited the same signs of strangeness, amounting almost to insanity, that were manifest in the subject matter. Reading the *Herald* was like the progress of a cart over cobblestones. Most sentences ran on endlessly. The first sentence contained no fewer than two hundred and eighty-four words.

I was more interested in certain personal data than in the fantastic announcement of the coming books. Certain facts of that mysterious life were disclosed here for the first time, though hardly any of them was very clear. Gurdjieff admitted having spent some of his life in an Eastern monastery in order to acquire certain occult knowledge. "I decided one day," he says, "to abandon everything and to retire for a definite period into complete isolation . . . and to endeavour by means of active reflection . . . to think out some new ways for my fertile researches. This took place during my stay in Central Asia, when, thanks to the introduction to a street barber, whom I accidentally met . . . I happened to obtain access into a monastery well known among the followers of the Mohammedan religion." Gurdjieff admits that he also devoted himself to the study of "supernatural tricks", and he relates how he acquired the gift of hypnotism. "I began to collect all kinds of written literature and oral information still surviving among certain Asiatic peoples, about that branch of science, which was highly developed in ancient times, and called *mekheness*, the "taking away of responsibility," and of which contemporary civilization knows but an insignificant portion under the name of "hypnotism" . . . Collecting all I could, I went to a certain dervish monastery . . . in central Asia . . . and devoted myself wholly to the study of the material in my possession. After two years of thorough theoretical study . . . I began to give myself out to be a "healer" of all kinds of vices and to apply the results of my theoretical studies to them . . . This continued to be my exclusive preoccupation . . . for four or five years . . . I arrived at unprecedented practical results without equal in our day."

Gurdjieff discloses that both through nature and inheritance there had been in him a predisposition towards supernatural knowledge. "Great Nature," he writes in his pompous style, "had benevolently provided all my family and me in particular . . . with the highest degree of comprehension attainable by man . . . " From his earliest days Gurdjieff appears to have had access to a knowledge not open to most men, and this may be partly responsible for his belief in his own infallibility. "I had . . . ," he says, "the possibility of gaining access to the so-called "holy of holies" of nearly all hermetic organizations such as religious, philosophical, occult, political and mystic societies . . . which were inaccessible to the ordinary man . . . I had read almost everything existing about these questions . . . a literature accessible to me because of quite accidental circumstances of my life far beyond the usual possibilities of the ordinary man."

Speaking of his former possessions Gurdjieff says that he had accumulated enormous wealth. It is not disclosed by what means, but he states: "I began to liquidate my current affairs, which were dispersed over different countries in Asia, and collecting all the wealth which I had amassed during my long life . . . " This reference to a long life as far back as 1912 focuses our attention on the subject of Gurdjieff's age. In another place he speaks of having finished certain researches before the year 1892. Both these facts indicate that in 1933 he must have been at least seventy, this being the year of the publication of his book. And yet the man to whom I had spoken that afternoon seemed little more than fifty years old. His looks, his figure, his voice, everything about him suggested that age.

* * *

Though Gurdjieff had adherents in England and in France, most of his credulous followers were in America. I was surprised at the number of people there who had attended his classes or seen his dances. Often when I mentioned his name, someone would come forward and give me some dramatic account, illustrated by a personal experience. Though these accounts varied, though some of the speakers swore by Gurdjieff and others almost cursed him, though some considered that he possessed greater and deeper knowledge than anybody alive and others called him a charlatan and a madman, they all agreed that there was something powerful and uncanny about him. Stories were reported to me of people who had given Gurdjieff their whole fortunes in order to help him with his work, and of pupils who were unable to tear themselves away from his abuse. I have never heard the word "possessed" used so often in connection with any other teacher.

And yet there could be no doubt that the man who exercised such a strong influence over his pupils had ceased to be the power he once was. Evasiveness, contradiction and bluff—formerly the weapons in a most complicated system — seemed to have become part of Gurdjieff's very nature. When his mother died in 1925 at Fontainebleau Gurdjieff placed on her grave a huge tombstone with the fantastic inscription:

> *'Ici Repose*
> *La Mère de Celui*
> *Qui se Vit par*
> *Cette Mort Forcé*
> *D'Ecrire Le Livre*
> *Intitulé*
> *Les Opiumistes'*

("Here lies the mother of one who sees himself

forced by her death to write the book *Les Opiumistes."*)

Mme. Gurdjieff was well over eighty at the time of her death, her end was not unexpected and could have hardly been a great shock to her son. The book which he saw himself "forced" to write has never been heard of.

It suddenly occurred to me that there was among Gurdjieff's present pupils not one of those who had gathered round him in Russia before the war. This was indeed of utmost significance, and it showed, too, why in his early days those who knew him had nothing but praise for him, while the opinions of his later pupils were, to say the least, most conflicting.

It was not only in New York that I met people who had been in touch with Gurdjieff. I came across them in several smaller towns and, of course, in California, where every uncommon metaphysical theory finds adherents. There were groups of people who had once been instructed by Alfred Orage and who now tried to follow Gurdjieff's chaotic teaching. Even if people had no longer any contact with Gurdjieff, they would become intensely interested the moment I mentioned his name. His indomitable personality never failed to exercise a strange fascination even over people who had denounced him long ago.

* * *

I suspected that Gurdjieff had no intention of giving any precise answers to the questions I had put to him, even supposing I were to meet him again. I could not conceive how a conversation of any significance could be successful in the atmosphere of an eating place in Fifth Avenue, with all its noise and bustle. The presence of Gurdjieff's pupils, whom I did not know, would be of little help in such a conversation. Nevertheless I decided one evening to visit him at his restaurant.

The Greek was sitting at a table quite near the entrance. Dressed in a dark suit, he looked more commonplace than on the first occasion I had met him. He was smoking a cigarette and writing in a copybook in front of him. The page was covered with large, slightly unformed English calligraphy. On another page the writing looked rather exotic and I assumed that it was Armenian. Gurdjieff did not recognize me at first, and I had to stoop down to him and explain who I was. After a few seconds he remembered me and asked me to sit down next to him. One of his pupils was with him.

I tried from the very first to ask Gurdjieff precise questions about his teaching. This would save time, and it would reduce the possibility of evasive answers. But I had hardly finished speaking when he got up and walked over to a lady who must have been standing there for some time, anxious to catch Gurdjieff's eye. In her face there was the same expression that I had seen in the face of the disciple during my first interview. When Gurdjieff had returned to our table I made another attempt to talk to him, but this time we were forestalled by a middle-aged man who came up to us. It was another of Gurdjieff's pupils. We exchanged names and the man sat down. Meanwhile Gurdjieff ordered coffee with lemon. This seemed to me a strange drink, but the waitress must have been used to the order, for she showed no signs of surprise, and returned with the drink a few minutes later. Gurdjieff squeezed out the juice of the lemon into the black coffee, and then dropped the lemon into the cup.

Within ten minutes several other pupils arrived, and our party now occupied three or four tables in a row. Gurdjieff was for ever getting up, walking towards the door, and talking to people who were coming and going. It was impossible to begin a connected conversation. Nevertheless I had a more favourable impression of him than at my first visit. He seemed simpler and less sinister. I noticed now for the first time a certain human quality in him. Even his English seemed better, and I began to suspect that its inferior quality during my first interview had been partly assumed. Had it been a part of Gurdjieff's method of provoking "genuine reactions"? I limited myself after a while to questions about his plans with regard to his new school, to the publication of his books or to other details of his work. But even so he remained evasive, and I could not record a single definite answer.

During one of his frequent absences from the table I began a conversation with the gentleman opposite me. He seemed Gurdjieff's main assistant, and I noticed that the questions I had been asking his master were making him uncomfortable. Eventually he expressed his anxiety: "I am afraid you have chosen a wrong method of questioning Mr. Gurdjieff. By asking him in such a direct and precise way you almost force him to answer yes or no. He is not used to that, and he does not care for such a form of conversation. Anyhow, I don't think you'll succeed very much. You ask him in a conversation of twenty minutes questions for the answers to which many of us have been waiting for a great many years. None of us dares to put to him such questions."

I thanked him for the information and decided that it would not indeed be of much avail to remain here any longer. As I was leaving for England in a few days' time, and had no chance of following the method of the disciples, it seemed that I should have to depart without receiving answers to my questions—but the frightened faces of the eight or ten people sitting round, and the hushed atmosphere the moment Gurdjieff addressed any of them, had been more explicit than any conversation could have been.

Gurdjieff's pupils did not try to disguise their feelings towards me. They probably considered me an intruder, and my presence was anything but welcome When they had met me at the beginning of the evening they had cast inquisitive glances in my direction as though fearing that a new disciple had arrived, upon whom their master might waste some of those favours that had hitherto been bestowed exclusively upon them. Once they were reassured that I was not a disciple, they seemed to feed their antagonism on my attitude towards Gurdjieff. They probably expected me to worship their hero, and were deeply offended at my failure to do so. Not one of them had given me even the conventional smile generally offered to a newcomer. Not one of them asked me the habitual questions which are put to break the ice, and they avoided helping me when they noticed my occasional difficulties in understanding Gurdjieff's English. It may be that their antagonistic reserve was affected by the presence of their master, under whose influence they were unable to show common politeness to a stranger. There was no doubt: I had overstayed my welcome, and I rose to go. No-one tried to persuade me to stay on, and even Gurdjieff did not utter a word of encouragement. I thanked him, bowed to the assembled company, and walked out into the bracing air of an autumn evening in New York.

* * *

When I arrived back in London I went to one of Gurdjieff's former followers in Europe. He was a fairly intelligent man, and earlier in the year I had had some interesting conversations with him about Gurdjieff. I told him of my experience in New York.

"Your account," he replied "does not surprise me. I have often heard stories like that. Even to me certain things about Gurdjieff were always as inexplicable as they must be to anybody unaccustomed to his wanton methods. And yet he has brought me—and many other people—nearer to truth than anybody else. Mind, emotions and body are no longer antagonistic. Though it is true that many of the things Gurdjieff does and says seem meaningless, yet while you are in the midst of your work, he will say something to you that will give you the answer to questions you have been long pondering. His sense of your problem of the moment and his knowledge of the moment at which you are ripe for the answer are uncanny. At times we had to wait for years, and it was as though Gurdjieff knew exactly how many doubts we had to conquer before we were ready for his answers. You would be wrong to judge his conduct according to ordinary human standards. There seems a richness within Gurdjieff which allows him to do things that would be wrong for your own limited selves. In a way he reminds me of the god Siva."

"The god Siva ?" I interrupted with surprise.

"Yes, Siva, the destroyer-god of the god-trinity, the god of many functions, the lord of the spirits of music —and, don't forget, the god of dancing."

This conversation only renewed and strengthened my conviction that the very teacher who may be of great help to one person may utterly fail to disclose himself to another. Even in the more recent years Gurdjieff's methods seemed to have been of some assistance to various people. Others were enlightened— where I was merely puzzled.

I could dimly discern that the essence of Gurdjieff's teaching contains a truth that everyone in contact with spiritual reality is bound to preach. But I failed utterly to accept his methods in that spirit of trust, of faith or of understanding, any one of which is essential for the absorption of spiritual knowledge. Sometimes the personality of a teacher is more impressive than his teaching—at other times the reverse is the case. If I found it impossible to accept Gurdjieff and to let him help me in moulding myself, it was because his personality, however strong, failed utterly to convince me. I had been unable to perceive in the man George Ivanovitch Gurdjieff the harmonious development of man.

Just as the manuscript of this book was going to the printers I received the following letter:—

Fifth Avenue House,
New York City.

Captain Achmed Abdullah
Sunday.

Dear Sir,

As to Gurdjieff, I have no way of proving that I am right—except that I know I am right.

When I knew him, thirty years ago, in Tibet, he was, besides being the young Dalai Lama's chief tutor, the main Russian political agent for Tibet. A Russian Buriat by race and a Buddhist by religion, his learning was enormous, his influence in Lhasa very great, since he collected the tribute of the Baikal Tartars for the Dalai Lama's exchequer, and he was given the high title of *Tsannyis Khan-po*. In Russia he was known as Hambro Akvan Dorzhieff; to the British Intelligence as Lama Dorjieff. When we invaded Tibet, he disappeared with the Dalai in the general direction of outer Mongolia. He spoke Russian, Tibetan, Tartar, Tadjik, Chinese, Greek, strongly accented French and rather fantastic English. As to his age—well—I would say ageless. A great man who, though he dabbled in Russian imperialistic politics, did so—I have an idea—more or less in the spirit of jest.

I met Gurdjieff, almost thirty years later, at dinner in the house of a mutual friend, John O'Hara Cosgrave, former editor of the New York World, in New York. I was convinced that he was Lama Dorjieff. I told him so—and he winked. We spoke in Tadjik.

I am a fairly wise man. But I wish I knew the things which Gurdjieff has forgotten.

Very faithfully,

A. ABDULLAH

62   GURDJIEFF

Postscript to Chapter 2

This is the end of Rom Landau's story. I think I can be certain that Gurdjieff played the part in Tibet that Captain Abdullah speaks about, but a great deal more information has been given to me about his political activities. Some are hard to describe, others seem fantastic. Here are the strangest. I will content myself with transcribing them without troubling to make up my mind whether I believe in them or not.

Gurdjieff has always refused to give the names of his companions who formed the group called "The Searchers After Truth," and explored the heights of primordial tradition; but those who have reason to know, assure me that one at least of these friends is known: his name is Karl Haushofer. He was later to found the "Géopolitique" and become one of the most important ideologists of the Third Reich. One finds traces of him in Tibet with Gurdjieff in 1903, and again in 1905, 1906, 1907 and 1908. Between 1907 and 1910 he lived in Japan. My informants also affirm that Gurdjieff never lost touch with Haushofer, and was responsible for introducing him, as Hitler's representative in the White Russian colony in France, to the dancer Gitkoff, reported missing since 1945. It was Gurdjieff who advised Haushofer to choose as emblem the inverted swastika.

In 1923 Haushofer founded an esoteric group modelled on similar groups in Tibet. This was at the time that Gurdjieff was settling in France. Haushofer's assistant was Dr. Morrel, who was later to become Hitler's personal physician and who, that same year, introduced into the group the future leader of Germany and his friend Himmler. The group was called the

"Thule Group" and its philosophy was founded on the famous book of magic of the Dzyan, which belonged to certain Tibetan sages; according to this book there are two sources of power in the world: the right-hand source, which comes from a subterranean monastery, a fortress of meditation, situated in a town called, symbolically, Agharti. This is the source of contemplative power. The left-hand source is the source of physical power, and comes from a town on the surface called Shampullah. This is the city of violence and is ruled by the "King of Fear." Those who succeed in making an alliance with him can dominate the world.

Through a large Tibetan colony in Berlin which kept constantly in touch with Haushofer, the "Thule Group" formed this "alliance" in 1928, and it was on this occasion that the inverted swastika was adopted. The following men were members of the Group at this time:— Hitler, Himmler, Goering, Rosemberg and Dr. Morrel, under Haushofer's direction. The members of the Group communicated in two ways with Shampullah and the "King of Fear" (symbolic names, of course): firstly, by electronic transmitters and receivers which put them in contact with a so-called "Tibetan" information centre through which they obtained valuable comments on India and Japan; secondly, by a kind of "game" which they played very often. Here are the details. The "authorities", through Haushofer, gave them a simple numerical code related to the letters of the alphabet. They then set out an equation which enabled them to re-arrange the figures according to variable parameters. Finally, to fix the parameters they drew lots from a kind of Tibetan tarot pack; the cards are round and engraved on a light, semi-transparent wood. This was the " game " played regularly between 1928 and 1941, or even later, by some of the leading men of the Third Reich. It seems that there are genuine documents in evidence of this. Some of my informants say they are prepared to confirm it publicly (one of them occupies an important position in the scientific world). They affirm that it was through this game that Hitler learnt that Roosevelt was about to die, and the exact date of his death, and further that he interpreted this " sign " as being beneficial for a thousand years. Hence his mysterious and rather baffling speech on the death of the President.

They affirm, too, that one of the conditions of the pact made between the " Thule Group " and the Tibetan " authorities " was the extermination of Gypsies. This extermination, never justified in documents or speeches, was carried out with extraordinary violence by Hitler and Himmler, who pestered the heads of the " Death Camps " to carry out wholesale executions. According to the most likely figures, seven hundred and fifty thousand Gypsies perished. Let me add that at the time that the Russians overran Berlin and directly after Hitler's suicide, fifteen hundred Tibetans and Hindus appeared in arms in the town and got themselves killed.

Finally, it seems certain that Stalin knew about the " Thule Group." (He had been a fellow-student of Gurdjieff's in the Seminary at Alexandropol). He declared in council that he felt it to be " inconceivable that, in the Twentieth Century, heads of States should indulge in such devilries."

At the moment of drafting this postscript the weekly French communist paper *Les Lettres Françaises* (of December 3rd, 1953) publishes two sonnets found on the body of Haushofer's son, assassinated in 1945 by the S.S. in the Moabit prison where he was detained for having taken part in the plot against Hitler. His father, Karl Haushofer, killed himself " officially " a few days after the son's arrest, but on this point we have no certainty. One of the son's sonnets struck me forcibly, after I had gathered all this information. Here it is:—

> *A profound legend of the East*
> *Tells us that the spirits of the power of evil*
> *Are held captive in the Marine night,*
> *Sealed by the prudent hand of God.*
> *Until fate, once in a thousand years*
> *Accords a single fisherman the power*
> *To break the chains of the prisoners*
> *If he doesn't at once throw back his catch into the sea.*
> *For my father, destiny had spoken.*
> *His will had lost the strength*
> *To push the demon back into its jail.*
> *My father broke the seal,*
> *He did not feel the Devil's breath,*
> *He let the demon loose on the world.*

IDIOTS' PASTURE

3

Have You Known A Man?

As I have said before, I have no intention of making a study of Gurdjieff's personality nor of presenting and commenting upon the whole of his doctrine. I only want to make plain the effects produced on the people who undertook this "teaching," and I think that my best plan will be to gather together some witnesses. I have, however, felt it necessary to make a rough sketch of Gurdjieff himself, but have outlined my portrait as lightly as possible. At the same time, before embarking upon my real subject I ought to indicate the main lines of the "teaching." This I shall do as carefully as I can.

Gurdjieff was—and still is—acknowledged by many people of sound judgment to be the possessor of various secrets relating to material and spiritual life, to the laws of the cosmos, etc. Perhaps he had acquired the "primary and absolute" knowledge that the "traditionalists" speak of, notably René Guènon.

Ouspensky lets this be understood and in his *Fragments of an Unknown Teaching* he gives a great deal of space to the exposition of theorems that are deduced from these secrets, and that give him the clue to a tremendously satisfying explanation of the Universe. I must not allow myself to write about this aspect of Gurdjieff's teaching because it has no bearing at all on the experiences of most of the disciples. Our experience was on quite a different level, on the level of psychology (I mean of course a very different kind of psychology from that practised to-day in the West). We were supposed to study ourselves; this was quite enough and would certainly last for years. We heard nothing of the theories, and even if we had, we knew that we must not allow ourselves to fall into the trap of imagining that they would be of any good to us at the moment. Nothing was any good to us yet—we had to wait for the future, the far-distant future. " We will see about that when you are bigger: when chickens have teeth and mermaids have legs"—when, that is to say, we had accomplished the miracle of struggling out of sleep, out of unconsciousness, out of the dispersed state that we are in at present and have only just begun to recognize. No—the things we heard were apparently very simple reflections on our every-day behaviour. This comprised the "teaching" as far as we were concerned, and Ouspensky was floating up in the clouds with his *Law of Three,* his *Principles of the Octave* and his *Table of Hydrogens.* If I keep to my original intention then, I shall only report the words that inspired our efforts and were responsible for our adventures as beginners. They were very simple words but one should not be deceived by this simplicity. Simplicity presupposes either extreme laziness or genius and there is only a hair's breadth between a truism and an overwhelming truth. It seemed to us that we were hearing overwhelming truths; however, when we tried to put them into words ourselves, for the sake of enlightening a friend or in order to shine in society, these truths turned out to be painfully obvious remarks. It is the old story of the roses changed into toads when plucked by the wicked—as soon as we uttered one of these illuminating words it lost its radiance.

As I knew only beginners, I can write about the "teaching" only in so far as it applied to beginners, that is to say to fools. Gurdjieff spoke this word with a mixture of scorn and kindness hard to describe. In the fool's pasture every harvest is disappointing, and when I tell you the things that we were told, these words, that for us were overwhelming truths, for you will appear to be platitudes. However, honesty demands that I confine myself to this harvest, and I shall therefore describe the main themes of the "teaching" as they impressed themselves on the minds of the elementary pupils and as they remain in my memory.

Ask your friends a simple question—"Have you ever known a man?" Be careful not to make any comment. Your question will be understood and a great effort made to answer it. Have I known a man? As soon as the question is asked, categories fade out of the mind and no need is felt for explanations. A man of social position? Cultured? Courageous? Intelligent? These distinctions suddenly lose their meaning (if the question has been asked authoritatively, and at a time when the mind of the hearer is receptive to the shock). Moreover—the distinctions appear ridiculous. I would be ashamed to have it thought that I attach any importance to them. I keep silent and think. I begin to measure the distance that separates *me* from a *man*. I do not really know what a man is but I have a blinding certainty that such a thing exists. He has weight, density, steadfastness and a radiance that I have not. Naturally I do not put this into words—I simply try to think. This all happens as though I were holding out my hand amongst a crowd of people that surge up in my memory, weighing those I have known one by one until the happy moment when I discover and recognize the one who makes the weight.

If you gather your friends' answers together you will have names and descriptions. Find out then what these men have in common. Never mind about their class or their profession, etc., the common denominator is elsewhere. You will often have heard—" He's isn't perhaps quite a man but . . ." and you will have noticed in passing this sudden and extraordinary illumination, this almost God-like assurance in weighing people up. You will be struck by the fact that all those questioned, whatever their education, trade, religion, philosophy, or political party, seem to know what is meant as soon as they are asked to describe a *man*:

" He had a beautiful expression, or rather one felt that he was responsible for his expression and this gave an impression of beauty. One felt that he could rely on himself in all circumstances."

" Everything he did really came from the man himself. We are very rarely master of our actions. It is they that order us. We do not *do*—things happen through us, but with him his actions were his own."

" He had adopted rules but he did not depend on them. He watched himself submit to them as one watches an engine to see that it is running properly. He was able to observe and to control himself from outside. He was free."

"He was always clear-sighted. He regarded things, himself and others always from a certain distance."

"He had will-power, but that is not saying much. He had the will to will and this faculty never varied in intensity."

"He was compact and solid. The quality of being can range from that of sponge to that of granite, and his made one think of granite."

"His energy was not the ability to be violently activated from the outside. It was a substance that he had accumulated within himself and that he could use as he pleased."

"Neither imagination nor fear had any hold on him."

"His words did not betray him; he did not waste his energies through idle speech."

"He was his real self in everything he thought, said, felt or did. He was there, the man himself, not his shadow."

"On seeing him one had the feeling that it is important to be alive."

You will quickly understand these approximations. They lift a veil from an almost supernatural idea of man that we nearly all of us have in our hearts. This is where Gurdjieff's teaching begins.

4

Which You Would You Change?

I would have liked very much to become someone of whom it could be said: "This is a man." I think I have always been painfully aware of not being a *man*. It was not that I felt myself lacking in will-power, intellect, talents, vital energy or capacity for feeling, nor that I felt unfortunate in the common meaning of the word. I felt I might become a "worth-while person" by following my own bent, as long as it led me upwards, as André Gide used to say. But, as I told myself, to be a worth-while person is not necessarily to be a *man*. There was I, surrounded by good, sincere Catholics, fervent revolutionaries, great intellectuals and potent creators, and all the time I was searching with a dull anxiety for a *man*, and not finding one. When I looked into myself I could not find one either. I did not quite understand what my desire was, but it cut me off from life and put me out of reach of its joys and troubles. I was as though dismembered by it and it made me see myself and others as without the power of being *men*. Bernanos wrote that there is only one thing that causes pain—not being a saint. This moved me, but I could not grasp clearly what a saint is. I searched amongst descriptions of saints but the descriptions were all of their moral virtues and I told myself that possibly moral perfections have very little to do with saintliness. I thought that saintliness is primarily a change of state, the change from a state of being an ordinary man to that of being a *man*, but nowhere could I find an account of this transition, of this journey. No-one could tell me how to obtain a ticket nor what happens on the journey—and it was this that I wanted so much to know. When I enquired a little deeper, the only explanation I was given was that I must *first of all* have faith. But I felt certain at that time that the pain of *not being* was faith — not faith in any particular creed, the choice of which seemed to me to depend on countless slight differences of feeling, education, race, etc., but the true faith of human kind. That is what my trouble was, this dull and nameless ache. I was told also of rules that had to be accepted, of monasteries, etc., but I felt strongly that if I experienced this ache by virtue of my humanity I should be able to pass from ordinary man to *man* in the common condition of mankind. So I used to reply that the way must lie in the heart of human life, in the heart of my own life, in expansion and not in suppression.

I felt there must be something in common between a Catholic Saint such as St. Bernard, a great Yogi such as Ramakrishna, a great poet such as Rimbaud and, on a different scale, the kind of person we confusedly call a *man*, (when our minds are for a moment half-opened) and that it was this something in common that I was searching for, that I had to find if I was to escape from my troubled state and from this demand that welled up in me with a strength and a persistence that I was bound to attribute to mankind as a whole.

I said to myself, there must be some simple trick to fit all conditions of life. I had a strong feeling against following the way of monks and yogis. I was not able to follow the way of the inspired poets as I knew I did not inhabit their world. My nature inclined me, rather, to follow the way of ordinary people, and that is why, to *force destiny*, I had written a book in which a man like you or me had changed his state without even wishing to do so. He suddenly found himself in possession of the trick and very surprised at what was happening to him, without his having taken any action. But I had taken my precautions: he produced nothing but emptiness around him and begot nothing but misfortune and death. I wanted an answer, and for this had sacrificed much of my vitality, that is to say, the characters in my book and all the emotional richness of my first twenty-five years. This book, for obvious reasons, was called *Saint Somebody*. In actual fact I *did* receive an answer; it was because of this book that Gurdjieff came and carried me off with him. For the fact is that one did not go to Gurdjieff, he came and sought one out when one had done something to force an answer. I had done this in my own way, by writing. But there are of course many other ways, all equally good.

What struck me, then, was the fact that there seemed to be no system for progressing from ordinary man to *man*. Try as I might I could find no way, and nothing seemed capable of causing a change of state in me, neither morals, religion, political parties, nor any of the opportunities afforded by history (and there were many for a boy of my age — twenty in 1940).

There were many ways of progressing from the ordinary man that I was already to a better made and better armed ordinary man, but that was all and that did not interest me very much. That is why I did not feel able to take part whole-heartedly in the activities of the world, nor to join any particular party, movement or religion. Neither was I in sympathy with the world's ideas and forms of thought. I did not feel very close to the men of my time and this made me very ill at ease in all situations and circumstances. My pride and sensibility were fruitlessly hurt by this discomfort and I began to rot rather than to ripen.

All this came to me, of course, in a confusion of disgust, revolt, loneliness, unadaptability, superiority and guilt. I had no clear thoughts about it but found myself languishing in an atmosphere of anxiety faintly illuminated by words such as: "*I* is another," "One must refuse to play a game in which everybody cheats."

Now the first sentence in the "teaching" that threw a little light for me and put some sort of order into my thoughts was this:

"Men, with very rare exceptions, are not completed beings." We are rough drafts of men, not men, and there is no straight-forward path from one state to the other. There is no kind of knowledge or effort on our part, neither psychology, the Churches nor anything else, that can help us to pass from prototype to completed man. We assume that adult man is in possession of all the necessary faculties for fulfilling his destiny if the wolf (that is to say — war, social injustice, etc.) does not get him. This is the view on which our present morals, philosophies and politics are based. It is the progressives' view, and very far from the truth. With all that nature has bestowed on us and all the benefits of civilization, we can at most hope to fulfil our destinies as prototypes, but that is far from fulfilling them as men.

There are very attractive and intelligent prototypes who do nicely in the end; they are the people we call " exemplary " and " superior "—but that is nothing. Nature creates men up to a certain point and then abandons them. It may even be that part of her work consists in lulling them into a state of self-satisfaction and preventing them from becoming aware of their unfinished condition.

The organs and faculties proper to a real man are, naturally, in us still in an embryonic stage, and we cannot develop these organs and faculties by ordinary means. No doubt we can proceed from bad to less bad by ordinary means, from a rough draft to a finished sketch, but not from less bad to good—not from a sketch to a man. It is not a question of refining but of changing. We can do nothing by following our own nature, which was not given to us to be polished; but this is the temptation of those above a certain level. If we spend our time polishing ourselves (by acquiring Christian " virtues," developing our personality, etc.) we end by falling asleep. In the same way a sculptor who spends years in working on a sketch, may become fascinated and forget that he meant to turn the sketch into a statue, that he meant to effect a change of state. Our nature was given to us to fight *against*, or rather in order that we should convert it into something else, something as different as a marble goddess is from a trivial pottery figure. This is the inner meaning of those trite words—" Life is a trial," that Gurdjieff re-stated in the words: " To be is to be different."

First of all one had to make a clean sweep of the concepts of psychology which in any case faded out when the question was asked: " Where is your fixed point ? " Neither academic nor popular psychology takes any account of this question. Search as one may, a fixed point can never be found in one's confounded self—always shifting, always crumbling, and blown here and there like leaves in the wind. Where is my fixed point ? In the end I found that my only fixed point was my great desire to change, but even this was not stable, it came and it went again. Honestly, I could not answer, and the question emphasized my lack of reality.

Yes, they used to say, you want to change, but *who* in you wants to change ? In order to change there must be something steadfast in you that steadily wants to change. Where is this something ? I was ashamed—I lacked this something. I realized that I had not even a name. Sometimes it was one Pauwels that wanted to change and sometimes another, and I saw that I had hundreds of Pauwels, some contented with their lot, others very anxious to make this journey, some enthusiastic, others recalcitrant. I could not say: Pauwels wants to change, because I did not really own my name. In other words I had hundreds of me's but not one Me with a capital M. Without a Me how can one have a name ? When I saw my name in print, on a book in the library or in a newspaper, I always had the uneasy feeling of being an impostor. I still do, and I cannot help thinking that most men who enjoy seeing their names in print and who can pronounce their own names in public without a qualm, are in some way insensitive.

I saw that I had to revise my ideas of psychology. From this business of the fixed point and "*who* in you wants to change?" I was led to see clearly that we believe, mistakenly, that we are studying man when all we are really doing is to define, quite uselessly, the ways in which we avoid the work of trying to become men. I understood at last that my "I" does not exist, or rather that it is dough, kneaded together with thoughts, feelings and moods, over which it has no control, for how can dough control the baker's hands? I was never the same person, always many different ones. Everyone of my thoughts, moods, desires and ambitions and all my memories, called themselves Pauwels, and every time I believed it to be the whole of Pauwels. But where is this whole Pauwels? I was made to see hundreds of separate little ones who either ignored each other, or were hostile. Where did this hostility come from? I did not know, but I felt that there were laws and influences playing from outside, as the wind plays with leaves, and that the figures of their dance depended on chance associations of ideas—a meeting, heat or cold, a glass of wine or a book. And now, just as I had found people who believed they knew the secret of how to effect a change, I discovered that in order to change I must know myself, and this seemed to be hopeless. It is true that I had some little "me's" stronger than others. It is thanks to them that I believed myself to be Pauwels, because they appeared, disappeared and re-appeared in groups on different unpredictable occasions—in some weathers and nervous conditions, or in certain atmospheres I came to realize, too, that these little "me's" that were stronger than the others and that forced themselves on my semi-consciousness, had no doubt only arisen through accidental events in my life, and appeared in circumstances that were independent of my own will. This Pauwels that was more of a Pauwels than the others, was still not a whole Pauwels. I saw at last that each one of these little " me's " when it finally came to the surface, after obscure interactions which took place outside my consciousness, claimed the right to call itself Pauwels and to act and speak for them all. For instance, an angry " me " took possession of my whole self. If I made a scene with the woman I loved and thus tortured a love that other " me's " felt with tenderness and serenity, the angry "me" spoke and spoiled everything in the name of them all. In that instant I would identify myself with the one " me " that came to the surface, heaven knows why, and in this way would involve all the other innocent " me's." Then another " me " would come uppermost, and again I would identify myself completely with it; a "me," for instance, that would give a solemn promise that Pauwels would drink no more alcohol — either for health reasons, or out of vanity or simply to appear interesting. Soon this " me " would disappear, and ten others, who had not been consulted, would re-appear in all innocence, with a great need of alcohol and many excellent reasons and excuses for taking it, and I would find myself in a painful state of embarrassment and remorse, and have to re-pay in shame what I had been let in for by the fleeting " me " who was afraid of liver-trouble or who wanted to show off his strong-minded temperance. It is our tragedy that any little " me " has the power to sign agreements that afterwards have to be faced by the whole man (if he exists). Think of your love-life and then consider this tragedy. Whole lives may be wasted in paying off debts contracted by accidental little "me's."

This was enough to make me realize that ordinary man cannot *do*. He does nothing, "it happens" through him, and what we call psychology prevents us from knowing the truth, which is impersonal and formless. It is possible that I have in me the seeds of the ability to *do* and to *be,* and no doubt there are ways of growing from seed to fruit. We shall see later. In the meantime I was despairingly convinced of the truth of what I had been told. I regarded myself coldly in any case, but after all that I had heard, to which I listened with a grim concentration, my self-regard became still colder. I felt, however, that once the interview was over and the door shut behind me, this coldness might vanish. One's self-regard has a horror of cold and in a few minutes is likely to warm up again. I persuaded myself in a very short time that the words I had heard were commonplace and on the level of ordinary language. The picture that had been painted now appeared harmless and I feared that it would probably take months of effort to retain these words in the light of their dangerous and overwhelming novelty. For this reason alone it was essential that I should join a group of people who, in well defined conditions, were attempting to develop and maintain a special quality of attention.

I was now about to discover that I possessed neither consciousness nor will, but this is another story, as Kipling says, who threw off so lightly that famous poem "If."

5

Are You Ever Awake?

At the beginning of my novel *Saint Somebody*, the poor hero, Jousselin, has just had a shock. His wife discovered that morning that he had deceived her and this leads to a rather stupid and sordid catastrophe. He is numbed by the shock; he wraps himself in cotton-wool and withdraws from the outside world. His inner reactions cease, all his perceptions reach him as though muffled by gloves. He is fixed as he was at the moment that his wife discovered his mistress's letter. Nothing stirs in his inner world. He sails a leaden sea in a dead calm. After the climax of the drama, as he is walking through the suburbs of the town where he lives. (Saint Yvette in the book, but in reality Athis-Mons where I lived as a young man) he says: " I like the path to the Town Hall. In the afternoon it smelt of hot dust and dried grass, burning in the silence of the heat of the day. A little further on, on the right, were meadows sloping down to the Seine, and on the left ran the dazzling white wall of a school, that scorched my face as I passed. I imagined a leafy coolness behind the wall, thick mosses, old oaks and strains of a harmonium coming from the deepest shade.

". . . I say this because, as I walked, I suddenly knew that I would never forget this moment, that it would remain forever in a recess of my mind. Not that there was anything very special about it; but sometimes one can catch oneself creating a vivid memory out of almost nothing."

I have not quoted this passage for the beauty of its style, as you can well imagine, but because what it expresses had now become very important to me. As I lived " poetically," I had always noticed that one could " catch oneself creating a vivid memory out of almost nothing." I know for certain that some particular instant will fix itself and live in my memory, complete and forever, and that is what happens. It may not be a particularly important moment, the moment for instance of my mother's death, my wedding day, the day I gave up teaching to throw myself into journalism or the time when the Germans found me, etc. It is hardly ever a moment that has " counted " in my destiny, or one that it would have been useful to remember in trying to summarize my life or to explain its unfolding. Who can tell me the meaning of these moments that will always be with me in their completeness ? Who can explain why it should be these and not others ?

Now, I was being taught that I have two memories, a true and a false, and that these inexplicably eternal moments belong to the true. The false memory is the one we use nearly all the time: I remember that such a thing happened, that it rained on my wedding day, for instance. I know this, but I have to call up the memory to live through it again and, moreover, I have to make an effort. Whereas these other moments, the time when I picked a branch of viburnum on the banks of the River Onge, the moment when, crouching in the sand at the end of the park in Athis I put a beetle into a jar, the moment when my hand brushed the rabbit-skin coat of a blonde in a passage in the printing-office — these moments without any apparent significance can be re-awakened in me in all their fullness by the slightest shock and without my having to make any effort. They live in me complete, in my head, nerves and body, and will always have the power to suspend time and to arrest me, fascinated, on the threshold of eternity.

It is probably these memories, and not the others, that pass before our eyes at the moment of death, and the well-known phenomenon of the dying " re-living their whole lives in a flash " is perhaps the flow of true memory. They re-live the moments that were outside time, before they themselves enter eternity.

I was being taught that we are hardly ever conscious, and that real memory is linked to real consciousness. Sometimes, by chance and in spite of ourselves, real consciousness comes to the surface and then at once the world around us takes on a solidity, a smell and a flavour unknown before, and our memory fixes this forever ; or rather, perhaps, we should say that in the rare moments when we are in a state of real consciousness, what happens to us happens forever, and we escape from time when we live these eternal moments. This is why, with our last breath, when our consciousness is at last fully aware of itself, these special privileged moments pass through our minds and appear finally in their true colours as the only landmarks in our lives and the only good that we have managed to acquire in so many days and hours.

I now had to learn that our real consciousness only awakens very rarely and for very brief moments, and that ordinary man has no control over it. From now on it was a question of trying to pass as often as possible and for as long as possible from an ordinary state to a state of consciousness. First of all I had to have a clear definition and demonstration of consciousness which it seemed to me that I succeeded in obtaining.

In the language of the teaching, the word " consciousness " is almost always used in the sense of intelligence, that is to say, mental activity. Occasionally it is used to express moral virtue for instance — "Mr. So-and-So has a high or beautiful consciousness," or else one supposes that a consciousness can be good or bad according to the acts or thoughts it produces. Finally, it can mean " states of consciousness," that is to say groups of thoughts, feelings, impulses and sensations.

We learnt that consciousness is not an attribute of man, but a state, and that this state, while extremely difficult to attain, is altogether independent of the mind's activities, or moral attitudes and of the various manifestations of the psyche. Neither " states of consciousness " as usually understood nor the workings of the intelligence, nor the weighing up of good and evil, have anything to do with the real " *state of consciousness.*"

Thus, psychology is the study of man *without taking into account whether or not he has attained a state of consciousness,* whereas our principal study was the study of the transition to this state. That is why we had to make a clean sweep of " psychology." The analysis of man had to be made with a fresh eye. What was this new " state of consciousness " ? This is where the Gurdjieff experience really began.

We were told to take a watch and to look at the big hand *while at the same time holding on to the idea of oneself* and concentrating on the thought " I am Louis Pauwels and I am here at this moment." Simply follow the movement of the big hand, we were told, while trying to think only of yourself, of your name, of your existence and of where you are.

At first this seems easy and even slightly ridiculous ; of course I can keep in my mind the idea that I am called Louis Pauwels and that I am here at this moment, watching the slow movement of the large hand of my watch. But soon I have to admit that this idea does not remain motionless for long in my head, that it takes on many different shapes and flows in all directions, like the objects that Dali painted. Then again I must realize that it is not an idea that I am being asked to keep alive and fixed in my mind, but a perception ; I am not being asked merely to think that I exist, but to know it in full consciousness. Now, I feel that it is possible that this *could* take place in me, and so bring me something new and important ; but I understand, as soon as I think about it, that everything happens as though our nature, when faced with an exercise such as this, turns against us and does its best to prevent the birth in us of this something new and important. I discover that hundreds of thoughts or shadows of thoughts assail me continually, hundreds of sensations, ideas and associations of ideas that have nothing to do with my aim and that distract me from my effort. Sometimes it is my watch-hand that attracts all my attention and in looking at it I lose sight of myself; sometimes it is my body, a cramp in the leg or a movement in the stomach, that distracts me from the hand and also from myself. Sometimes I believe I have succeeded in stopping my inner film show and in eliminating the outside world, but then I find that I have been plunged into a kind of torpor in which the hand, myself and everything else has disappeared. In this state the images, feelings and ideas continue to weave themselves together but as though behind a veil, or in a dream that goes on by itself while I sleep. Sometimes, at last, for a fraction of a second, *I am looking at the hand and I am myself,* totally and completely; but in the same fraction of a second I congratulate myself, my mind applauds its success and in so doing irreparably impairs it. In the end, upset and very exhausted, I tear myself away from the experiment and I feel that I have just been through the most difficult minutes of my life and endured the most gruelling test. How long it seemed! It was in fact not much more than two minutes, and in those two minutes I was only really conscious of myself for three or four almost imperceptible flashes.

I had to admit now that we are hardly ever conscious of ourselves, and hardly ever aware of the difficulty of being conscious.

A state of consciousness to begin with is, we were told, the state of a man who knows that he is hardly ever conscious and who therefore can find out, little by little, what obstacles in himself prevent him from making the required effort. By the light of this little exercise I knew now that a man can, for instance, read a book, and be bored or enthralled by it without for one second being conscious of the fact that he *is*, and therefore without his reading making any real impression. His reading is just a dream added to his other dreams, a flow in the continual flow of the unconscious. Our real consciousness can be, and nearly always is, completely absent from everything we do, think, want or imagine.

I understood then that there is very little difference between our state when asleep and our normal waking state, in which we speak and act, etc. Our dreams have become invisible, like the stars when the sun rises, but they are still there and we continue to live under their influence. All that we gain, when awake, is a critical attitude in the place of mere sensations, better co-ordinated thoughts and actions and livelier impressions, feelings and desires, but we are still in a state of unconsciousness. It is not a matter of a real awakening but of a " waking sleep," and it is in this " waking sleep " that almost the whole of our lives are lived. They taught us that it is possible to wake up completely and that in this state of consciousness of oneself one can gain objective knowledge of the flow of one's feelings, thoughts, desires, etc. In this state I would be able to make the necessary effort to examine, to check from time to time and to modify this flow, and the effort itself would, they said, create in me a certain substance. This effort would not lead to any specific results but the very act of making it would create and accumulate in me the substance of my own *being*. They told me that as I should now possess a fixed *being* I could attain to " objective consciousness," which would mean a completely objective, an absolute knowledge, not only of myself but of everyone, of everything, of the whole world.

Later, we were given many more exercises. We were told, for instance, to be aware of our right arm at a precise moment during the day and for as long as possible. This may seem ridiculous, but it was certainly not so for us. Some people thought that the object of the Teaching was simply to strengthen their powers of concentration and so to help them in all their different activities. "If I learn to concentrate on my right arm, for instance, at times when my mind is attracted by other things, I shall be cultivating my powers of attention and this will be useful to me in my studies, my business, my relationships and my love affairs." But this was actually an undertaking on a very different scale. I want this to be clearly understood. "Paying attention" was of little importance. In order to *know* my right arm, from the shoulder to the fingertips, at a quarter to six exactly, while reading my newspaper in the underground and despite my desires, joys and troubles of the moment, I have to dissociate myself from what I usually call my personality and it is in this act of dissociation that the exercise consists. To remain aware of my right arm I must refuse to identify myself with the article that I am reading, with my present mood, with the noise, the smells and the conversations around me. It is soon brought home to me that I am in a permanent state of identification and that I am constantly engulfed by my associations of ideas, sensations, feelings, etc. As soon as I give way I *lose my arm*. To help me retain my awareness I am not allowed to fold my newspaper and imagine that I am in a dark and silent room. This is strictly forbidden. I must manage with things as they are, and this means that I must remain aware of my arm in spite of the fact that my desire is awakened by a woman's body pressing against my legs. I must not deny my desire but must struggle not to be engulfed by it, even for a second. I must keep it at a distance, and then all that normally goes with it — images, psychic sensations, emotional attitudes — all this is at once pushed back and annihilated. I have *sacrificed* my desire to my arm and in so doing I have shorn my desire of all that was foreign to it, and have made of it an extra instrument for self-remembering. It is the same with the newspaper article, the people, the sounds, the posters that pass before my eyes, etc. In the effort that I make to keep the awareness of my right arm there is also the effort to keep myself at a distance from the outside world as well as from myself, and at this distance *I can see objectively* what is going on in and around me ; I have reality restored to me in all its purity and all that I see becomes an opportunity of sacrifice indefinitely renewed.

At the same time, this apparently ridiculous effort has begun to give birth to a big "Me" behind the hundreds of restless and identified little " me's." A certain substance is deposited in me, a minute grain of *being*.

We learnt, through many exercises of this kind, that our ordinary waking state is not the real one, and we discovered the great themes of all traditional religious teachings through these humble efforts of *self-remembering*, as we called it. To be, one must die to oneself. We understood this clearly and also that, to be conscious of oneself if only for an instant, to feel the big " Me," one must have refused to identify oneself with all that one calls one's personality. We rediscovered the theme of sacrifice by understanding that in the refusal to identify oneself with, for instance, a sexual desire, the desire itself was freed from all that did not belong to it and restored to its purity, and that it then became a purified object *thanks to which* a state of consciousness could be attained. I have taken a sexual desire as an example, but of course what I have said would apply equally to anything within us or any act, sight or re-action, etc. Everything, whether inside us or outside, can become an object of sacrifice to attain *being*, and as we sacrifice, we purify and create. We create ourselves and in so doing we restore to a state of purity the thing which enables us to create ourselves. If I talk to the woman I love and kiss her, I must not identify myself with my love, nor with her, nor with my words, nor my kiss, but while loving, talking and kissing I must constantly remember myself and remind myself that I *am*, and thus I restore my love, my words and my kiss to a state of purity.

We learn that consciousness as it is understood by philosophers and psychologists and as our nature encourages us to understand it, is nothing but the illusion of consciousness. I imagine that I am *naturally* conscious of myself, and when I look at a tree, what I call my consciousness takes note of the tree but does not *naturally* find it necessary to take note of itself. We learnt that this consciousness is merely that of the man who has *not yet reached* the real state of consciousness, a purely psychological and empirical awareness as opposed to the transcendental consciousness that we wished henceforth to attain. A man with true consciousness would look at the tree in the following way:

I watch myself looking, I remember myself as I look and in the difficult act of noticing, not the tree but my perception of it, of creating a relationship between the tree and a compact and permanent Me attained through the *sacrifice* of all the elements of my personality set in motion at the sight of it, my real consciousness begins to appear and is born of this effort. At the same time the tree passes from a relative existence to an absolute one, it discloses its real *being*. I no longer see the tree or examine it, I *know* it, we are born to one another.

In this way the whole world says to us, as Dona Musique says to the Viceroy in Claudel's " *Le Soulier de Satin* ": " Don't prevent me from existing," and it is in sacrificing what we normally call our consciousness to a state of Consciousness that we fulfil the world's amorous prayer, and in fulfilling it pass from illusion to real existence.

We learnt that those who pass from a purely psychological consciousness of themselves and of the world to a state of Consciousness, pass at the same time from relative and scientific knowledge to absolute knowledge. My friend Raymond Abellio makes this clear and helps me to recall my own memories in the following fragment of an unpublished work he has just sent to me, written in the course of our Gurdjieff experiences together:

" As far back as I can remember," he writes, " I have always been aware of colours ; my eyes took in blue, red and yellow — I had latent awareness of them. Of course my " eyes " did not enquire about them, how could they have asked questions ? Their function is to see, not to watch themselves seeing, but my brain was as though asleep ; it was not the eye of my eyes but only a prolongation of them, and I used to say, almost without thinking: ' This is a good red, or a dim green, or a brilliant white.' One day a few years ago, as I was walking among the vines that overhang the shores of Lake Léman and make this one of the most beautiful places in the world, so beautiful and so grand was it that my " Me " melted at first into this beauty and then, quickly recovering itself, became excited, and a sudden and very extraordinary thing happened. I had very often seen the yellow-ochre of the hillside, the blue of the lake, the purple of the mountains of Savoy and beyond, the sparkling glaciers of the Grand-Combin, but I knew for the first time that I had never *taken them in*. I had however lived there for three months and from the first moment I was moved by this landscape, but my only response to it was a vague excitement. The philosopher's "Me" is certainly stronger than any landscape. The poignant feeling of beauty is only the growing realization by the "Me" of the infinite distance that separates us from this beauty. But suddenly, that day, I knew that I myself was denying the landscape, that it was nothing without me. 'It is I who see you, and who sees myself seeing you, and who, in seeing you, creates you.' This inner cry is the cry of the demiurge as it creates the world. It is not only suspension of an old world but projection of a new. And, truly, in that instant the world was re-created. I had never seen such colours. They were a hundred times more intense, more subtle, more 'alive.' I knew that I understood colour for the first time, that I was re-born to it, and that never before had I really seen a picture or penetrated into the world of painting. But I knew, too, that in self-remembering, in perceiving my perception, I held the key of this transfigured world, which is not a mysterious other-world, but the real one, the one from which 'nature' excludes us. This has nothing to do with paying attention. Transfiguration is full, attention is not. Transfiguration is recognized by its immediate adequacy. Attention tends towards eventual adequacy. One cannot, of course, say that attention is empty — it is avid, but avidity is not the same as fullness. As I went back to the village that day the people I passed were for the most part 'attentive' to their work: they seemed to me, however, to be sleep-walking."

The Russian philosopher Ouspensky in his book "*Fragments of an Unknown Teaching*" tells of similar experiences. They are for him the basis of all initiatory transformation. It is this transformation that is referred to in Yogi teaching when it speaks of the discrimination of the spectator or of the spectacle. This discrimination is not natural but transcendental, and it is significant that if we speak of this discrimination to a "natural" man he brings it down to the ordinary level of attention with the words: "It is I who . . ." The transcendental "Me" present in the transfiguration is not merely a figure of speech but of actual content; not only a word that in philosophical speculation can be used in the third person as well as in the first, it is an absolutely voluntary and primary act, an act-principle by which the whole being is seized and which overflows critical knowledge. It is a lived experience. One cannot assert that this transcendental "Me" is within anybody's reach — it is not. It depends on a certain level of consciousness, on a form of asceticism that raises this level and gives the consciousness a "corrosive" action in regard to the "old world."

It was this asceticism that we were pursuing in order to reach the required level of consciousness. We began to know how to watch ourselves think, feel, act, etc., and so to discover which elements in us were harmful and which useful to the accomplishment of this voluntary, absolute and primary act of which Abellio speaks;

an act in which there is consciousness of consciousness in face of an object re-established in its objective reality, in which there is simultaneous awareness of one's *being* and of one's sacrificed and purified inner world, simultaneous awareness of *being* and of the exterior world.

Through many exercises that I shall not describe here, through talks and also no doubt through hidden influences working on us from certain members of the " school," we learnt to conquer in ourselves the natural obstacles that prevented us from attaining a state of consciousness. It was becoming possible for us to put our inner house in order — to re-arrange and grade our little " me's." We learnt to distinguish in ourselves the chief functions of the human machine: the functions of thought, feeling, instinct (all the inner workings of the organism), movement and sex. We learnt to relate to the correct " centre " all the movements, moods, associations of ideas, desires, gestures, etc., belonging to what we used to call our " personality " and that we now had to envisage as a machine to be completely dismantled and put together again in such a way that it would *produce* consciousness. Other functions would then appear, linked to the new states, functions of which ordinary man is deprived; for the attainment of the state of consciousness towards which all our efforts were directed is, we were told, only the first step. This would no doubt take us many years and perhaps we should die before attaining it, but we had to realize that the completion of man does not end there.

We aimed to become men already very different from ordinary men in the kind of knowledge we possessed of ourselves, in the understanding of our position on the ladder of possibilities, and in the acquisition of a *permanent centre of gravity*. This phrase, that was often used in the "school," meant that the idea of attaining unity, consciousness, a permanent "me" and will — that is, the idea of our development — would one day become more important to us than anything else. We would then have within us, our "Guardian Angel," and would understand the significance of this expression.

This *state of consciousness* that we now experienced only in flashes, what might it not be if it became a permanent state? What extraordinary transformations would take place in man? To what degree of knowledge might he not attain? By occasional descriptions they allowed us to catch glimpses of the stages to completion, but I could not convey them here without losing myself and making nonsense of them.

I hope I have said enough to clarify the general direction of the Gurdjieff teaching, the kind of "work" we did and the heights to which we aspired.

For my own part I felt, not without excitement, that I was first cousin to the Devil.

Provisional Conclusion

My mother died in terrible circumstances and soon afterwards, my father. I could never decide, later on, between the different emotions that could have been responsible for my want of suffering at this period. Was it courage or egoism? The "sacrifice of pain" or a cowardly refusal to suffer? A heroic struggle against "negative emotions" or a shameful hardness of heart, that kept me from weeping? I often experience the moments of these deaths again in my dreams and, after five years, I still sob in my sleep for having *felt* nothing at the time. Instead of growing in stature, I believe that on the contrary I was shrivelling up, and some of the dryness of that period still remains.

As my work intensified and increased in precision I felt I was approaching ever nearer to anguish, pride and scorn. Sometimes I seemed at last to reach the extreme limit of "self-remembering." Sometimes, thanks to the right arm exercise, I believed that I succeeded in achieving a big, compact and steadfast " Me." I felt this too after a session of the " Movements " in the Salle Pleyel, or while lying stretched out on my bed after " re-arranging " my limbs and organs, or, again, while kneeling with my arms crossed, and gazing fixedly at a black spot on a sheet of white paper. I would achieve this big "Me" by the sacrifice of all identifications and the suspension of all the " natural " reactions of my personality. It would happen in a flash. I was reaching a state of consciousness in which my *being* could know itself in its absolute reality. It was born to itself at the centre of my transfigured personality, the elements of which, when arrested for a moment, could be likened to those of a church ; from the greatest pillar to the smallest ornament everything is unified, and serving a single purpose. Then anything that I become aware of is seen in its entirety, whether it be an object, a being or an idea ; it exists objectively and is known in an absolute and ineffable way. Supposing this were permanent! I experienced it only for a thousandth of a second, but this was an instant of the only true life, and a promise of eternity.

I knew that I *did not exist* apart from these moments, and the strength of this feeling in addition to the powerful means of self-observation that I had been taught (and that through a kind of sullen obstinacy I practised longer than I should) was responsible for my *watching myself not living* nearly all the time. This was agonizing. I felt I knew what living with death would be like and sometimes I awoke at night thinking that my last moment had come. I watched myself identifying — being swallowed up by ideas, moods, people, things, work and gestures. I watched my rebellious personality going through motions that were certainly no concern of mine but the sight of which dismayed me. From the depths of my despair I despised myself as much as I despised everyone else, whom I knew to be in the same state of non-existence. Nothing about them seemed to me real, neither their goodness, intelligence, sufferings, desires and ambitions, nor their wickedness and stupidity. We were all non-existent but I was alone in recognizing it, and so I had a feeling of superiority of which they were unconsciously aware and which caused them to love or, more often, to hate me. But it was my profound anguish that gave me this air of superiority, and physically and morally I was so nearly exhausted that all my attention and energy were focussed on the difficult task of keeping myself alive somehow, and I had no resources left for easing my relations with others. As I no longer attached any importance to myself, apart from the importance that my horror lent to the abyss of non-existence, I was apt to indulge in actions, words and writings that put a further strain on my relationships. Thus, broken friendships, ruined love-affairs and violent enmities became more and more frequent and I was considered an unscrupulous adventurer and a monster of pride and egoism.

I was alone at a time when solitude was torture to me, and in the anguish of *not-being* my inhibitions and nightmares became ten times more insistent. While I was writing the first chapters of " *Les Voies de Petite Communication* " this inner strain was at its height. I was carried off to hospital as thin as a rake and blind in one eye. The central vein in the retina of my left eye had burst. In the course of the following weeks of examination in hospital not a trace of anaemia could be found. I was dying in " good condition," but nevertheless I was dying.

Due to my fear of death, after I left hospital, I tried to lay hold of pleasure and pain at the same time, and seeking pleasure I spoiled love. With the Teaching in mind, I was careful not to be taken in by desire. I told myself that to love one must *exist,* that I was as yet nothing, and therefore logic demanded that I should separate sex from love. *While awaiting the possibility of love* I took licentiousness to be my proper course and practised it in order that I might at least feel myself to be alive. I dragged along with me the person I should most have " respected " according to current morality; I suffered from the knowledge that I was risking her ruin and the end of our love, but I was tasting life in two forms, as pleasure and as suffering. Although I was using the Teaching in the wrong way, the profound demand it made on me held me to it, a demand that the fear of death over-shadowed but could not extinguish.

I was still awaiting Knowledge, though the approaches to it had brought me to the verge of death ; and although ordinary knowledge seemed to me derisory yet I strove after it. I used what I " knew " to enjoy myself in a world that bored me, partly in order to hold and at the same time to lose it.

In the following years of my strange convalescence I still hoped to find guardians amongst the people in the Teaching, but there were no guardians and the " master " himself vanished in death.

Later, I came to understand that love, the complete giving of oneself to another, love, in its moments of illumination, is also able to lead to the state of consciousness and Knowledge that I had been seeking with Gurdjieff. A state of grace is to be found at the extreme limit of self-abandonment as well as at the extreme limit of self-remembering. But I discovered, too, that love has the same set-backs, barren periods and risks as we encountered in the Gurdjieff adventure; that there are many ways to the one state that we really want to attain, and that while awaiting our own way, our saving grace is a feeling of hope and thankfulness for a world so rich in ways to true existence.

This is the conclusion that I would like to have reached at the end of the book, but I am not sure of being able to reach any conclusion at all.

NOTES ON A SECRET BOOK

7

Music And Writing

Mr. Rom Landau tells us that he was able to look through a small book of Gurdjieff's called: "*The Herald of Coming Good.*" It must have been printed in 1933 at the author's expense, with help from his disciples. Gurdjieff took great care to efface all traces of himself; for instance he brought back and burnt all the programmes produced for the performances of music and dancing in the Hébertot Theatre. These programmes started off with a detailed but quite false description of the Institute for the Harmonious Development of Man, which he had just founded at Fontainebleau-Avon. It is likely that the only edition of "*The Herald of Coming Good,*" a clumsy little book according to Rom Landau, was destroyed as soon as possible. In spite of all my researches I have not been able to find a single copy.

After he settled in Paris, in 1934 Gurdjieff devoted himself to writing. He composed many thousands of pages of music, as he considered a special kind of oriental music with esoteric notation to be one of the most effective disciplines for attaining knowledge of the laws of cosmology and of the inner life.

"Objective music," he said, "is all based on 'inner octaves.' And it can obtain not only definite psychological results but definite physical results . . . There can be such music as would kill a man instantaneously. The Biblical legend of the destruction of the walls of Jericho by music is precisely such a legend of objective music. Plain music, no matter of what kind, will not destroy walls, but objective music indeed can do so. And not only can it destroy but it can also build up. In the legend of Orpheus there are hints of objective music, for Orpheus used to impart knowledge by music. Snake charmers' music in the East is an approach to objective music, of course very primitive. Very often it is simply one note which is long drawn out, rising and falling only very little; but in this single note 'inner octaves' are going on all the time and melodies of 'inner octaves' which are inaudible to the ears but felt by the emotional centre. And the snake hears this music or, more strictly speaking, he feels it, and he obeys it. The same music, only a little more complicated and men would obey it.

"So you see that art is not merely a language but something much bigger. . . . Mechanical humanity can have subjective art only. Objective art* requires at

---

* "The difference between objective art and subjective art is that in objective art the artist really does 'create', that is, he makes what he intended, he puts into his work whatever ideas and feelings he wants to put into it. And the action of this work upon men is absolutely definite; they will, each of course according to his own level, receive the ideas and the feelings that the artist wanted to transmit to them. There can be nothing accidental either in the creation or in the impressions of objective art."

least flashes of objective consciousness ; in order to understand these flashes properly and to make proper use of them a great inner unity is necessary and a great control of oneself."

These innumerable pages of music will probably never be published. They belong exclusively to the " groups."

Gurdjieff's artistic side took the form of music and choreography. He was also interested in the art of carpet-making in so far as the traditional weaving, traces of which still remain in Persia, was a method of incorporating rhythms and tunes. Writing did not interest him. However, since giving up the Institute for the Harmonious Development of Man, he had applied himself to the writing, in Greek, Armenian, Russian, bad English and pidgin-French, of a fantastic and lengthy work in which he purported to give the whole of his mystical experiences and the knowledge he had accumulated during the course of his life in the monasteries of Tibet and Asia Minor. " He who speaks does not know ; he who knows does not speak," says Lao Tsu.

Nevertheless, Gurdjieff who was supposed to know, decided to speak. Everything leads one to suppose that he spoke only to increase the obstacles surrounding the *Knowledge* in question and to deepen the mystery.

The pages of this inordinately long book had been type-written in a lingua franca by confidential disciples and were kept in a cupboard in the flat in the Rue du Colonel Renard. One American woman had paid a thousand dollars for the privilege of reading twenty pages and she was not the only applicant. Towards the end of his life Gurdjieff seemed to have given up teaching, either from fatigue or from distaste for other people. The faithful were only summoned to his flat for the dinners and the readings from this manuscript. While he sat on the sofa drinking and smoking and bursting with laughter over a passage that his audience did not find funny at all, an unfortunate pupil faced by twenty or thirty people sitting cross-legged on the floor, would stumble through the reading of this extraordinary work, stuffed with untranslatable puns, coarse jokes, learned meditations, wisdom, eccentricities and genius. The atmosphere of the room, the special power and quality of concentration, Gurdjieff's presence and the confusion of the reader he appointed, all lent a depth, a richness and a flavour to the text that perhaps it did not really possess, unless it had been written purposely, to produce disturbing undertones in just such circumstances as these.

After Gurdjieff's death part of this book was translated into English and published for the English and American pupils in 1950 with the title " *All and Everything* ". A few who were not disciples got hold of this massive and difficult work and tried painfully to read it. I think it may be useful to give their impressions. None of them, with the exception of Mr. Kenneth Walker, had followed Gurdjieff's teaching or been in permanent contact with him, so I think their opinions will be of especial value. I propose to include here some of the first pronouncements on " *All and Everything* ". Firstly, an extract from Kenneth Walker's book " *Venture with Ideas* ". Secondly, an essay especially written by M. Denis Saurat. Thirdly, an article by Gorham Munson that appeared in 1950 in the American review " *Tomorrow*."

8

Mr. Kenneth Walker's Story

... All that it is possible to do is to give the impressions which Gurdjieff created in me and these can be summed up in the generalization that for me he represented the outcome of the work. By this I mean that he had achieved greater consciousness, control and unity than those possessed by other men. It is true that the consciousness of another person cannot be measured objectively but the greater a man's consciousness, the more control he is able to exercise over his various functions. Everything Gurdjieff did seemed to originate from within. When he became angry, as he sometimes did, his anger had the appearance of being deliberate and it was laid on one side as soon as it had served its purpose. The dark eyes would then regain their twinkle, the stern olive-coloured face would relax and the conversation would be resumed at the point at which it had been suddenly broken off. He never fumbled in his thoughts or his movements. The latter were always purposeful and made with the strictest economy of effort, like those of a cat, and his immense capacity for work was due to this ability of his never to waste energy. It was particularly noticeable that he had obtained complete mastery over his body.

. . . Sometimes we went to his flat to listen to music and then Gurdjieff would bring with him his special instrument, an unusual form of accordion. Balancing this on his knee, he presses backwards and forwards a hinged flap on the back of the accordion with his left hand and thereby obtains a rather spasmodic supply of air. His right hand rests on the keyboard and, sometimes improvising and at other times remembering, he calls out of his instrument music of a kind that I have never listened to before. It is in a minor key and at one moment it calls back to my memory the song that the Mohammedan dockers chanted when, many years ago, at Suez, our ship's coal bunkers were being replenished and at other times it is more reminiscent of the mournful music I listened to as a child as the sea surged backwards and forwards through the narrow entrance of a cave. Gurdjieff told us very little about the music he had collected during his travels but it was obvious that it came from several sources. Some of it was clearly occupational in origin, songs sung by peasants while carrying on their crafts. There were for example the traditional songs chanted by the old carpet makers of Central Asia as they squatted on the floor of some large barn, combing, spinning and dyeing their wools or weaving them into well-known local patterns. Gurdjieff described how of a winter evening a whole village would take part in this work in which everybody had his allotted task to do, each with its own musical accompaniment. Another source from which he drew inspiration was the sacred music he had listened to in the various monasteries he had visited, monasteries of many kinds, Greek Orthodox, Essene and Sufi. I have little personal knowledge of music and I can say only two things of the music he played, first that it was very old and second that it had a strong emotional effect on most of his hearers.

... The more I saw of Gurdjieff the more convinced I became of his uniqueness. He had qualities which I had never seen in anybody else; profound knowledge, immense vitality and complete immunity from fear. He was old but he was still capable of working for a longer time than anybody else.

Few people realized how busy he was between our visits. Not only had he his French followers to look after but there was a number of indigent Russian refugees to be fed in his flat. Many a person in trouble made his way there for help and advice, for Gurdjieff was a familiar figure to the frequenters of the neighbouring cafés.

... One of the most striking features of these last reunions was the number of young people who crowded round his table, especially after his return from America. Those of his followers who were parents seemed to have realized that the moment had come for taking their children to Paris. They might understand very little but they wanted them to be able to recall in later years having, a long time ago, met a very remarkable man in France, a certain Mr. Gurdjieff. To ensure their being able to do this, children, ranging in age from three to fourteen, were now being brought to Paris and invited to his flat. There they sat at his table warmly welcomed and specially entertained by him.

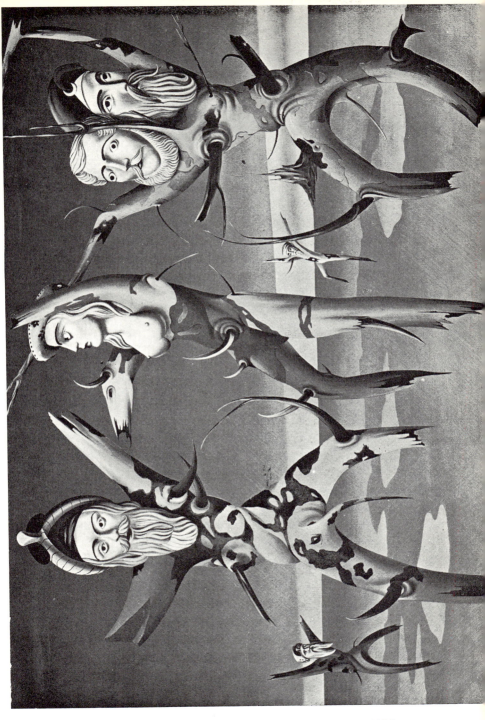

Felix Labisse: *L'inconstance de jason,* 1955

Felix Labisse: Verdelet, 1956

Felix Labisse: Mythomecanique, 1958

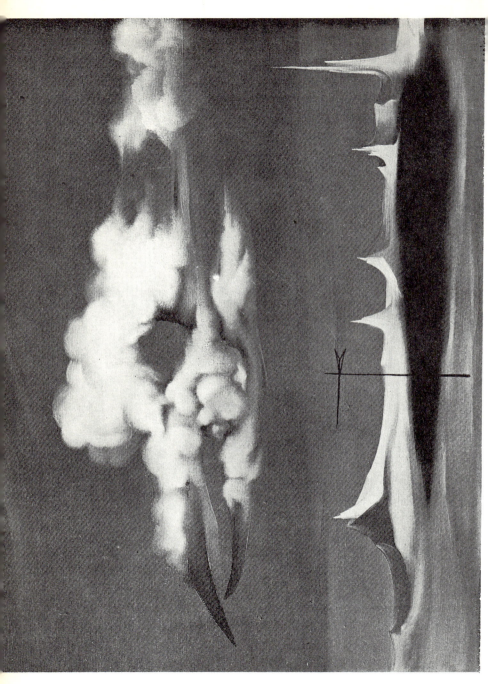

Felix Labisse: Charadrius, 1959

Felix Labisse: Libidoscaphes faisant surface dans la baie de Rio, 1962

Felix Labisse: *Jeune figue posant pour Leonard de Vinci une annonciation, 1946*

Felix Labisse: L'etat d'urgence, 1962

Felix Labisse: La fille prodigue, 1943

He had the simplicity of a great man and he enjoyed their presence at his table, loading them with presents and sometimes causing their parents embarrassment by the amount of food he pressed on them. Some of the children were shy, but most of them were at their ease, laughing at his jokes and promptly replying to his questions. For him, very young people were of far greater importance than the rest of us, for they were representatives of a future generation of men and women, a generation which had not yet been ruined and which, by right teaching and upbringing, might possibly be saved. I like to remember these youthful gatherings, for when I look back on them I recall not only the children, but Gurdjieff in a new rôle, Gurdjieff as grandfather, dispenser of gifts and enjoyer of fun.

. . . The key to the understanding of much that has been misunderstood in him is undoubtedly supplied by a study of his book *Beelzebub's Talks with his Grandson*, now published under the title, *All and Everything*. First novels are usually autobiographical and although *All and Everything* is not a novel but an allegory, it contains much that throws light on its author. The chief character, in this allegory Beelzebub, was born in the far distant planet of Karatas and he was fashioned in a form quite different from that of a man, possessing hooves, a tail and, until he was deprived of them as a punishment, horns. Yet as one continues to read, the description of Beelzebub slowly fades, however one struggles to retain it, and the picture of a human being with an immense head, a sweeping moustache and dark observant eyes takes its place. Instead of watching Beelzebub travelling through the geography and history of this earth, one can only see the wanderings of Gurdjieff. It is Gurdjieff whom one espies sitting at 'Chaihanas' sipping tea with some fellow traveller and discussing with him the strange ways of men. It is Gurdjieff who descends on to the earth at the time of the Babylonian civilization to attend the debates between the great scholars of the day as to whether man has or has not a soul. The author of the book is always proving too strong for his own characters and is continually speaking instead of them and edging them off the stage. So when Beelzebub replies to a question of his grandson about the difference between right and wrong it is Gurdjieff and not Beelzebub who is speaking.

'And which of these manifestations,' asks Hassein, 'do they [the earth beings] consider good and which bad?' His grandfather answers that there are two independent understandings on the earth concerning right and wrong. 'The first of these understandings,' he says, 'exists there under the following formulation: Every action of man is good, in the objective sense, if it is done according to his conscience, and every action is bad, if from it later he experiences remorse.' Beelzebub then explains to his grandson that there is a second earthly understanding of right and wrong, which 'passing from generation to generation through ordinary beings there, gradually spread over almost the whole planet under the name of morality'. Beelzebub evidently thinks very poorly of this morality for he adds that its distinguishing mark is that it has the 'unique property which belongs to the being bearing the name chameleon.'

Mr. Gurdjieff always laid great stress on conscience and he develops this theme very fully in the chapter of his book in which he describes the arrival on the earth of a Divine Messenger, Ashieta Shiemash, sent from Above on a mission to man. He recounts how the saintly Ashieta Shiemash during a preliminary period of fasting ponders over the best method of discharging his mission and comes to the conclusion that it is useless for him to appeal to the ideas of which his predecessors have always made use, Faith, Hope and Charity. It is useless because the mentation of men has degenerated so badly that they are no longer able to grasp the true meaning of these sacred 'being-impulses', Faith, Hope and Charity. He decides therefore to appeal to something else that has not entirely atrophied in them — their consciences. 'Thanks to the abnormally established conditions of external ordinary being-existence here [on the earth], this factor [conscience] has gradually penetrated and become embedded in that consciousness which is here called ' subconsciousness', in consequence of which it takes no part whatever in the functioning of their ordinary consciousness.' Ashieta Shiemash decides to try to awake this submerged and quiescent conscience in the hope that it can be made to participate ' in the general functioning of that consciousness of theirs in which they pass their daily, as they say, " waking existence".' By this means he may be able to bring about the salvation of mankind. The chapter concludes with a description of the successful discharge of this mission and with an account of the period of peace and goodwill on earth which followed it.

There were two other words, besides conscience, of which Gurdjieff made constant use, the words duty and responsibility. He said that on arriving at a certain age every man had certain duties to perform ; he must justify his existence by service to his fellow creatures and to his Creator. A child was exempt from duties and responsibilities but on attaining manhood he must learn to discharge faithfully both of these obligations. In an early chapter of his book he recounts how the young Hassein was overcome 'with a sense of indebtedness' to those who in the past, through their labours and their sufferings, have brought about the conditions which he, as a newcomer, enjoys. His grandfather replies that he does not as yet have to repay this debt.

"The time of your present age is not given you in which to pay for your existence, but for preparing yourself for the future, for the obligations becoming to a responsible three-brained being. So in the meantime, exist as you exist. Only do not forget one thing, namely at your age it is indispensably necessary that every day, at sunrise, while watching the reflection of its splendour, you bring about a contact between your consciousness and the various unconscious parts of your general presence. Try to make this state last and to convince the unconscious parts — not as if they were conscious — that if they hinder your general functioning, they, in the period of your responsible age, not only cannot fulfil the good that befits them, but your general presence, of which they are part, will not be able to be a good servant of our *Common Endless Creator* and by that will not even be worthy to pay for your arising and existence."

It was not only in his writings that Mr. Gurdjieff stressed the importance of the obligation which the mature man must faithfully discharge. I recall very vividly an evening on which he inquired my age and, having learnt that I was the oldest person present, except himself, he turned to the others and said: 'You notice that I do not treat everybody in the same way.

I treat seniority with respect and so also must you.' Then speaking directly to me he added: 'And you on your part must discharge your responsibilities as an older person. When people apply to you for help you must give them what they expect of you, for you also have to make payment. Always bear in mind that every age has its appropriate duty to perform.' It was indeed a general principle of the work that the more senior the standing of the member of the group, the more was expected of him; a lapse that could be pardoned in another person could not be pardoned in him; an effort that was sufficient elsewhere was not sufficient for him. All manifestations of personality and of self-love in an older person were received with a special scorn.

And it was with man's personality that Gurdjieff was always at war, for it was this that prevented his making contact with the deeper and more real parts of his being. It is on this note that his book *All and Everything* begins and on this note that it closes. In the last chapter he recounts how Beelzebub, having completed his mission, returns triumphantly home. As the spaceship is nearing its destination his grandson puts a final question to him. 'How would you answer,' he asks, 'if God were to summon you into His presence and inquire of you what means could be adopted to save the inhabitants of the earth?' To this question Beelzebub replies:

"The sole means now for the saving of the beings of the planet Earth would be to implant in their presence a new organ . . . of such properties that every one of these unfortunates, during the process of existence, should constantly sense and be cognizant of the inevitability of his own death as well as of the death of everyone upon whom his eyes or his attention rests. Only such a sensation and such a cognizance can now destroy the egoism completely crystallized in them that has swallowed up the whole of their Essence and also that tendency, namely, which engenders all those mutual relationships existing there, which serve as the chief cause of all their abnormalities unbecoming to three-brained beings and maleficent for them themselves and for the whole of the Universe."

I am convinced that Gurdjieff followed the dictates of his conscience and that when he sinned he sinned only against the moral code which 'has the unique property which belongs to the being bearing the name of chameleon'. When he offended conventional morality he did so openly for no person cared less for his own reputation than he. If told that somebody had criticized him adversely for something he had done he would laugh and say that this was as nothing compared with what some people thought and said of him.

As I looked at him for the last time and thought of all he had achieved in the course of his long life and how much I owed him, the oddities in his behaviour which in the past had puzzled and even troubled me were forgotten. What trifles they became when viewed in relationship to the whole man. What Horatio had said of Hamlet's father, the dead king of Denmark, I could truly say of him,

"He was a man. Take him for all in all
I shall not look upon his like again."

9

A Study by M. Denis Saurat

I do not think that Gurdjieff should be looked upon as a master whose object was to instruct disciples in a doctrine, but rather as a teacher trying to shape the intellect and character of a chosen number of pupils, whom he regarded as children under his care. One does not tell children the whole truth, one gives them carefully prepared parts of the truth that one hopes will further the development of their souls, and sometimes one even invents stories, such as Father Christmas, to encourage the children to express themselves. In his book, *All and Everything*, Gurdjieff says, when speaking of a great sage of the earth (page 901):

"I had full moral right to tell him the truth about myself, because by his attainments he was already ... a three-brained being of that planet with whom it is not forbidden us from Above to be frank. But at the moment I could in no way do this, because there was also present there the dervish Hadji-Bogga-Eddin who was still an ordinary terrestrial three-brained being, concerning whom, already long before, it was forbidden under oath from Above to the beings of our tribe to communicate true information to anyone of them on any occasion whatsoever . . . This interdiction on the beings of our tribe was made chiefly because it is necessary for the three-brained beings of your planet to have 'knowledge-of-being.'

"And any information, even if true, gives to beings in general only 'mental knowledge' and this mental knowledge always serves beings only as a means to diminish their possibilities of acquiring this knowledge of being.

"And since the sole means left to these unfortunate beings of your planet for their complete liberation (from their errors) is this knowledge-of-being, therefore this command was given to the beings of our tribe under oath concerning the beings of the earth."

This almost hidden passage on Page 901 (that most readers never reach) gives us the clue to Gurdjieff's behaviour with his pupils. His aim was to induce them to discover truth for themselves as, according to Gurdjieff's general doctrine, this is the only kind of truth of any value. Cardinal Newman gives us the essentials of this doctrine on the many occasions in which he makes his famous distinction between "notional assent" and "real assent." A man gives "notional assent" to something that his mind understands and accepts, but he hardly ever acts on this assent, which is purely intellectual, abstract and fruitless. "Real assent," on the other hand, comes not from intellect but from immediate contact with being, and this "real assent" includes not only intellect, but also

desire, will and action. Newman would not have agreed with Gurdjieff that intellectual acceptance is fatal to real knowledge, but at heart Gurdjieff's thought is not far removed from Newman's, nor from that of many of the poets, Keats amongst others, who says in the "*Ode to a Nightingale*":
"*Though the dull brain perplexes and retards,*"
for it is his intellect that prevents him from taking in the beauty of the nightingale's song.

In Christian theories of grace there is, indeed, the same idea. It is not through the intellect that one reaches faith, on the contrary, intellect is inimical to faith. Faith is direct contact with God and comes through grace. In Gurdjieff's thought this theory applies to everything, not only to God, of whom he hardly ever speaks. In order to know things, one must discover them for oneself and all that we are told by others is only a veil.

The fact that Gurdjieff gives free rein to his sense of humour follows from this theory. In the way he presents things he is above all a humorist. I do not mean that he is humorist and nothing else, on the contrary, I maintain that he is an extraordinary highly developed spiritual teacher. But the presentation of his doctrines and above all, perhaps, his actual behaviour towards his disciples, is dictated by his sense of humour. This can be seen in the first few pages of his book.

The first chapter is called: *The Arousing of Thought,* and on the next page he says: " In any case I have begun just thus, and as to how the next will go I can only say meanwhile, as the blind man once expressed it, ' we shall see '."

This excellent theory and the equally excellent practise of never telling the truth are both evidently beyond human strength; Gurdjieff himself inevitably tells, from time to time, and even perhaps quite often, what he believes to be the truth.

His enormous book is a startling mixture of humorous stories, deliberate lies told in all seriousness, and ideas of which he himself is profoundly convinced. This means that one reads it at one's peril and that one would need to be cleverer than Gurdjieff to see through his diabolical method and to separate these three geological layers that he does his best to confuse.

But on the other hand, one can conceive the immense pleasure of embarking on this adventure, a pleasure that would be intellectual, moral and even spiritual. It seems to me that the best way would be to start with a prejudice against the book and to resolve, like Descartes, not to take anything that is said seriously unless one can verify it by one's own inner experience.

Perhaps I may add that according to my own personal contract with Gurdjieff (it is true that this was only one afternoon's talk through an interpreter thirty years ago), and to my later observations of many of his disciples, the method that I advocate of reading his book would have his entire approval. Gurdjieff was not proud of his disciples and he tried hard to discover amongst them even a handful of promising ones. It is touching, by contrast, to see how much affection and respect the disciples felt for him, and it is quite possible that Gurdjieff under-estimated them. We must remember that Gurdjieff came from the East and never understood very well the European type of mind and of civilization, but he saw our faults clearly and it is perhaps this fact that could be of most value to us.

All and Everything is a critical study of certain fundamental points of our civilization, and of our ways of thinking. If we could understand the book it would be of immense value, but that is the great difficulty. Gurdjieff's sense of humour is different from ours in the West and we often cannot tell if he is joking or not. Wit is a dangerous intellectual game and should only be practised on unimportant subjects because even if one carries it only a little too high it will be found that no two people have exactly the same sense of humour. Many misunderstandings arise from this fact, not only between nations but also between people and especially between men and women. So Gurdjieff is very hard to understand, even when what he says seems to him to be perfectly clear.

All this is, in fact, quite superficial and I am only describing the intellectual atmosphere of the book. I must now state clearly that Gurdjieff is a very great spiritual teacher. He evidently knows things that the ordinary man of culture does not know. He has a quite exceptional and very surprising conception of the spiritual world. One can only take in fragments here and there of this conception, but these fragments are of a very high quality. Everyone interested in philosophy and metaphysics should read Gurdjieff closely; I mean that all who read the Christian mystics and know the Father's will, and those who follow recent trends in psychology, will find many interesting ideas and possibly even new facts in this great book, which at first seems nothing but a hotch-potch.

I can only attempt, here, to give a very short résumé of the general scope of the work. It would appear that the world we live in and our solar system owe their existence in part to a mistake. During the creation of the world, some personage very high up in the hierarchy of beings committed a signal blunder. This was not pre-ordained and the catastrophe arose from a momentary stupidity on the part of a very intelligent being. The first result of the accident was that the two moons that circled the earth began to recede in a dangerous manner and if this movement had not been stopped these disorderly satellites would have caused trouble and distress in the rest of the solar system. The superior beings who rule the physical universe then behaved with the utmost selfishness. Wishing to hide their mistake from the supreme being, they made a sacrifice of mankind. They invested man with a special organ that caused him to perceive reality the wrong way round and to attach pleasure to things that in themselves are neutral. This organ, implanted in human life, set off vibrations in outer space that acted as a brake on the runaway satellites. Thus after a certain length of time the two moons were permanently fixed in their new orbit. The disastrous organ could then be disposed of but, unfortunately, men had by then formed habits of thought under its baleful influence which persisted after its removal and so they continued to see things the wrong way round. This is the cause of all their moral and political errors and especially of their wars. Thus, things can happen that God has neither wanted nor foreseen. and that he personally can do nothing about. This God is evidently not the supreme God, as he only rules over a small portion of the Universe, but unfortunately for us it is the part that we live in. He tries to help us as much as he can and whenever circumstances allow, he sends us superior beings incarnated as prophets who come to reveal a small number of ultimate truths. These prophets naturally always fail and are usually killed, because they attempt to make man give up his wrong ways of thinking and acting. Occasionally however a slight improvement is made. This sad story is told by Beelzebub, one of the superior beings, to his grandson, who is still a child and the whole book is in principle adapted to his childish mentality.

One of the principal errors to be corrected is the idea that all men have souls. There are in fact very few beings with an immortal soul. It is true that all beings are necessary and those who strive especially hard in the pursuit of virtue or intelligence can acquire a soul that may be more or less immortal, but on the whole mankind differs very little from the animals. Both the theory of evolution and the theory of incarnation contain little more than errors of perspective. Christianity is a little nearer to the Truth. The idea of a supreme God comprising the Father, the Son and the Holy Ghost is perfectly true, but even this God is subject to certain limitations. Behind the Trinity there appears to be something called the Sun Absolute that *emits* laws, perhaps through the Holy Ghost. The Son and the Holy Ghost together, recover in space the loss sustained by the Sun Absolute through its creative activity. A huge proportion of this loss is caused by mankind, and part of the Son's work is to recover as much as possible of this substance or divine force that is wasted by us. But the success of this enterprise is prevented by our vices, and in particular by our sexual behaviour which is quite contrary to the right ordering of the world. Above all, humanity is degraded and the spirit more and more debased by the practise of abortions and contraceptives, that have brought human beings lower than the animals. Truly, animals that live according to nature have more soul than degraded human beings. The "Nature" of our earth is a kind of interior divinity who has the power, nevertheless, to foresee and even to create the future up to a certain point and who treats our present humanity as we treat pigs that we fatten up, kill and eat. After all, that is what ordinary man is for.

On the other hand a man who has evolved passes, at his death, into a kind of purgatory. Paradise and Hell are errors caused by the unfortunate organ whose functions were really connected with the moon. But the idea of purgatory is entirely true; even the best souls that have developed on Earth require lengthy trials after their terrestrial life, before they can become true spirits.

One might say, in fact, that for Gurdjieff this world is a hell with occasional glimmers of hope, a hell from which a few of us may escape to pass into purgatory, there to become purified, so as to raise ourselves gradually to the rank of higher spirits.

It is hard to say how much faith Gurdjieff expects us to attach to this phantasmagoria. I think I can say with certainty that he was quite sincere in his expression of the general idea that the European mind of to-day completely distorts the truth by its way of looking at things, and even in some cases affirms the opposite of the truth. It follows that he was also sincere in his criticism of our intellectualism and of our Western civilization. But this criticism, that could have been so useful is not presented coherently throughout the book; we can only perceive fragments of it so to speak. It is most marked against America and all that comes from America, whereas France is treated with noticeable sympathy.

An interesting idea to notice and probably to

examine closer is the idea that Buddhism, as a religion, is slowly invading the West. According to Gurdjieff the different kinds of occultism of the nineteenth and twentieth centuries all derive from Buddhism: theosophy, spiritualism, psycho-analysis in its different forms and nearly all contemporary psychology. Gurdjieff was certainly a great connoisseur of Buddhism. Some highly educated Orientals with whom I have discussed Gurdjieff go so far as to maintain that he was simply a Buddhist who for personal reasons settled in the West and tried to teach us some of the simplest of the methods and truths known in the Far East. I can say nothing about this and Gurdjieff's book shows no prejudice in favour of Buddhism, on the contrary he seems expressly to condemn the spread of Eastern ideas towards the West. He told me himself that he aimed at achieving a synthesis of Western science and technique on the one hand and Eastern spirituality on the other, but he did not necessarily mean Buddhism, and was even of the opinion that all religions found in Asia to-day are degenerate forms of an ancient revelation. He affirmed that he had discovered truth, in collaboration with a dozen other seekers who had travelled together first over Asia and then over the rest of the world. In addition to oral witnesses, they consulted books, and studied archæology and the modern sciences. This group of seekers managed to persuade themselves that they had more or less reconstructed the true and ancient revelation. Having achieved this, the members of the group had scattered throughout the world, each one to act as he thought best, with no more than a friendly contact with the other members. No work was undertaken as a group. After a few expeditions to the United States Gurdjieff himself had decided to settle in France, to take disciples and to write books, the first of which, *All and Everything* appeared in 1950.

Finally, in order to correct certain things that have appeared in the Press, I should like to say that I am not and never have been a disciple of Gurdjieff's. The brief contact I had with him has left an impression on me of a very powerful human personality and in addition, an exceptional moral and spiritual sensibility. By this I mean that he appeared to be activated by the highest moral intentions, moreover that he knew what few men know about the spiritual world and that he was a true master in the realms of mind and spirit. Thus, without pretending to understand him perfectly, I feel a great deal of sympathy for him and even a kind of affection.

My own personal evolution followed quite different lines from his. In his book, which should not be accepted as a systematic statement, I find many ideas that seem to me right and a few that seem profound. But these ideas came to me from elsewhere, and those I find in this book are merely welcome confirmations. It seems to me that this is the attitude he would have preferred to find, for in spite of an occasional violence and rudeness, he had the greatest respect for the personality of others, when he could detect personality in them, and behaved and expressed himself with a courtesy and tact that were undoubtedly reflections of the depths of his soul.

10

An Article by Mr. Gorham Munson

The iconoclasm of this book is so violent that Nietzsche's iconcolasm seems by comparison feeble. To quote his own words, the author has wished " to destroy mercilessly, without any compromises whatsoever, in the mentation and the feelings of the reader, the beliefs and views, by centuries rooted in him, about everything existing in the world." The first surprise is to discover that the hero of this series of adventures is none other than Beelzebub, the prophetic divinity of the Old Testament, the Prince of Demons of the Evangelists. In *All and Everything* Beelzebub, who was born on the planet Karatas, enters the service of His Infinity on the Sun Absolute; from there he thinks he notices something "illogical" in the behaviour of the Universe. Being young, head-strong and rebellious he tries to intervene in the ordering of things, and to punish him for his unfortunate attempt he is exiled to a distant solar system—our own. His conduct on Mars,

Saturn and our Earth is so meritorious that, after many centuries, His Infinity forgives him and allows him to return to his native planet. We first meet him on the interplanetary space-ship travelling towards Karatas; to pass the time he tells his grandson Hassein, the story of his six descents to Earth. The first descent was during the Atlantean civilisation and the last one lands him in America in 1921.

Beelzebub is an extraordinary creation; he has been given a cosmic point of view, and a historical perspective that goes back almost as far as the origins of mankind. He speaks of human communities as a much-travelled Parisian might speak of African settlements, and his historical knowledge extends into the past as far as the time when a collision separated two fragments from the Earth, the Moon and another satellite unknown to astronomers. All said and done, Beelzebub is a wonderful story-teller, much better even than Shéhérazade.

He manages to discuss almost everything that has exercised the human mind in the past. Here is a very incomplete list of the subjects he broaches to enlighten his grandson: the civilizations beyond the Gobi Desert; the distortions incurred by Buddhist teaching; the real significance of the Last Supper; the re-instatement of Judas; the esoteric meaning of the architecture of the Mont-Saint-Michel; perpetual motion; the mysteries of electricity; Bolshevik rebellions in ancient Egypt; the riddle of the Sphinx; polygamy in Persia; objective music that can cause a boil to appear on a man's leg; the persecution of Mesmer; the bad effects of the cult of Sport in Britain, and of American food; the experience of emptiness on Saturn; the fact that

Leonardo da Vinci succeeded in discovering nearly all the secrets of objective art.

On reading *All and Everything* one soon realizes that it is a strange kind of allegory. The book most like it that I can think of is *A Tale of a Tub* by Swift. What is the key of this allegory? The author tells us in the Epilogue, where he describes man as a mechanical being, without real freedom, who nevertheless, thanks to a special training, can harmonize his " three brains " and acquire initiative and will-power.

It is safe to predict that at first *All and Everything* will not make much of a stir and will probably be considered a heavy book, but I believe it will endure, attract more and more readers and prove a rich source for future writers.

Part Two

THE FOREST PHILOSOPHERS

1

Gurdjieff Leaves Russia

THE REVOLUTION broke out in Russia in 1917. The face of the world was about to change. I must guard against the temptation of linking such an important event in the world's history with the sudden change of attitude in Gurdjieff, which occurred in the same year, but we still know nothing of the activities of secret societies on the eve of the Bolshevik Revolution. It seems most unlikely that we ever shall, when we consider the conspiracy of silence and the falsifications that have prevented all work on the esoteric explanation of the French Revolution from being published. Be that as it may, Gurdjieff made a sudden *volte-face*. After 1917 we feel we are in the presence of a caricature of Gurdjieff. It is no concern of mine to find reasons for this change nor even to try to describe it. Twelve men were affected by the transformation, suffered from it and yet were unable to form a clear view of its nature. It was as though Gurdjieff himself suddenly *withdrew* from view, shielded himself behind publicity, money, and " schools." The twelve men are now all dead, and the only one to have spoken is Ouspensky, and he only in guarded terms. The Gurdjieff of the second phase still exerts a peculiar force, and his influence on our contemporaries will be a thousand times greater than that of the earlier Gurdjieff. In the same way Bolshevism, itself a caricature of the revolutionary hope and the great desire for the " liberation of man," triumphs and, to the extent that it accentuates its own exaggerated features, increases its hold on the modern world. The thought sometimes occurs to me that the Caucasus has produced two great men who, with full knowledge of what they were doing, both chose to present the world with a caricature of the power with which they were invested—I mean Stalin and Gurdjieff. (They were at school together). But enough of this.

I repeat that it is the later Gurdjieff with whom we have to deal, bearing in mind that I am not trying to portray the whole man, but to give as accurate an account as possible of his influence on European intellectuals during the last years of his life. If it is really a caricature that emerges, we must realize that we live in an age when only a caricature of a master will be accepted as a true portrait — an age in which, as Jean Paulham says : " Everything that we call occult science is today rather *less* advanced than it was in the thirteenth century; there are fewer facts, as though nature had her own way of secreting and concealing." We have here another sign of the extraordinary obscurity of the modern world. I say again that, notwithstanding the fact that he chose to appear among us as a caricature of himself, still Gurdjieff remains one of the few figures that stand out from the general level of mediocrity.

In 1917, Gurdjieff took refuge in his own country—the Caucasus. He rented a small house on the outskirts of the town of Essentuki. He assembled his twelve best disciples, chosen during the course of four years of apparently pointless meetings in the cafés of Moscow and St. Petersburgh. The twelve men left everything they had to follow him, without much hope of ever being able to return to a country in the grip of civil war.

"I always have a very strange feeling," said Ouspensky, "when I remember this period. On this occasion we spent about six weeks in Essentuki. But this now seems to be altogether incredible. Whenever I chance to speak with any of those who were there they can hardly believe that it lasted only six weeks. It would be difficult even in six years to find room for everything that was connected with this time, to such an extent was it filled."

During the six weeks, Gurdjieff gave them the whole range of the physical and mental exercises designed to lead to the second consciousness, and revealed all his most secret doctrines. "He unfolded to us the plan of the whole work. We saw the beginnings of all the methods, the beginnings of all the ideas, their links, their connections and direction. Many things remained obscure for us; many things we did not rightly understand, quite the contrary; but in any case we were given some general propositions by which I thought we could be guided later on."

Now, one afternoon, at the end of the six weeks, he suddenly announced that he wanted everyone to leave, and that he was going away, by himself, to the Black

Sea coast. They could not believe it. "Everything is just beginning for us," thought the disciples. "He has set us on our way, telling us it will take at least ten years' work under his guidance before we can begin to see the goal he has described to us.—It's impossible." But they had to believe it. "All but a few of us announced that they would follow him wherever he went. G. consented to this, but said that we must look after ourselves, and that there would be no work, no matter how much we counted on it. All this," adds Ouspensky, "surprised me very much. I considered the moment most inappropriate for 'acting,' and if what G. said was serious, then why had the whole business been started ? . . . If G. had started work with us such as we were, then why was he stopping it now ? . . . I had to confess that my confidence in G. wavered from this moment."

Ouspensky, whose whole life was changed by the "teaching" has never said any more about his break with Gurdjieff.

After several months on the Black Sea, and another period at Essentuki, during which time Gurdjieff explained various dance movements designed to give greater control of the body, Ouspensky, aware of the great change that had come over Gurdjieff in the summer of 1917, decided finally to leave him — "The decision to leave G.'s work and leave him exacted from me a great inner struggle. I had built very much upon it and it was difficult for me now to reconstruct everything from the beginning. But there was nothing else to do. Of course, all that I had learned during those three years I retained. But a whole year passed by while I was going into all this and until I found it possible to continue to work in the same direction as G., but independently."

A little while later Gurdjieff left Russia for Tiflis, where he opened his first *Institute for the Harmonious Development of Man*. This was no more than a rehearsal for the big show that he meant to put on either in London, Berlin or Paris.

" During the summer and autumn of 1919," says Ouspensky, " I received two letters from G. . . . He wrote that he had opened in Tiflis an ' Institute for the Harmonious Development of Man ' on a very broad programme and enclosed a prospectus of this 'Institute' which made me very thoughtful indeed. The prospectus began in this way:

' *With the permission of the Minister for National Education, the Institute for the Harmonious Development of Man, based on G.I.G.'s system, is being opened in Tiflis. The Institute accepts children and adults of both sexes. Study will take place morning and evening. The subjects of study are: gymnastics of all kinds (rhythmical, medicinal, and others). Exercises for the development of will, memory, attention, hearing, thinking, emotion, instinct, and so on.*'

" To this was added that G.I.G.'s system—

'*. . . was already in operation in a whole series of large cities such as Bombay, Alexandria, Kabul, New York, Chicago, Christiania, Stockholm, Moscow, Essentuki, and in all departments and homes of the true international and labouring fraternities.*'

"At the end of the prospectus in a list of ' specialist teachers ' of the Institute for the Harmonious Development of Man, I found my own name as well as the names of 'Mechanical Engineer' P., and still another of our company, J., who was living at that time in Novorossiysk and had no intention whatever of going to Tiflis.

"G. wrote in his letter that he was preparing his ballet 'The Struggle of the Magicians' and without making any reference at all to past difficulties he invited me to go and work with him in Tiflis. This was very characteristic of him. But for various reasons I could not go there. In the first place, there were very great material obstacles, and secondly, the difficulties which had arisen in Essentuki were for me very real ones. My decision to leave G. had cost me very dear and I could not give it up so easily, the more so as all his motives were to be seen. I must confess that I was not very enthusiastic about the programme of the Institute for the Harmonious Development of Man. I realized, of course, that it meant that G. was obviously obliged to give some sort of outward form to his work having regard to outward conditions, as he had done at Essentuki, and that this outward form was somewhat in the nature of a caricature. But I also realized that behind this outward form stood the same thing as before and that *this* could not change. I was doubtful only of my own ability to adapt myself to this outward form."

Then, as though suddenly seized by a passion for moving, Gurdjieff left Tiflis and installed himself in Constantinople. After a few months he gave up his new Institute there and started one in Berlin; this one, too, came to an end, and he moved to London, where he met Ouspensky's pupils at the many lectures that his former companion was giving at that time. He had to leave England for reasons that have been explained before, but, by an extraordinary intervention on the part of Raymond Poincaré, he obtained permission to settle in France.

It is at this moment, in 1922, after five years of preparation, that the real game is about to begin.

2

Paris, New York, Fontainebleau

On December 13th, 1923, the following notice appeared in the Paris theatrical newspaper *Comœdia*:

"Professor Gurdjieff may be unknown in Paris, but he is famous throughout the world. The first performance by his Institute, which will be given tonight in the Théâtre des Champs-Elysées, is to present his 'movements.' Later there will be performances of music and demonstrations of strange truths learnt from religious ceremonies of the ancient East.

"The Institute for the Harmonious Development of Man, as the Gurdjieff Institute is called, will introduce us to discoveries made by Gurdjieff in all parts of the world and during the course of many years.

"It is mainly the Orient, both ancient and modern, that has interested Professor Gurdjieff, and it is Oriental art that we shall see demonstrated in exercises, rhythms and sacred and profane dances, including dances of dervishes, fakirs and monks, some of which are still intimately connected with religious ceremonies.

"For the first time we shall see dances from Tibet and Afghanistan."

In April, 1924, in New York, Mr. Carroll, a reporter on the *New Evening Post,* announced that the first performance in America by pupils of the Gurdjieff Institute had just been given in a hall in the west of New York, led by Professor Gurdjieff himself. He wrote as follows:

"First there were dances by a group of men and women in flowing garments and soft shoes. It was really fantastic, as each person danced in a different way. The orchestra produced strange music in which drum-beats predominated. The movements were symbolic and not at all sensual, for it would seem that we were witnessing the manifestations of a cult in which sensuality has no part.

"It is impossible to describe these dances which, it seemed, came down to us from ancient religions. A woman explained that in bygone times the object was to make the dancer perform real acts of grace, praise and supplication. We were shown, in this connection, whirling Dervish dances that might have come straight from the circus.

Gurdjieff directed the dancers, signalling the start with a wave of his arms and stopping them suddenly. They had to keep as still as statues in the positions in which they were stopped. They seemed to be under some hypnotic power.

"The music was a kind of exaggerated jazz, and had been transcribed by M. de Hartmann according to Gurdjieff's instructions. He had memorized the melodies and rhythms from hearing them in various

Eastern monasteries and religious communities during his 'search for Truth.' He asserts that the music dates back to highest antiquity and is transmitted by inscriptions in certain temples.

"The last part of the programme was devoted to different turns — some of them tricks and some natural phenomena — derived from religious ceremonies and based mainly on hypnotism and magnetism.

"These dances can, we were told, lead to higher consciousness, and were practised for this reason by Eastern mystics. The result is obtained by the complete subjugation of the body; in this connection, the dances and movements we had seen were revealing. They teach those who practice them to become aware of all the functions of the body, whereas in normal life we are hardly aware of more than a quarter of them. For example, according to Gurdjieff, one could be taught to regulate the circulation of the blood and to control the glands as easily as waving an arm or kicking a leg."

Finally, Rom Landau, many years later, wrote as follows:

"One of Gurdjieff's main methods is a queer system of dances, the aim of which is not to give the dancer a chance to express his subjective emotions, but to teach him the collaboration of his three different centres through 'objective' exercises. Every movement, pace and rhythm is minutely prescribed. Each limb has to be trained in a way that permits it to make independent movements, not at all co-ordinated with those of the other limbs.

"We all know that our muscles act and react in certain ways because they have always been used to making the same kind of movement. This does not mean that such movements necessarily and always fulfil the real 'ambition' of the muscle. To illustrate this point, let us consider for a moment the difference between our own and the Eastern way of sitting. The Eastern fashion of properly crossed legs and straight spine is much more restful than sitting on chairs with legs dangling down and with the weight of the body wrongly distributed. One can sit in the Eastern position for hours without being interrupted by restlessness or aching limbs, and one rests much better that way than by lying down on a bed. And yet hardly any of us can do it. Why? Because our muscles act automatically.

" Gurdjieff's dances were meant to break the muscular conventions of the dancers. By creating independent movements instead, he endeavoured to attack the mental and emotional convention of his pupils as well.

" Gurdjieff himself wrote the scenario and the music of the dances. Some of the music was based on dervish dances, of which he seemed to possess a very thorough knowledge. He has written thousands of compositions, most of which served as music for the dances.

" When, in 1924, Gurdjieff took a group of his pupils to the United States, the performances of 'objective dances' roused a certain interest. Many people were attracted by their novelty, for these dances had nothing in common with the methods of Dalcroze, Rudolf Steiner, Isadora Duncan, or any of the newer reformers.

" The British author, Mr. Llewelyn Powys, described the visit of Gurdjieff to New York and the effect of his dances in a book, *The Verdict of Bridlegoose* (1927), in which he writes: 'The famous prophet and magician Gurdjieff appeared in New York accompanied by Mr. Orage, who was acting for him as a kind of Saint Paul ... I had an opportunity of observing Gurdjieff while he stood smoking not far from me in the vestibule . . . His general appearance made one think of a riding master, though there was something about his presence that affected one's nerves in a strange way. Especially did one feel this when his pupils came on to the stage, to perform like a hutchful of hypnotized rabbits under the gaze of a master conjurer.'

"I heard very similar opinions from many different sources. People told me that the dancers looked like frightened mice; but they added that it was useless to judge the dances themselves by common aesthetic standards. And yet I came across people who had admired them even for their aesthetic beauty, though there were none of the usual attractions of stage presentation. The dancers wore simple tunics and trousers. One of them told me that the impression of being hypnotized came from the intense concentration that each performance required. Not only had their bodies to act; each one of their three centres had to be controlled consciously, and the required co-ordination of the three centres could only be achieved by the greatest effort of concentration."

Thus, the interest of French and American intellectuals was strongly aroused by the curious public performances in Paris and New York. At the same time, in London, Ouspensky was attracting many writers, artists and psychologists by his series of lectures on the theories and methods he had learnt from Gurdjieff. In rather less than a year, the Western *intelligensia* were *disturbed* by Gurdjieff. The dances and movements were no doubt only the outer manifestations of the work on oneself that was carried on in the Priory at Avon. Great trouble had been taken to advertise the dances, and at the same time, confusing and ambiguous reports had been broadcast, in order to attract as much attention as possible. Gurdjieff cared nothing for material success and had spent recklessly on the production of his " shows." He had arranged for a fountain of scent to play during the two hours' performance at the Champs-Elysées Theatre. In 1917, Gurdjieff had given up working in secret with his few carefully-picked companions. He had chosen, instead, to disturb the Western mind, bound by countless conventions, at whatever cost to his own dignity, and to adopt for the time being, a provocative role.

Behind these noisy demonstrations, as Ouspensky says, the same esoteric researches were undoubtedly proceeding as when he was travelling in Asia, or secretly teaching in his little house in Essentuki, but the method had changed and become almost a caricature of what one would have expected to have been secret.

This mixture of secrecy and showmanship upset his old disciples but caused intense interest amongst the Western intellectuals, dissatisfied with the values of the modern world, after the upheavals of war.

I myself have practised some of the movements and I know how much effort they require. They are the result of a kind of crucifixion of the self. Imagine making contradictory movements with all your limbs; this in itself is very difficult and assumes a certain mastery of the body. Imagine doing, at the same time, extremely complicated mental calculations with rules that *outrage* the rules of ordinary arithmetic (for instance, sums in which one plus one makes three, two plus two makes five, three plus three makes seven, with additions and subtractions all on this same repellent basis). The slightest slip in these calculations, on which the timing of the movements depends, can throw out completely the *ensemble* of the choreography. Finally, imagine concentrating all your emotional powers on a given theme (say, for instance, " Lord, have mercy on me " and *feel* this from the bottom of your heart) and you will then have some idea of the " work " involved in these dances. Every note of the music that accompanied them could be interpreted, according to the highest religious traditions, as symbolic of one of the countless situations of the self in the cosmos. We came away from these sessions shattered, and curiously drained of our ordinary " me's," extremely receptive to " something else " and as though invested with a divine freedom. We were, in fact, de-humanized. I know of one woman who failed to " recognize " her husband when he came home from one of these sessions, and, feeling suddenly abandoned and bereaved, retired to her room to weep and wait until he should " return."

There will be fuller descriptions of these " movements " further on. At the moment I only want to make it clear that the interest aroused by the exhibitions in Paris and New York did not depend solely on the unusual character of the dances. The more intelligent amongst the spectators were well aware that underlying the dances was a method of shattering the foundations of classical psychology and an astonishing example of revolt against what we Europeans so improperly call the " human personality." It was this that aroused in them such a passionate curiosity to know what was going on in the Priory at Avon.

WHAT WAS SEEN BY OUTSIDERS

3

Mr. G. E. Bechhofer's Article

A month after these manifestations in New York, the American review, *The Century*, revealed to the general public some aspects of Gurdjieff's personality and of life at the Priory. Mr. Bechhofer's essay, which was to end his contact with Gurdjieff and the disciples, was introduced by the editor in the following words:—

"In these post-war years of intellectual and spiritual disillusionment thousands of men and women the world over are exploring strange paths and, with inarticulate desires, clutching at every passing cult that promises to pull their lives together and reinvest them with meaning. Nothing seems too bizarre to enlist disciples.

"One of the most picturesque cults of the day is Gurdjieff's Institute for the 'Harmonious Development of Man' for which he has recently been recruiting pupils in the United States. We present here the story of this cult, first because it is a fascinating narrative and second because it is one symptom of our disordered time."

Of all the mystics who have become prominent in Europe during the last twelve years or so, and especially since the war, when their numbers have been doubled, I cannot recall that any has attracted so much interest in so short a time as George Ivanovitch Gurdjieff, the founder of the " Institute for the Harmonious Development of Man," at Fontainebleau, near Paris. I exclude Rasputin from this statement, both because his " mysticism " was of a somewhat peculiar nature and because his notoriety was due to his political rather than his intellectual influence.

Although Gurdjieff's institute has been in existence in France for little more than a year, there is hardly any member of intellectual and professional circles in England, to mention only one country, who is not agog to hear the latest details concerning it. The wider public first became interested when Katherine Mansfield, the writer, died there; immediately people were interested to know what mysterious sort of place this was where the clever young authoress had preferred to pass the last months of her life.

And yet reliable information has been lacking. Except for one or two uninformed articles in a London daily paper and a reply to these in a weekly journal, no account of Gurdjieff's institute has, I believe, yet appeared in print. I shall endeavour to set down here the main theories that underlie Gurdjieff's methods and the form they take in practice.

Although, as will be clear from this article, I am by no means a devotee, I have had exceptional opportunities to keep in touch with Gurdjieff, to recognize the influence he has had over many people of widely differing types, and to realize how skilfully he has kept his colony in existence in the most difficult and varying circumstances.

My first meeting with Gurdjieff was in a remote part of the world. It came about from my renewing an old acquaintance with P. D. Ouspensky, a Russian mathematician, author and journalist, at Rostov-on-the-Don, in the days when General Denikine, the anti-Bolshevist leader, occupied the city.

Now, Ouspensky, as Gurdjieff's chief spokesman and his introducer to English circles, needs a few words of description. When I first knew him in Petrograd at the beginning of the war, he had just returned, as I had also, from a long journey to India; he was well-known as a writer on mystical and theosophical subjects; his book, *Tertium Organum*, which has recently been translated into English, had served to popularize the idea of the fourth dimension in Russia; he was a contributor to several important papers, a vegetarian, but an excellent companion.

When we met again five years later in a tumbledown barn in Rostov, our joint home with a third man, who was dying, although we did not know it, from small-pox, we naturally exchanged accounts of how we had spent the meantime.

It was clear, from what Ouspensky told me that Gurdjieff's coming into his life had been the principal event of the period. He recounted to me how he had come across Gurdjieff in Moscow, and at first had been sceptical of his claims, but had at last been convinced of his great powers and knowledge. Ouspensky and a number of Gurdjieff's other pupils followed the master to Essentuki, a watering-place in Northern Caucasus, where the whirl of the Revolution caught them. When life became intolerable there, they dispersed in various directions. Gurdjieff and a faithful group went to Tiflis, in the Transcaucasus.

When, after a few weeks, terrible weeks in which Denikine's hopes were shattered and his forces driven into the sea amidst indescribable circumstances of horror and despair, I crossed the Black Sea and came to the Transcaucasus, it was natural I should immediately pay a visit to Gurdjieff.

I found him without much difficulty in a small house in Tiflis, where a sign-board announcing the " Institute for the Harmonious Development of Man " hung outside the store which it occupied.

He was altogether Eastern in appearance, short, swarthy, almost bald, but with long, black, moustaches, a high brow and piercing eyes, quite unlike the tall, fair, European of cultivated Ouspensky. He spoke a halting and broken Russian, his native languages are Armenian and the Greek of the Transcaucasus, but his intellectual language, his thinking language, so to speak, is Persian, a fact that may be noted later in connection with his ideas. He received me kindly and I spent many hours in his company then and in later months, either at the house watching him drill the dozen or so members of his institute in exercises and dances that will be described later, or chatting with him on the verandah while he cut out and sewed costumes for a ballet he hoped to produce at the Tiflis Opera-house, or dining with him in admirable Georgian and Persian restaurants beside the swift waters of the wild Kuva River, and near the famous hot baths from which the town takes his name. Once, even, we went together to the baths, and a naked Persian massaged us with his hands and arms and feet much in the manner that, five years afterwards, I saw Gurdjieff employ to massage some of the members of the institute at Fontainebleau.

Once, too, I attended a lecture he gave; it was, I thought, a rather vapid and half-hearted affair, its solitary point of interest being the disputable statement that the mind of an infant is like a clean gramophone record on which every experience is traced, to be brought out again when circumstances arouse an association.

Even in those days he demanded and received absolute obedience from everyone of his pupils. His word was law, and he reigned as a tyrant among devoted slaves.

In essence, it seems to me, nothing has altered from those early days at Tiflis to the present magnificence of Fontainebleau. The scale of the enterprise is enormously larger, the number of pupils is much greater, and they work in a far wider range of occupations; and now Ouspensky gives the semi-public lectures which attract strangers to the Institute. But to one who, like myself, knew the baby institute at Tiflis, there is little new about Fontainebleau.

A few months afterward I met Ouspensky again in Constantinople; he announced to me the forthcoming arrival of Gurdjieff and selected members of his colony. Next Gurdjieff and his party made their way to Berlin, where the institute was again re-opened and the dances, exercises and lectures continued.

Meanwhile, two years ago, Ouspensky suddenly

arrived in London. I understand that the co-operation of a radical editor, interested in mysticism and an old acquaintance of Ouspensky, and that of a society lady in England, the wife of a dull but very successful newspaper proprietor, made this possible. The former provided an intellectual welcome for Ouspensky, the other the means for his journey. The two of them, the editor and the lady, whipped up an audience for him, and we used to meet, either in her studio, an appendage to her splendid house, or in a theosophical lecture-room in Kensington or in a doctor's house in Harley Street. In the audience one saw doctors, psychologists, psychoanalysts, editors, writers, civil servants, theosophists of both sexes, clergymen, and a sprinkling of the men and women who are always attracted by the lure of the mysterious. The psychologists, of course, had an additional technical interest in the lectures. They had realized that psycho-analysis would never accomplish what its earlier exponents had claimed for it, and they hoped now to find in Ouspensky's doctrines hints of a new line of psychological investigation that might do what they had in large part failed to accomplish.

For some reason or other the attempt to conduct an institute at Berlin was abandoned, and the little colony of mystics moved to Paris. Here Gurdjieff hired a Dalcroze school and continued his work of training the others in dances and physical exercises. And, presumably encouraged by Ouspensky's success in England, he now decided to come to that country.

It was difficult for Russians to get permission to live in England, and so a delegation, consisting of one or two of the interested psychologists and the radical editor, representing Ouspensky's congregation, reinforced by a friendly specialist, and backed by the influence of the society lady, interviewed an official in the British Home Office and requested that Gurdjieff and his colony be allowed to come to England and establish an institute. But the Home Office was at that moment terrified of Bolshevists and suspected them in all groups of Russians. Permission was refused to the colony, but it was said that Gurdjieff would be permitted to enter England alone.

Following this rebuff, Gurdjieff set about finding suitable premises for an institute in France. After much trouble he discovered what he wanted in the priory at Avon, near Fontainebleau, thirty miles out of Paris. This is a large old house, that had once been inhabited by a royal mistress and, later, by Dreyfus's advocate; it was from the latter that the estate was bought, consisting of the priory itself, with large gardens and many acres of woodland, set in a beautiful valley on the fringe of the forest. There the colony was duly installed, while Gurdjieff went to London to inspect the disciples that Ouspensky had collected there for him.

To these he must have seemed a strange figure as he looked them over, addressing them in imperious phrases of broken Russian which Ouspensky translated, and treating them with every sign of superiority; however, they promptly accepted him as a person from a higher psychical world, living on a plane of consciousness far above their own. Several sold all that they had and gave him the proceeds for the Institute, and prepared to follow him back to Fontainebleau, among them two psycho-analysts, who disposed of their Harley Street practices; a radical editor also resigned his post, sold his share of his paper, and gave this also to the cause. Others gave according to their means, which, in the case of one or two rich people, represented a considerable sum. And then one little party after another went to live in the institute, convinced that they were on the threshold of a new vision which would lift them beyond the limits of everyday consciousness and make them, finally, beings of a higher order.

Thus, at the end of 1922, "The Institute for the Harmonious Development of Man" began serious work at Fontainebleau with sixty or seventy disciples. Of these perhaps nearly half were Russians from Tiflis and Constantinople, men, women and children; one or two survived from the earliest Moscow days. Others were Russians from Berlin and London, people whose means of livelihood had been removed by the Revolution and who, besides being attracted by anything avowedly mystical, realized that life in the institute was probably not less agreeable than that of Russian emigrants outside.

Most of the remainder were English, if I am not mistaken, the only two French people in the colony were the wives of an English and a Russian pupil; no French men or women seem to have felt an independent call to the new faith. The inhabitants of Avon accepted the institute as an economic asset, but dismissed it otherwise as being simply a *maison de fous* a mad-house.

Among the English, as among the Russians, women predominated, most of them theosophical types. Of the men, the most important were the editor, two psycho-analysts, and two members of the civil service. There were also a few young men, patients of the psycho-analysts, to whom the latter had suggested a visit to the institute.

Of course, there were a few people who did not fit

into any category, as for instance, the society lady who arrived in state every now and then, in the earlier days of the institute and used to perform the harmless, if not very psychical, service of carrying cups of coffee out to Gurdjieff in the grounds. But, alas ! after fluttering for a while like a charming butterfly through the austere halls of Fontainebleau, she soon tired of it and, ever in search of new experiences, flew away, so I am told, to seek spiritual comfort by working for the cinematograph !

Visitors, Russian and English, used also to come to see their friends among the colonists; and frequently people, as it were, on probation from Ouspensky's circle in London, would help to crowd the institute's buildings.

On my visits to the institute, I have usually made my headquarters in Fontainebleau or Paris, but more than once I have been admirably lodged in the priory itself, in a room next to Gurdjieff's own, with my needs attended to by some of the hard-working colonists. I have often been pressed to enter the institute, partly for my own spiritual salvation, which has always exercised my friends, but principally in order that I might act as interpreter between Gurdjieff and his English pupils, and between the English and the Russians generally.

But I have preferred to remain an intimate and disinterested spectator, keeping in touch with all the members of the institute, from Gurdjieff to the latest joined Englishman, and thus collecting gradually a mass of impressions and information, which I am here, for the first time, setting on paper and endeavouring to summarize.

The reader may be interested to know, in brief outline the principles on which Gurdjieff's " Institute for the Harmonious Development of Man " is based. I may begin by pointing out again that, to me as to all the other English people acquainted with the institute, it is Ouspensky and not Gurdjieff who has been the exponent of the philosophy. But we have his definite and repeated declaration that he has learned his ideas from Gurdjieff, who brought them back with him from long journeys in the interior of Asia where he studied in mysterious monasteries, Mongolian and Tibetan, and other secret places of the East.

The philosophy can be described from several angles. I shall concentrate on that side of the theory that finds direct expression through the work of the institute. First, then, civilization, in developing certain of man's faculties, has wholly atrophied or destroyed other higher ones. Those faculties that remain are grouped around three main centres; the intellectual centre, which thinks, plans, formulates; the emotional centre, which feels, likes and dislikes; and the physical or instinctive centre, which acts, moves, creates. In every man, one or other of these centres predominates; he is predominantly intellectual, emotional or physical.

Next, as men are now, every human thought, feeling and act is a purely mechanical reaction to outside circumstances. It is not I who think, but someone thinks through me; it is not I who feel, but someone outside me determines my feeling; it is not I who act, but exterior conditions call forth the appropriate action. Man is like a ship out of control, following a devious course through the waters of life, according to the various currents that carry him with them and appoint his course.

How may a man become master of himself? It is this that Gurdjieff sets out to answer.

First he must learn to know himself as he is, namely a tripartite machine, wholly subordinate to circumstances. To realize this, he must observe himself at every and any moment of his life, when he is working or resting, happy or unhappy, vigorous or weary; he will soon see that it is not he, but outside circumstances that control his actions, emotions and plans.

The next thing for him to do, when he has realized his lack of self-mastery, is to get to work to harmonize his three centres. They ought to enter equally into everything in which he is concerned; when this is the case, he will be harmonized. Then he will be immune from reactions and he will himself be responsible for his acts. He will no longer be rudderless, automatic, a toy of the outside world.

Since the path to this is first through self-observation and self-awareness Gurdjieff sees to it that in the institute you shall be constantly observing yourself under variable conditions. Thus he sets his intellectuals to hard manual labour, so that they may observe themselves under that unaccustomed strain. If a bricklayer were to join the institute, he would presumably be set to loafing or reading, so that he might observe himself. Gurdjieff starts out also to break you of your habits, which are the strongest mechanical processes to which you are subject, and, he says, the more petty the habit, the harder it is to be got rid of. He does this by showing you your particular habits and making you aware of them.

The editor, to take an extreme example, was an inveterate smoker; Gurdjieff promptly cut off his tobacco. If anyone expresses a preference for sweet food, he is suddenly put on an unsweetened diet or is surfeited with food that is all sweet, until he sickens of it. In this way, and, of course, in others more subtle, Gurdjieff seeks to teach his pupils to cast off their habits and so become more and more masters of themselves.

How long does the process take until the disciple reaches the state of self-mastery, self-awareness, fourth-dimensional consciousness? This depends on the innate capacity of the subject and on the extent to which he permits Gurdjieff to help him.

All personal barriers must be broken down. If a man is proud, Gurdjieff humiliates him deliberately before all the other pupils. If he has a special affection or aversion, it has to be eradicated. There is, for example, a man in the institute who, when he entered, hated the sight of blood; he was at once set the task of slaughtering the animals for the stock-pot. There is another very important method that Gurdjieff uses to promote the harmony of the centres—dancing. He endeavours to teach his pupils to become aware of their body as of their mind, and in their exercises and dances they learn how intimately both are bound together. This is why the institute devotes much time to ballets and group dancing as well as to physical exercises.

To sum up, then, the aim of the institute is the development of the innate faculties of its members by first breaking down the artificial barriers of their personality, and then by developing and harmonizing their various mental and physical centres, the means of doing this being self-observation; a practical course of dancing; manual and physical exercises, psychical analysis of every kind; and a series of tests, mental and physical applied by Gurdjieff to fit each individual case.

From this fourth-dimensional plane of consciousness —we are at present on the three-dimensional plane— the harmonized man may proceed even further, developing, or, rather, recovering the control of, newer and ever superior psychic centres.

The reader would perhaps like an example of the difference between an ordinary three-dimensional and a harmoniously developed four-dimensioned mind. Here it is. I meet Jones, whom I dislike, in the street. Immediately I feel a sense of hatred for him, an emotional act called forth mechanically and outside my power to prevent. I clench my fist as if to hit him, which is a physical act of the same nature. But I decide that it would be indiscreet to attack him, as he is much bigger than I, or a similar intellectual process. If, on the other hand, my three centres were balanced or harmonized, I should regard Jones with equanimity, I should not instinctively clench my fist, and, even if he hit me, I could, as did one who was according to Gurdjieff, a great fourth-dimensional mystic, " turn the other cheek." I should, in short, be master of myself.

To the fourth-dimensional man, all worldly problems are clear, for his mind is simultaneously aware of cause and result. For this reason his power over things and men is enormously superior to that of the most powerful ordinary man.

How are we average people to reach this blessed state ? Can we do it by observing ourselves in the seclusion of our homes ? No; this may even be dangerous, since to attempt to alter so fundamentally the working of one's mental mechanism may bring results as unforeseen and irremediable as if one attempted to alter the processes of, say, an internal combustion-engine without properly understanding it. It is therefore essential that the work of harmonization should not be undertaken otherwise than under the care of a teacher who has learned in the occult schools of the East to diagnose and set straight the individual shortcomings of each human machine that presents itself to him.

This, according to Gurdjieff is the reason for the institute. Gurdjieff is such a teacher; he is supposed by most of his disciples to be himself a fourth-dimensional man, with his centres balanced and harmonized, and to be able to assist others toward the same desired condition.

It may be well to illustrate the practice of these ideas during a typical day at Fontainebleau. The inmates wake at about eight or nine o'clock of the morning. This may sound a fairly late hour for so monastic an institution, but you must remember that they probably went to sleep only at about four or five o'clock. It is one of Gurdjieff's doctrines that out of the seven or eight hours' sleep of the normal man half are wasted in the process of " falling asleep," whereas the only period that matters is passed in " deep sleep." This last can be gained equally by spending less time abed, and being more prepared to fall quickly into it from fatigue.

Looking round any of the rooms, you will be astonished at their bareness. The beds are rough couches—I am speaking, of course, of the colonists', not of Gurdjieff's—covered with one or two coarse blankets. There may, perhaps, be a trace of a fire on the hearth, but the chimneys are so foul and fuel is so scarce that a fire is almost more trouble than it is worth. There are sometimes one or two stoves lighted in the corridors, but the priory remains damp and chilling in the colder months of the year.

There may be a ragged scrap of carpet on the floor; two rickety chairs and a fragment of a mirror are probably all the remaining furniture of the room. Physical comfort is not catered to in the institute.

The two or three inmates of the room, then, throw on what clothes they have removed for the night and stumble drowsily downstairs to their work. They may be tending the pigs or cows or sheep, or whatever other animals Gurdjieff may recently have bought. (It may be stated in parenthesis that animals do not prosper there. The institute may perhaps know about the welfare, physical, moral, and psychical, of human beings, but it certainly does not know how to keep animals in good condition.) Or they may be engaged in carting stones in wheelbarrows from one end of the estate to the other. If they carry too many, as the editor and another man did one day when I was with them, they are told that it does not matter; they can carry the surplus back again.

They may, instead, be building a wall for a new structure that Gurdjieff has in mind, perhaps destined for a theatre, a Turkish bath or a new pig-sty. There are always new buildings going up. I remember when Katherine Mansfield was alive, Gurdjieff proposed to build a balcony on the cowshed, so that she might lie there and inhale the odour, which, he assured us, would help to remedy the consumption from which she was suffering.

Worse still, they may be set to cleaning out the sties or the poultry-yard. Or they may have to cut trees or repair a fountain, or perform any other of a thousand tasks. It may even, indeed, be the turn of one of them to be the waiter and dish-washer for the mess; all the inmates take this duty in rotation. The women, who mess apart, have a similar rotation of service in the scullery. It should be noted that, except for a few married couples with children, the sexes are strictly and effectively segregated in the institute; virtually the only time they meet is at the dancing and at the work, in which the women perform tasks nearly as onerous as the men's.

While our friends are at their work, they may look up suddenly to find Gurdjieff, in his round, brimless Caucasian hat of black fur, and his dark, shabby clothes, standing beside them, cigarette in mouth.

"Skorry ! Queeker ! queeker ! " he snaps in his broken Russian and English. " Work ver' good; make you better; you start think better; ver' good ! " Or he himself will take a hand at the work, impressively demonstrating how it ought to be done.

I used to hear what a wonderful worker Gurdjieff was. Rapt disciples told me with bated breath of the abnormal speed and skill with which he built paths, for example, or sawed wood, laid bricks and designed ovens and even a kippering-kiln. But recently I have noticed an element of doubt in these accounts. The paths wear badly, the walls crack, the ovens do not function, and the kiln no longer kippers. Is it possible that Gurdjieff is not the super-artisan he was supposed to be ?

Perhaps, but there is also another explanation for these mischances, which has often been put forward by the editor.

"It is a test," he declares, explaining that Gurdjieff

could, of course, do it all much better if he wished, but he is anxious to test the faith and devotion of his pupils.

At last, at mid-day, comes dinner. The workers troop into their mess and sit down with hearty appetites. They receive a meal consisting of one course only, usually a soup with a little Russian porridge, of which they may eat whatever quantity they desire. The only times I have eaten in the institute I have shared Gurdjieff's own fare in the comfortable old kitchen of the priory; thus I am not in a position to speak of the quality of the pupil's soup. Some favoured ones are allowed also a mouthful of rice pudding, or similar delicacy. I was much impressed, in the mess, by the eager, almost greedy glances that were turned upon the fortunates by the others. It was all rather like being back at school, except that I was the uncle and the others the children.

Sometimes, of course, Gurdjieff commands some of his students to fast altogether. In these cases they continue to work, but go without food for whatever length of time, days or weeks, he declares necessary.

After dinner comes a short rest, and then a return to labour until the evening when, with the exception of those on special duties, the colonists retire to their rooms until the dancing begins. Then at nine or ten in the evening they gather in the largest room of the priory and begin anew the long series of exercises that they have been rehearsing monotonously for months beforehand; in the case of the Tiflis survivors, for years. Occasionally, but rarely, Gurdjieff varies the proceedings with a lecture that is rather a number of replies, more or less oblique, to questions put to him by the more inquisitive or sceptical of his pupils.

The dances are of two kinds, exercises and ballets. The former consist of various motions of the limbs and certain tests of endurance, such as walking round the room with arms outstretched, which some of the more experienced colonists can continue to do for more than an hour without a pause.

Another kind of exercise is derived from the Dalcroze method. In the middle of a complicated movement Gurdjieff suddenly shouts "Stop!" Instantly everyone becomes still in the attitude he or she is in, however uncomfortable it may be; and so they stop until he releases them. This, of course, is designed to help them to contemplate themselves in action. Still another exercise combines physical motions with mental arithmetic; proficiency in it is again largely a matter of practice.

The ballets, on the other hand, are claimed by Gurdjieff to be for the most part reproductions of sacred dances of the East. Each of them has, therefore, according to Gurdjeff, a secret significance not usually obvious to the layman.

It is understood that Gurdjieff has seen and studied these dances in his wanderings through the East, and that he reproduces them exactly as he saw them, and with the original music, which is played in the institute on a piano by a Russian musician who has been with him ever since Tiflis.

The dances are, from the outsider's point of view, the most interesting aspect of the institute's activities. The audiences at the public performances Gurdjieff gave last Christmas in Paris recognized the skill with which Gurdjieff presented his company. The drilling of the twenty or more performers was unusually good;

during the whole programme hardly any movement was made out of time with the others. Whether this was due, as an admirer suggested to me, to every individual performer's deep understanding, conscious or unconscious, of the mystical meaning of the dances, or, as seems quite as probable, to the long and systematic training they have received night after night at Gurdjieff's hands, is a matter on which opinion must differ widely.

Technically, too, the dances are interesting; Gurdjieff has apparently a fine memory for what he has seen or heard and a considerable gift of improvisation. In his own field I should rank him high among contemporary ballet-producers. It is true that, from the stylistic point of view, the movements contain too many broken movements, but this is a minor defect easily to be overcome.

With a rehearsal of the exercises and some or all of these dances, then, the night's work at Fontainebleau ends in the small hours, and the weary colonists go off one by one to bed. But sometimes, on very special occasions, a birthday, for instance, of some popular member, a feast is given by Gurdjieff to the colonists in the composition of which his Asiatic tastes have full play. Dozens of dishes, bearing anything from a sucking pig to Turkish delight, and innumerable bottles are stood upon the floor, and then, squatting on carpets, all the members of the institute sit round and take a welcome respite from their daily duties. But on the morrow the work begins again.

The decision to court publicity by giving the performances in Paris has changed considerably the atmosphere of the institute. It was a curious experience for me, in the dressing-rooms of the Champs-Elysées

Theatre, to hear these philosophers discussing whether they had been sufficiently applauded. I gather that the previous local exhibitions in the institute itself failed to impress local French visitors; but now that Gurdjieff has taken a select group of performers to the United States, I presume that public performances will be one of the principal means of attracting new members to the institute and calling attention to its activities, a curious fate indeed for so esoteric a body.

It is certainly much easier to understand the psychology of the members of the " Institute for the Harmonious Development of Man " than that of the master, Gurdjieff.

So far as the Russians are concerned, for many of them, as has already been pointed out, life in the institute is not worse than life outside; moreover, being Russians, they are mostly prepared to accept without question the mystical claims Gurdjieff or anybody else puts forward. They willingly suffer any humiliation at his hands and by his orders, and repay his severity with a devotion unsullied by any trace of scepticism.

It is all the more curious that some of the Russian men, but not the women, take every opportunity to dodge the manual tasks they receive; they believe, one must presume, in the efficacy of faith more than good works. I remember in this connection an amusing remark of the English editor about a glaring dereliction of duty on the part of one of the senior Russians: "Poor fellow," the editor remarked to his English neighbour and to me, as they rested wearily on their wheelbarrows, " I suppose we must forgive the old man. After all, he has had his centres balanced ! "

This joke shows fairly well, I think, the half-tolerant,

half-sceptical tone that is typical of the English members' attitude towards Gurdjieff and his institute.

They began their careers there without anything more than a hope to find his claims justified. To give him a fair chance of success with themselves, they conscientiously carried out all his instructions and, like mystical *Micawbers,* waited patiently for something super-conscious to turn up.

Before long, I fancy, doubts began to develop among certain of them. It was indeed easy to foresee that if Gurdjieff failed, it was most likely to be on the practical side of his work. It is, after all, not very difficult to maintain an obscure mystical prestige, but the presence of two such experienced doctors as the English psycho-analysts was a constant menace to Gurdjieff's position. I have no means of knowing whether they still acknowledge his claims, though it is an open secret that they have both left Fontainebleau, but one of the severest trials that he has had to face during the last year was his dispute with one of the two.

It occurred as the result of a painful seizure on the part of one of the women colonists, during which, according to one of these English doctors, she vomited blood; according to Gurdjieff it was not blood. The doctor, without examining her, stated that he thought she was suffering from an intestinal ulcer; Gurdjieff denied this, and offered quite a different diagnosis. A month or so later the lady was operated on in London, and the cause of her illness was shown to be indeed an internal ulcer. When the doctor put this to Gurdjieff, the latter merely rebuked him for his lack of trust; and when he spoke of the incident to the editor, his room-mate, the latter merely insisted that, as usual, it had all been a " test ". Gurdjieff, he suggested, knew perfectly well that she had vomited blood, but it was part of his method to make the doctor think he (Gurdjieff) did not know!

It would be wrong to imagine from this naive incident that the editor is a man without experience of the world and one who sees everything and everyone through rose-coloured spectacles. He is, on the contrary, a remarkably lucid and well-informed writer, possessed of a vast experience of men and affairs and, at times, of a mordant wit. Few readers of this article would fail to recognize his name, were I to mention it here. He has, in his career, followed many ploys, of which theosophy was the first, and is now, in its Fontainebleau form, apparently the latest. But even he, I presume, is still only willing to believe in the authenticity of Gurdjieff's claims; he is, however, giving him a larger run than most of the other Englishmen have done.

Not greatly, I imagine, did Katherine Mansfield's attitude differ from his. When I saw her last, a few evenings before her death, a frail, fated figure, watching the dances at the institute, she assured me that she was entirely happy there. She was so confident of recovery that she told me her plans for her next book, and for the one after that and, I rather fancy, for yet another. She did not suggest that Gurdjieff and his colony would appear in them, but it seemed to me, perhaps quite wrongly, that the old sardonic smile in her eyes hinted that sooner or later she would turn these experiences into laughter.

She would have enjoyed, I am sure, Freud's remark, when he heard that the institute housed two psychoanalysts who had been well-known exponents of the theories of his rival, Jung. "Ah," said Freud, " you see what happens to Jung's disciples ! "

In general, however, may we not say that the institute seems to leave its members pretty much as it finds them ? They gain in physical strength but lose in mental poise, becoming almost the automatons of their master. They learn to dance and grow rusty at their old trades. They break their old habits and form new ones. The more they change, the more they remain the same. Or so at least it appears to the onlooker.

Are we to consider Gurdjieff as a true mystic, a genuine initiate of the esoteric doctrines of the East ?

Perhaps; but this is not a thing that may be either proved or disproved. There is, after all, a certain amount of presumptive evidence to bring against the hypothesis. In the first place, would a teacher of an admittedly secret faith blazon his mission from the house-tops, as Gurdjieff has done ? Secondly, it is hardly to be believed that a real initiate, if such exists, would advertise his name and his features in connection with the sacred law. And yet, on the cover of a Russian pamphlet Gurdjieff issued a few years ago about his Tiflis Institute, not only is his name prominently displayed, but even his face is portrayed in the centre of the mystic geometrical figure that symbolizes the base of the occult wisdom.

Thirdly, it is difficult to imagine that a true mystic would demand fees from his disciples. Whereas many of the Russians are supported by him, it must not be overlooked that he in turn has received very considerable sums from English sympathizers, nearly sufficient, indeed, to cover the expense of purchasing the priory and its estate, as well as the cattle, carpets, motor-cars and other things he has acquired. Whether the remainder has been made up by smaller contributions from his English paying guests or by thank-offerings for the healings he undertakes independently in Paris, no one but himself appears to know. In any case, I do not think we may accept as proved the hypothesis that Gurdjieff is a mystic, charged with a mission by a higher occult authority in Asia.

The second and opposite notion, that he is a deliberate charlatan, is not for an instant to be credited by anyone who has come into personal contact with him. He is much too interesting and picturesque a figure to be a mere swindler; besides, there is the interesting philosophy that he and Ouspensky have set out, and the really admirable dances that we saw at the Champs-Elysées Theatre. No, this crude suggestion does not explain Gurdjieff, or even begin to explain him, and need not, therefore, be discussed.

A third theory within the bounds of possibility is that Gurdjieff suffers from a form of megalomania in which he sincerely believes that he has done and can do all that he claims. And, indeed, that many of his statements are patently absurd may be seen from some paragraphs in a pamphlet that was distributed last Christmas to the audience at the Paris theatre which were wholly misleading and untrue.

" The number of persons who are interested in the fundamental ideas of the institute is sensibly increasing; it has not far short of 5,000 adherents, scattered throughout the world, among them persons of every nationality and religion.

" In the principal establishment of the institute are to be found physicometric, chemico-analytic, and psycho-experimental cabinets, intended for independent research and also for the verification of theories and theses which appear dubious or arbitrary.

"The general programme of the work of the ' Institute for the Harmonious Development of Man ' calls for the study of harmonic rhythm, arts and crafts, and languages; parallel to this is conducted a profound study of man and the universe in all their relations according to the materials provided by European sciences and the ancient science of the East. These studies demand the application of new methods, hitherto unpublished, of conceptions and perception; they enlarge the horizon of human conceptions and simultaneously contribute towards regularizing the processes of thought and conscience.

" The Institute possesses also a Medical Section charged with the correction of functional irregularities pre-existing in the patient, the disappearance of which is necessary before his harmonic development can be effectively undertaken."

Finally, another paragraph mentions the existence of a *Journal of the Institute* published in " appropriate characters " and containing reports of all the lectures, discussions and incidents of life in the institute. One wonders how Gurdjieff can have brought himself to permit the publication of claims to so many things that at best can only be hoped for in the future. The 5,000 adherents may safely be cut down to 500; the physicometric, chemico-analytic, and psycho-experimental cabinets, like the journal in appropriate characters, are as unknown, I imagine, to everyone else familiar with the institute as they are to me; the profound study of man and the universe in all their relations is pure verbiage, while the " Medical Section ' consists merely of a few pieces of electrical apparatus of ordinary type and is certainly insufficiently equipped as yet for the important purpose it is said in the pamphlet to perform.

I foresee that each of these three theories about Gurdjieff will continue to have its adherents. Perhaps none of them is correct, and others may have to be brought forward to provide a satisfactory explanation of his motives in founding his " Institute for the Harmonious Development of Man." Still, whatever his purpose, the results have certainly been curious enough to merit the attention that has been given to them during the last few years.

4

*An Account by Denis Saurat of His
Visit to Gurdjieff in 1923*

One Saturday morning in February 1923 Orage came to meet me at Fontainebleau station.

Orage is a big man from Yorkshire, with distant French connections—hence his name. For fifteen years he has been a powerful personality in the English literary world. He edited the "New Age," a half literary and half political weekly which, between 1910 and 1914, had been the centre of the liveliest intellectual circle in England.

Orage might have been the greatest critic of English literature, a literature which suffers much from a lack of criticism, but which revives each time a new writer of genius arises. But he sold the "New Age" and is now at Fontainebleau; literature no longer interests him.

I was astonished when I saw him. When I knew him before he was rather fat, supporting his 190 lbs. on a large, bony frame. The figure that came to meet me was thin, almost gaunt, with an anxious look. An Orage who seemed taller, whose movements were stronger and quicker—a healthier man, but unhappy.

Orage is one of Gurdjieff's disciples. Gurdjieff had set up in the Priory a community " rather on the lines of a Pythagorean community" as Orage said vaguely, "only much more strict."

Strict was right. When I asked him about his health and physical transformation, Orage replied by telling me about his life. He went to bed at about midnight or one o'clock and was up and working again at four—hard labour it was, excavating and building in the Park; quick meals snatched in the short intervals between work. Every now and then the workers would be summoned before the Master for gymnastic exercises, then back to work, digging huge trenches or filling them in. "Sometimes Gurdjieff makes us spend a whole day digging out an enormous trench, and the next day he makes us fill it all in again." I asked why, but Orage did not know. What is Gurdjieff? I asked—but Orage did not know that either.

Two years ago there had been talk in London about Ouspensky, who was working on a book called "Tertium Organum," implying that he only acknowledged two predecessors—Francis Bacon and Aristotle. Mankind was about to change its course. Ouspensky had formed a group of pupils over whom he exercised absolute control. He then gradually made known the fact that he himself was only the precursor of some-one much greater, who would come from Russia or even further East. This was Gurdjieff. In the meanwhile, Ouspensky instructed and prepared the way. He had even invented a new method of teaching. The true doctrine was too abstruse to teach directly, the disciples would not have understood it. He therefore made the disciples do the speaking; one of them asked a question and then explained it. For instance, a pupil might ask : " Is the soul immortal ? " Then, according to the quality of the explanation of this question, the master would reply, giving as much of the truth as he thought the disciple could absorb.

This had been going on for several months when Gurdjieff arrived in London. Now Gurdjieff knew neither English, French nor German. He gave his orders in Russian (he only spoke to give an order) and these were translated by one of his followers.

He was said to be fabulously rich; he seemed to have access to an inexhaustible supply of the world's gold. He wanted to found a University of Occultism and to reveal the One Doctrine, not to the world, which he despised, but to his chosen disciples. This is where politics intervened. Lloyd George was flirting with the Soviets. Gurdjieff and his party were opposed to the Soviets but were not White Russians either. The English authorities, at Moscow's request it was said, refused to give them permission to remain in England; but because Lloyd George had refused, Poincaré would consent, and, in fact, hoping thus to cause the downfall of the Soviets, Poincaré granted Gurdjieff the necessary permits. So he had bought the chateau and park at Fontainebleau with the intention of establishing there his school of Occultism.

But who, amongst the disciples, would be admitted ? Several hundred Londoners were members of Ouspensky's groups. One day Ouspensky sat at the end of a large room, while all the men and women who aspired to immortality were made to file slowly past him. It was said that only the chosen would have a chance of immortal souls. Among the chosen were Orage and Katherine Mansfield. Gurdjieff did not speak as he knew no English, but he could pick out at a glance the likely candidates for immortality and, by a sign, he extracted from the queue those who were to go to Fontainebleau. They were usually rich, but he occasionally picked some-one poor.

Orage told me all this as he led me to the Priory. Katherine Mansfield had died a few weeks before. I had come to see Orage because his letters had worried me. It was he who had persuaded Katherine Mansfield to come here, having received almost a promise of her recovery. He was going to show me the place where she passed her last days—an extraordinary place.

Gurdjieff undoubtedly had supernatural powers. He had appeared to his disciples in Moscow or in Petrograd, or, at any rate, somewhere in Russia, while his body was wandering hundreds of miles away. Ouspensky had seen him.

But since Orage had been at Fontainebleau Gurdjieff had not spoken a word to him. The group exercises were supposed to be a necessary preparation for initiation. Gurdjieff directed them in Russian. The Russians present used to say, with a doleful, but at the same time triumphant expression, that Gurdjieff constantly lost his temper and that his language on those occasions would have made even Lenin blush. There were about seventy Russians there, and twenty English. Not a single Frenchman.

There was a cow-shed and five or six dirty cows. There are no servants in a Pythagorean community, and men of the world, even literary critics, are not much good at looking after cows. These cows produced milk for the hundred disciples. Katherine Mansfield was tubercular and lived in this cow-shed. Cows, too, are often tubercular, and milk carries the germ.

The ceiling was high—this cannot have been a cow-shed before the master came. Less than six foot from the ceiling, a Russian with a gift for carpentry had constructed a platform; there was a ladder up to it, and a mattress with cushions on it. This is where Katherine Mansfield lived. The master had said, it seems, that the emanations from the cows would cure her illness—not only the smell of the cows and the cow-shed, but spiritual emanations. Katherine Mansfield died and no-one dared to ask the Master why. Besides, he could speak no English and it would have meant asking one of the Anglicized Russians and all the Russians were terrified and tame, much more so, even, than the English.

There were several doctors amongst the disciples. They said that in any case their medicine could do no more for Katherine. At least, said Orage, she died serene and even happy.

Another Russian, with a gift for painting, had decided to contribute to Katherine Mansfield's last pleasures. He had painted a large number of crescent moons, suns and stars in very bright reds and blues, on the plaster just above her platform. He had not as much gold paint as he needed but made do instead with red and blue. Katherine gazed at these stars and crescents as her last days passed by. At least the cows helped to keep her warm; it was very cold that February and the château was barely heated.

We had lunch in the large dining-hall of the château. The furniture was shabby. The cooking was done by the disciples. In principle, everyone had to feed himself; in practice the disciples took it in turn to cook.

In actual fact, some of the women were in charge. The food was quite passable. There were other visitors; some White Russians, a former minister of the Tzar. The talk was of occultism.

It seemed (but no-one knew for certain) that Gurdjieff had revealed that few human-beings have immortal souls. A certain number have a kind of embryonic soul. If this embryo is cultivated according to the laws, it may develop and reach immortality. If not, it will die. Gurdjieff alone knew the right methods. But everyone he had brought with him here had, at least, an embryo. During the file-past, in London, the master's second sight had discovered the possible candidates. That was a great comfort—everyone had at least a good chance of immortality. At any rate the disciples. The visitors looked at each other anxiously. There were about twelve of us. Most of Gurdjieff's subjects had no fixed hour for their meals.

The door opened suddenly. A large, powerful-looking man burst in. He was dressed in a fur-lined overcoat with the fur outside, but was bare-headed. His head was completely shaven. His expression was one of habitual ferocity, mixed, at this moment, with a tenderness that was evidently fleeting, as he held in his arms a large lamb. His tenderness was for the lamb. With great strides he crossed the room, without even glancing at us, and went out by another door. We all realized who it was. The disciples much moved, said: " It is always so. He does not look but he has seen you. He knows you all perfectly."

Orage wanted to show me the Park, so after lunch we strolled down the avenues. Gurdjieff had bought an aeroplane-hangar from the military authorities. The disciples had dismantled and re-erected the hangar.

This huge, dirty black building looked out of place in the garden. The park was, indeed, scarred by trenches. " Gurdjieff keeps us hard at it. The soul cannot develop unless the body is in perfect equilibrium. They teach us mastery of our muscles; we can manage the heaviest work, and we can also move our left arm in a different rhythm from our right. We can beat four with the right and three with the left, at the same time."

At the end of one avenue, in a large hollow, we saw a kind of huge native hut, made of bricks and mortar. Orage explained that these were the Turkish Baths. Men and women went there separately. Complete chastity reigned, but there were married couples living normally as well. Gurdjieff neither preached nor practised asceticism, but his pupils were worn out by hard labour and by fear.

All of a sudden we caught sight of Gurdjieff. He was standing a few feet away from the bath-house. Nearby, workers were mixing cement. Gurdjieff took a great handful in his bare hands, rolled it into a ball and threw it into the hut. He bombarded the interior of the hut with balls of cement in rapid succession. We approached. The boiler, constructed by pupils with no experience, had burst. We could see a crack through which were being sucked long, thin tongues of virulent flame. No-one knew what to do. Gurdjieff arrived. The heat made it impossible to get near the furnace. So Gurdjieff attempted to stop the crack with balls of cement. He aimed well. He started at the top of the crack, and the balls made a curious sound as they struck the burning casing. His unbuttoned overcoat flapping around him got in the way, so presently he took it off. He did not look at us. Some pupils watched him from a distance with a kind of horror. The cement-mixer looked like a slave.

We were embarrassed. I had the impression of witnessing something obscene. We left.

I was asked to spend two nights. That evening after dinner, while I and some of the English were in Orage's room, Gurdjieff sent us a large bottle of vodka. They all said this was a quite unusual honour. These people were helpless, a prey to a mixture of shame, fear and unavowable hope. I suggested that we should throw half the vodka out of the window to make Gurdjieff think we had drunk it. The fact was that none of us wanted to drink more than a few drops and we felt quite incapable of doing justice to the whole bottle. But my suggestion was not followed—they were all afraid.

We talked late into the night. A few people there were well-known in London; there was a distinguished doctor from Harley Street, a lawyer and several writers. Someone came to tell me that Gurdjieff would see me on the following afternoon and would have an interpreter. There was great consternation! He had never received anyone before, they said. The English begged me to ask all sorts of questions; he had not spoken to any of them since their arrival, several months ago. They did not know what they were doing there. The Russians only gave them vague indications. They were all at the end of their tether and demoralized by manual labour that was too hard for them. Later on that evening we were told that Gurdjieff had ordered a "mystical night" for the following Sunday, in the hangar transformed into a temple, and that he had authorised the presence of a reporter from the "Daily Mail." They were all dumb-founded. Was this mystic secret that they knew nothing about going to be revealed to the " Daily Mail "?

Sunday, February 18th, from two-thirty to four-thirty, with a Russian interpreter, Madame de Hartmann, who spoke good English. I must condense the long conversation:

Me: " What results are you trying to obtain here? "

G.: " Better health, wider intelligence, and a complete break with people's normal routine."

Me: " Have you already attained your objective with some people ? "

G.: " Yes, in four or five years some of the disciples have reached the goal."

Me: " Do you know that several amongst them are near to despair ? "

G.: " Yes—there is something sinister in this house, and that is necessary."

Me: " Their ambition is to become immortal ? "

G.: " All have ambitions, few satisfy them. (Sardonically). Each one possesses a ' me ' and an essence. Many would like to transfer their ' me ' into their essence and so become immortals."

Me: " What is the object of all this manual labour and must it go on for long ? " (The English had begged me to ask this.)

G.: " To make them masters of the exterior world. It is only a temporary phase."

Me: " Are you trying to give them occult powers ? "

G.: " Yes. I am trying to give them all powers. There is no difference between occult powers and other powers. The occultists of to-day are all wrong."

Me: " You do not form part of a school ? "

G.: " No, we are a group of friends. Thirty years ago, twelve of us spent many years in Central Asia, and we reconstructed the Doctrine; by oral traditions, the study of ancient costumes, popular songs and even certain books. The Doctrine has always existed, but the tradition has often been interruped. In antiquity some groups and castes knew it, but it was incomplete. The ancients put too much stress on metaphysics, their doctrine was too abstract."

Me: " Why did you come to Europe ? "

G.: " Because I want to add the mystical spirit of the East to the scientific spirit of the West. The Oriental spirit is right but only in its trends and general ideas. The Western spirit is right in its methods and techniques. Western methods alone are effective in history. I want to create a type of sage who will unite the spirit of the East with Western techniques."

Me: " Are there sages of that kind yet ? "

G.: " Yes—I know a few European learned men who have reached that goal."

Me: " Apart from questions of method, do you teach a positive doctrine ? "

G.: " Yes. Few human-beings have a soul. None have one at birth. Those who do not acquire one, die: their atoms are dispersed, nothing is left. A few make themselves a partial soul and are submitted to a kind of reincarnation which allows them to progress. And, finally, a very small number succeed in acquiring immortal souls. But this number is really very small indeed. Most of those who have achieved any success have only managed to acquire partial souls."

Me: " Do you believe in Free Will ? " (Neither the interpreter nor Gurdjieff seemed to know what Free Will meant. My explanations produced the following answer from Gurdjieff) : —

G.: "Everyone does what he wants. Nothing can stop him. But men do not know how to will."

Gurdjieff had an astonishing courtesy. He gave not the slightest impression of being a charlatan during this conversation. He seemed to be trying to explain himself in as rational a way as possible, and did not refuse to answer any questions. His ferocity seemed changed into strength. I asked him if he still saw any of the friends with whom he had reconstructed the Doctrine. He replied that he saw three or four of them.

"What are they doing?"

"Carrying on their ordinary professions."

"Are they teaching?"

"No, I am the only one who teaches. That is my profession." The disciples said that he described himself as a dispenser of solar energy, which they did not pretend to understand. "Is there a God?" I asked, and was told: "Yes, and Gurdjieff's relationship with him is that of a somewhat independent, obstinate and touchy minister with his King." Women, they said, had no possibility of really acquiring a soul except through contact and sexual union with a man.

In the evening, before the big *séance*, I gave the Englishmen the results of my enquiries. They were extremely disappointed. What annoyed them most was that Gurdjieff should have said that the Doctrine could be found in books. "In that case" said the doctor from Harley Street, "if the tradition can be found in books, what are we doing here?"

"It means" said another, "that there is no secret tradition." And they decided that this could not be so —either I had not understood or else the interpreter had interpreted wrong. The only comfort was that their manual labours would not go on for ever. They were much struck by Gurdjieff's admission that there was, by his own will, something sinister about the house. They wondered a bit if they were being duped, but even if it were so they preferred to remain victims. At the same time, they were afraid of being exploited by Gurdjieff for occult purposes. They had full confidence in his power, but were not so sure of his intentions towards them.

Ten o'clock, in the hangar. An enchanted atmosphere. Carpets that looked extremely valuable covered the floor and the walls. The man from the "Daily Mail," who attached himself to me, assured me he was a *connoisseur* of carpets and that these must be worth more than a million. The walls and floors were, indeed covered, and in places there were several layers. A large couch with cushions ran the whole length of the walls, about three feet from the ground, on which were reclining many men and women, awaiting mystical experiences. There was music, purporting to come from Central Asia—and anyway, very strange; there was perfume, and, in the middle of the room, a fountain played, with coloured lights.

The dances started under Gurdjieff's direction. They were slow dances, and the dancers were placed rather far apart. At a word of command, everyone stopped and remained motionless until the signal came to go on. Those who were out of balance when the command came, were not allowed to finish their movement and fell heavily to the floor from the normal effects of gravitation. Having fallen, they had to keep still.

The "Daily Mail" man was justly frightened. The perfumed atmosphere, coloured lights, rich carpets and strange dances—it was Oriental romanticism at last realized on earth. To reassure the journalist I told him that I was a professor in Bordeaux University and that all these people were mad. He thought about it for a moment, and then seemed much relieved; his confidence in himself came back. But, next day he treacherously recounted my words of comfort to Orage, who was greatly upset and only forgave me ten years later."

[It is interesting to note that thirty years separate this visit of M. Saurat to Gurdjieff, the account of which appeared in the "Nouvelle Revue Francaise" in 1933, from his criticism of "All and Everything" that I have included in the first part of this book.]

5

Knowing and Being

Such are the stories told by the week-end visitors, the tourists, who came to the Priory. Now I shall try to give some impressions of the day-to-day life of a few of the inmates of Avon. Whatever the conclusions reached separately by each person, everyone, whether visitor or practitioner, was equally struck by the diversity of the teaching: manual labour, rhythmic exercises, dances, lectures, conversations, mental exercises, etc. No-one had the slightest doubt that Gurdjieff's view of the structure of the personality, of the relation between man and the world, and of many other things, was original and in no way reducible to current vague "spiritualist" systems. This view, which has been clearly and learnedly developed by Ouspensky, presupposes a sound philosophical system in which psychology, theology, cosmology, ethics and aesthetics are firmly linked and which, as expounded by Ouspensky, deserves quite as much notice as any of the most important European philosophies. Now, it was impossible to penetrate Gurdjieff's system of thought without first passing through an experience that involved the whole of oneself, without first reaching a level of physical and mental initiation on which what we call "intelligence" and "culture" are denied. This is why psychologists, doctors, writers and every other kind of academic intellectual could be seen pushing wheelbarrows, looking after cows, dancing and generally engaged in "un-learning." It was not possible to approach this teaching from the intellectual standpoint that we normally adopt in any philosophical enquiry. It became necessary to change our idea of *knowledge*. This, amongst many other less important impressions, was abundantly clear to the visitors as well as to the disciples.

"There are," says Gurdjieff, "two lines along which man's development proceeds, the line of *knowledge* and the line of *being*. In right evolution the line of knowledge and the line of being develop simultaneously, parallel to, and helping one another. But if the line of knowledge gets too far ahead of the line of being, or if the line of being gets ahead of the line of knowledge, man's development goes wrong, and sooner or later it must come to a standstill.

"People understand what 'knowledge' means. And they understand the possibility of different levels of knowledge. They understand that knowledge may be lesser or greater, that is to say, of one quality or of another quality. But they do not understand this in relation to 'being.' 'Being,' for them, means simply 'existence' to which is opposed just 'non-existence.' They do not understand that being or existence may be of very different levels and categories. Take for instance the being of a mineral and of a plant. It is a different being. The being of a plant and of an animal is again a different being. The being of an animal and of a man is a different being. But the being of two people can differ from one another more than the being of a mineral and of an animal. This is exactly what people do not understand. And they do not understand that *knowledge* depends on *being*. Not only do they not understand this latter but they definitely do not wish to understand it. And especially in Western culture it is considered that a man may possess great knowledge, for example he may be an able scientist, make discoveries, advance science, and at the same time he may be, and has the right to be, a petty, egoistic, cavilling, mean, envious, vain, naïve, and absent-minded man. It seems to be considered here that a professor must always forget his umbrella everywhere.

"And yet it is his being. And people think that his knowledge does not depend on his being. People of Western culture put great value on the level of a man's knowledge but they do not value the level of a man's being and are not ashamed of the low level of their own being. They do not even understand what it means. And they do not understand that a man's knowledge depends on the level of his being.

"If knowledge gets far ahead of being, it becomes theoretical and abstract and inapplicable to life, or actually harmful, because instead of serving life and helping people the better to struggle with the difficulties they meet, it begins to complicate man's life, brings new difficulties into it, new troubles and calamities which were not there before.

"The reason for this is that knowledge which is not in accordance with being cannot be large enough for, or sufficiently suited to, man's real needs. It will always be a knowledge of *one thing* together with ignorance of *another thing;* a knowledge of the *detail* without a knowledge of the *whole;* a knowledge of the *form* without a knowledge of the *essence.*

"Such preponderance of knowledge over being is observed in present-day culture. The idea of the value and importance of the level of being is completely forgotten. And it is forgotten that the level of knowledge is determined by the level of being. Actually at a given level of being the possibilities of knowledge are limited and finite. Within the limits of a given being the *quality* of knowledge cannot be changed, and the accumulation of information of one and the same nature, within already known limits, alone is possible. A change in the nature of knowledge is possible only with a change in the nature of being."

This lesson upset all the preconceived ideas of those at the Priory. In this fact, it seems to me, lies the importance of the Institute at Avon in the history of contemporary ideas. If this seems a rash statement, it is because we look at these things only from a rationalist's point of view or else from the cautious point of view of the Church. The fact is, that since the middle of the nineteenth century, there has arisen in Europe a method of knowing that runs counter to the conventional methods of our civilization. This counter-current has grown continually from its beginnings in the romantic occulists down to the introduction of Oriental philosophy (Zen Buddhism, for instance, or the Vedantas). It has been developed by the traditional metaphysical philosophers from Claude de Saint-Martin to René Guénon; it has been much enriched by the contributions of the great German writers from Nietzche to the phenomenologists like Husserl, who laid the foundations of a science of being, by revealing for the first time the heart of " mysticism." Even the avant-garde physicists and mathematicians have added enormously to this counter-current. It is from such indications that it would be possible to trace the real history of contemporary ideas, and in such a history Gurdjieff's thought would occupy an important place.

The Gurdjieff movement entered an apparently less " scandalous " phase after the closing of the Institute for the Harmonious Development of Man, and the decision not to attract any more public attention. It was at this time that I and many others, whose stories you will read in Part III, were drawn into it. But, during this first period of Gurdjieff's activities in the West, when everything seemed to be expressly arranged to shock the largest possible number of intellectuals, to repel the mind and the philosophical, psychological, moral, religious and aesthetic ideas of the Western " elite," he displayed a kind of scornful amusement, a light-hearted wilfulness, a supreme contempt for all our conceptions of " classical " knowledge, for human personality, liberty and respect — an extravagantly strange attitude that can only be attributed to a quite abnormal *vital energy*.

The year 1923 was a milestone in France. At exactly the same time the surrealist movement was secretly coming into being, and was openly tearing down the tenets of psychology, the conventions of language, the conceptions of Man's position in the so-called " civilized" Western world; this is not unconnected, at a certain level, with Gurdjieff's much publicised work of *revolt*.

André Breton wrote:— "It is living and ceasing to live that are imaginary solutions. Existence is elsewhere." I am well aware of the important distinctions between the aim and methods of Gurdjieff's teaching, nevertheless I would like to point out to those who are sensitive to *signs*, that the year 1923 is an important year in the history of the clandestine ideas that I have mentioned before.

I believe these considerations to be necessary, difficult though it is for a man with no serious philosophical training or facility in the use of abstract language to formulate them. If you have been able to follow them, in spite of my clumsiness, you will be interested in the following article, which was published in the important French daily paper—*Le Temps*. Mr Levinson, who, under another name, knew Gurdjieff well, I am told, devotes two columns to the defence of the Western intellectual conventions and ways of thought on which our "modern civilization" depends. One should bear in mind that this paper was, for half a century in France, the guardian of conformist opinion, so this long and vehement defence takes on a special significance in its pages.

Doctor Miracle

"At the present time there is an extremely interesting show; M. Gurdjieff, the healer and mystagogue, is arranging demonstrations by his Institute for the Harmonious Development of Man. He presents thirty young men and women, dressed up in white Oriental clothes, who suggest a picture of a slave-market at the time of the Barbary pirates. They perform gymnastic movements, sometimes altogether, sometimes in groups. The movements have, in fact, been taken from Oriental rites and liturgical dances; the pupils cross the lower part of the leg " outside " and then force a kick; they flutter their hands; they raise and drop their outstretched arms all in one piece, with wrists and fingers rigid. To be sure, the interest of this limited number of movements is relative, the exercises attributed in the programme to Kashgar being not at all unlike the ceremonies from Afghanistan; and both sets bearing a strong resemblance to the exercises and rhythmic games of the Dalcroze Institute, whose ' popular Oriental dances ' we have already seen on their posters. Instead of searching out these 'working dances' in distant Turkestan villages, the ideas might just as well have been discovered in a popular German book called *Work and Rhythm*. The thing that strikes one most in these movements, apart from a few chance undulations, is the strong effect of the rhythm, an effect that appears to be hypnotic, for the pupils turn and stamp as though bewitched. They remind one of the primitive Slavs in the *Sacre,* of Nijinsky, and of the mechanical dancers in *Les Noces.* They perform grimly, like a gang of convicts or prisoners, without a smile, and give one a horrible feeling of sadness, as one is instinctively repelled by the spectacle of Will succumbing to suggestion. At the end of each turn the performers seem to collapse inwardly and to become ugly and dull. I gathered from the programme that the miraculous doctor is supposed to straighten out and exalt the personality; what he does in fact is to give his puppets the illusion of freedom.

" One very successful exercise particularly annoyed me. The pupils would all be moving together in a tumultuous and complicated dance when they are suddenly halted by an imperious ' Stop ' from M. Gurdjieff. They have to remain motionless in their often unstable positions until the master sets them free with another word of command. It seems like something out of the *Arabian Nights* ! For although the halt could have been pre-arranged, thus making the trick easy, the effect was none the less powerful and intense. What would I have done in such circumstances, if this brutal command to stop had been flung at me ? I should have fallen out of line and turned my back on the placid and implacable face of the magician, for I am Western European and not a dog to be ordered about. Let those who will be hypnotized.

"I had already heard about the Gurdjieff Institute in intellectual circles; lawyers, doctors, statesmen, already converted in advance, were looking forward to a pilgrimage to the Institute with the eagerness of neophytes. It would seem that the European *élite* is in haste to abdicate — the cultured have ceased to be proud of their heritage. They fly from the clear gaze of Athene and wish only to fall asleep, like Vivian in Merlin's garden. They want an enchanter, a dispenser of dreams. I am not casting doubt on M. Gurdjieff's knowledge and honesty and I acknowledge his immediate power, but were he the Grand Panjandrum or simply a quack, his influence would still be the same. The man himself is not in question, but the symptoms are frightening.

"From all sides Asia is on the march against us. She has already invaded Germany. Spengler prophesies the end of the West, and all that will survive, according to him, is a fierce desire for domination. Count Kayserling, on his return from India exchanged his Chair of Philosophy for a School for Sages. In Prague and Belgrade, Russian refugees have founded the "Eurasian" doctrine, they try to turn their sick countries towards the East, to some new Mecca. The Asiatic invasion has already crossed the Eastern boundaries and is permeating the Latin countries. Magic is besetting scientific thought — mystification is clouding the truth. We are disillusioned about everything and turn to the spells of snake-charmers.

"It is, however, Europeans who have irrigated the Indian fields, fought against pestilence and built civilizing railways up the slopes of the Himalayas. It is the 'Sahibs' who have crossed the Sahara in track-laying vehicles, who built the Villa Rotonda and wrote the *Divine Comedy.* Is our heritage really so negligible? Has our way of thought nothing to put beside the mystical experience of the East? Have we given knowledge to the backward races only to become, in our turn, their dupes? Certainly we are seldom in harmony, but rather in a state of disequilibrium, which causes us suffering but also leads to action. Our great leaders were all men of action. And now we choose to give ourselves up to hypnotizers and to those who promise us Nirvana. Where will M. Gurdjieff's methods lead to in the end, if they are as successful as his rhythmical teaching already proves to be? They will exclude from ordinary life with its struggles, victories and joys, a few people who are given up to a sterile 'harmony.' We all of us have, however, a task to fulfil, we have to reconstruct our house, the great Western civilization. But no doubt the nymphs of Fontainebleau Forest, whose dances Corot evokes, will prove the best protection against the white-robed, silk-sashed phantoms that haunt the Priory, and are commanded by the mysterious Persian, M. Gurdjieff."

There are still two or three real alchemists in Paris. One of them spoke to me about Gurdjieff in terms comparable to Mr. Levinson's. The latter however defended the West in the name of the "modern" mind and the Cartesian convention, whereas the alchemist defended it in the name of a certain aspect of occultism that properly belongs to the Latin races. Thus the two criticisms are radically opposed.

This is what the alchemist said: —

"Since the beginning of the Romantic movement there is a progressive invasion of Europe—rapidly increasing to-day—by forms of Eastern thought presented in such a way as to hasten the spiritual collapse of the West. Now, all spiritual actions have their repercussions in the material world. Sooner or later, spiritual invasion means physical invasion. Behind these " masters " and " doctrines " the East and the Middle East are plotting the conquest of the white races who, little by little, are proving themselves incapable of managing any longer either their spiritual or their material capital. A man such as Gurdjieff was appointed from Above to work, in a specified area, at the disintegration of the West. These plans have been maturing for centuries. It is a matter of transforming the face of the world, and it is in relation to plans on this scale that Gurdjieff's actions must be seen."

As I write these lines I do not know what to think either of Mr. Levinson's accusations, the alchemists, or of the accusations of the priests, for whom Gurdjieff is a prefiguration of Anti-Christ. But I feel sure that Gurdjieff's work should be placed in the counter-current of which I spoke earlier. Its study has been unjustifiably neglected and will repay our attention.

THE WAY THE DISCIPLES LIVED

An Article by Dr. Young

Doctor Young was a well-known English psychiatrist, follower of Jung. When Freud (Jung's rival) heard of his presence at the Priory, he exclaimed in a falsely pitying tone:— "You see what happens to Jung's disciples!"

In an article written for the New Adelphi in September 1927, Dr. Young gives a full account of his experience with Gurdjieff. First of all he tells his reasons for joining the Institute for the Harmonious Development of Man, as follows:—

"At the outset I would point out that every form of occultism implies its own particular psychology. Also, I think it may be said that every form of occultism aims at self-development through deepening, or expanding the limits of, self-consciousness, or however you like to express it. Now it is obvious that this laudable object cannot be attained merely by embracing the ideas of a system, however rapturously. The all-important factor of the exercise and proper application of will must enter, if anything is to be achieved. If it does not, then the ideas, however beautiful and intriguing, in the end become merely 'dope.' I need not remind you how many people make the classical Adlerian 'escape' into occultism, and how difficult it often is to cure them of this 'dope habit.' Such people constitute the pseudo-occultists of our time and of all time. So it may be said that 'pseudo-occultism' only exists by reason of the 'pseudo-occultists.' I even venture to think that the term occultism will tend to disappear altogether with the realisation that the essentials of its matter (in so far as it contains true psychology—and ruling out speculative theory) are implicit in the interpretations and findings of modern psychology.

"However that may be, I said above that the all-important factor in self-development by any system whatever was necessarily the will. The insistence, in the Ouspensky-Gurdjieff doctrine, on the need for development of the will through ceaseless application to the 'work,' in the specific sense, impressed me deeply. I was not so overwhelmingly satisfied with the results of my analytical therapy that I could afford to ignore any ideas or theories bearing on the question of will, because it seemed to me that 'failure of will' was *the* 'bête noire' in neurosis. Roughly, the neurotic symptom from the Freudian standpoint is the disguised expression of an effect which is too painful to be *faced*. From the Adlerian standpoint, it is an 'incomparable arrangement,' by which the patient avoids *facing* a certain aspect of what we call reality. In the broadest sense in both systems, it is a question of failure to *face up* to reality. Now it by no means follows that, when it is made clear to the patient by analysis what aspects of reality he had been unconsciously avoiding, that he will at once be able to cope with it. This is particularly evident in the case of obsessionists, as I have proved to my own satisfaction again and again. A washing obsessionist, for example, cheerfully subscribes to the theory or origin of her washing, but when called upon to make the slightest new adaptation, always falls back on her washing. In effect she says: 'I cannot marry, or do this, that or the other, because, you see, I wash." To put the matter in a nutshell, analytical knowledge is not necessarily effective knowledge. Now I think it will be generally agreed that what I have called 'failure of will' is often bound up with an endocrine deficiency or dyscrasia, sometimes acquired and sometimes apparently so fundamental as to justify the term 'primary plasmic insufficiency,' which corresponds to Adler's organic inferiority. Unfortunately, the science of endocrinology was not, and is not yet, so far advanced as to enable us to remedy such dyscrasias with anything approaching to certainty or precision, even granted that our powers of diagnosis may be able to divine the true nature of such complicated conditions. My problem, then, was how to overcome the difficulty of 'failure of will' by means of a definite psychological method. What I learnt in the early stages of my acquaintance with the system which was afterwards tried out at Fontainebleau gave me reason to hope that here was something which I had been seeking. It must not, however, be supposed that I embarked on this adventure chiefly, or even mainly, to improve and expand my psychological and therapeutic technique. I cannot lay claim to such a purely impersonal motive. It may be that I was a little discouraged by the less consistent and more ambiguous results of analytical therapy in contrast with the precise and concrete results of surgery, which I had practised a good deal, both before and during the war. This state of mind was helped neither by the paeans of joy and jubilation which issued from the ranks of those who acclaimed the successes of a cut-and-dried technique, nor by the acrimonious discussions which seemed to centre round the maintenance of a dogmatic standpoint rather than round the need to cure patients. This vital point for physicians seemed often to be lost sight of, so that I was inclined to sympathize with the sceptic who changed the old quip, 'the operation was successful, but the patient died,' into 'the analysis was successful, but the patient committed suicide.' I was ever mindful at that time of Jung's story of the patient who came to him from another doctor, and, speaking of the latter, said: 'Of course, he never understood my dreams, but he took *so much trouble* with them.' In brief, psychopathology seemed to me to be claiming too much for itself as a science, thereby stultifying itself, and too little for itself as an art, thereby impoverishing itself. Perhaps I was stale. This is just the condition in which one is ripe for a spiritual adventure. So I went on it."

Here, then, was a man already past his prime, who suddenly interrupted his career, closed his consulting-room and, at the risk of shocking his many patients and being derided by his colleagues, went off to live with the curious " Forest Philosophers."

After twenty years of surgery, he had set out, with

Jung, to discover an entirely new method of healing. From surgery to psychoanalysis is a considerable step. Taking into account the atrophy to which most medical specialists early succumb, one cannot but admire the courage and flexibility of a man who, in middle life, could forsake the scalpel for the analysis of dreams, could abandon a science already sure of itself for one that was still in its infancy. Now, after a few years of the study and practice of psychoanalysis, he asked himself the one vital question, the question that neither Jung nor Freud (for even stronger reasons) dared to ask, the question about Will. I do not, of course, mean the will as described in the text-books of classical psychology but, if I may use such an expression, the Will to will, the primary source of man's freedom.

"Will" Gurdjieff says, "is absent in ordinary man, he has desires only; and a greater or lesser *permanence* of desires and wishes is called a strong or a weak will. Real will is a power, not merely composed of various often contradictory desires belonging to different " I's", but issuing from consciousness and governed by individuality or a single and permanent " I." Only such a will can be called "free," for it is independent of accident and cannot be altered or directed from without."

Dr. Young concluded that psycho-analysis would not be able to develop without a new psychology of will, and it seemed to him that such a psychology had been perfected and applied by Gurdjieff. So with no hesitation and in a spirit of scientific curiosity, he packed his bags and took a ticket to Fontainebleau, prepared to try a new experience in perfect humility. I know of few better examples of open-mindedness.

"I scented the possibility of a substantial addition to my knowledge of psychological problems by accepting a discipline calculated to force one to experience oneself in a new way or from a different angle. It is an axiom that in experiencing a thing one experiences one self. If the circumstances of one's life are uniform, one experiences one's self in a uniform way; in other words, one becomes stale. Staleness tends towards a mechanical state, and ultimately to petrifaction. Of course, one can devise means, if one is ingenious, of experiencing oneself in a new way. An enthusiastic disciple, for example, used to stand on his head, propped up against the wall, and try to think out a problem. He found that he could not at first. But he persisted and succeeded, thereby overcoming mechanism, which only allowed him to think in an ordinary uninverted posture. Whether there is any ultimate value in that particular form of achievement is open to question, but the principle holds good that the soul must experience itself in new ways in order to grow. It is needless to say that the new ways must be significant, and not trivial. As I understand it, this is the *sine qua non* in any attempt at all-round self-development. The idea of the Institute, then, was to provide an artificial milieu so arranged that the pupil would be forced to experience himself in radically new postures, both physical and psychological. The new postures were to be brought about by 'shocks,' as they were called. Instead of the shock bringing about insanity, as the novelists put it, 'shocks' were to produce sanity ! It was to be one more attempt to put into practice the age-old maxim: Know Thyself. 'Shocks' there were in plenty, and by no means always premeditated or arranged by M. Gurdjieff."

Dr. Young then gives a short account of Gurdjieff's basic doctrine. He enumerates the four possible states of man: the sleeping state, or subjective dreaming which is our normal state; the waking state, or objective dreaming, the state of those who realize that they are "asleep" and try to awaken; the state of real self-consciousness, and, finally, the state of higher consciousness. Dr. Young's classification is not complete, but it is based on Ouspensky's first lessons in London.

Dr. Young continues:— "Self-consciousness was postulated as being so radically different from waking consciousness (so-called objective dream-state) that it might be said to belong to a higher dimension, although it was not stated in such terms. I may stand open to correction on this point, but, so far as I can remember, the criterion of this hypothetical state was that in it one would foresee all possible results of one's action, much as the greatest chess-players can foresee all possible results of their moves, but substituting the world in general for the chess-board. A much-to-be-desired, if exalted state, you will admit. So much to be desired, indeed, that the idea of the possibility of it is all too liable to become a neurotic power-fiction for the simple-minded. Nevertheless, as a guiding *fiction* for self-integration it is as good as many and better than most. The practical import then, of the postulation of the state of self-consciousness may be formulated thus: " Work upon yourself, by means of self-remembering in the most rigorous sense, *as if* it were possible to attain to a state of being able to control not only your actions, but the effects of your actions, that is, to foresee the results of your action." The work, if properly understood, means death to all day-dreaming. In so far as there cannot be psychological stasis, that is, if there is not progression there must be regression, so there must be continual effort."

Then, having recalled Ouspensky's first lectures, Dr. Young describes his experiences at the Priory.

7

Dr. Young's Experiences at the Priory

During the period of the lectures and meetings in London, M. Ouspensky had spoken of a remarkable man called Gurdjieff whom he had known in Moscow as the composer of an original kind of ballet, and whom he had met again in Constantinople after the Revolution. He averred that Gurdjieff had travelled widely in the East, in Turkestan, Mongolia, Tibet and India, that he had an intimate acquaintance with monastic life in those countries, that he had acquired an unrivalled knowledge and repertoire of their religious exercises and dances, and a profound understanding of their application to psychological development, and that he wished to found a school in which his knowledge would be incorporated and applied in accordance with the psychological system which M. Ouspensky was expounding. The latter also stated that Gurdjieff, who was then in Dresden, had a trained staff of instructors in physical exercises and all sorts of handicrafts, and counted among his entourage a number of distinguished artists, musicians, doctors and philosophers, most of whom were refugees from the Bolshevik régime, and who had already formed the nucleus of an institute in Dresden.

Gurdjieff came to London, twice, I think; he was an enigmatic figure, but, on the whole, he created a favourable impression. A few timid people were scared away—perhaps by his completely shaven head. There was a project for founding the Institute in London, which fell through on account of passport difficulties. The Dalcroze Institute in the Rue de Vaugirard, in Paris, was taken temporarily during the summer vacation of 1922, and there, in August of that year, I, with a number of English people, joined up. The exercises were soon in full swing. They were of a kind I had never seen before, and certainly fulfilled expectation in that they were directed towards overcoming the inertia or limitation of body habit. I found them difficult and stimulating, probably on account of their strenuousness. I can, perhaps, best convey an idea of their strenuousness by reminding you of a game which was probably familiar to us all as children. It consisted in trying to massage the stomach with a uniform circular movement of one hand, and at the same time to pat the top of the head rhythmically with the other. Most people find this very difficult; the movements usually become irregular and blurred, and end in a chaos. The will finds it difficult to combine two such unaccustomed movements and to keep them clear-cut and regular, at the same time. The exercises were mostly devised on these lines, and some of them each of which had its own distinct rhythm. To attempt required the combination of four different movements, these exercises involved a great strain, and to continue for any length of time was very fatiguing. One became intensely aware of the inertia of a body, perhaps otherwise well-disciplined (as by athletics), when called upon to make these unaccustomed combinations of movement. The struggle against this inertia, then, was one of the means to be employed in order to "wake-up."

The other main activity of this period in Paris was the making of costumes which were to be worn in the public exhibitions of the exercises and dances given later at the Institute. Gurdjieff cut out the materials with great skill, and the members were employed in sewing, hand-painting and stencilling designs on them. Metal ornaments for such things as buckles and belts were also fashioned with varying degrees of skill. Other things were made or improvised, dancing pumps and Russian boots, for example, which called for a knowledge of various handicrafts. Not having this knowledge, one had to pick it up as best one could, which meant overcoming one's awkwardness and diffidence, and sometimes, be it confessed, one's indifference or even dislike. This work was carried on with feverish activity, and occupied, together with the exercises, thirteen or fourteen hours every day. The keynote was "Overcome difficulties—Make effort—Work." There was little time for meals during the day, but at night there was a fairly substantial meal. You may imagine that this kind of communal work, together with misunderstandings that arose from language difficulties, called upon one's exercise of the virtues of self-remembering, non-identifying and non-considering to the utmost.

My impressions were very mixed. The people fell short of the standard of culture which Ouspensky had led me to expect. However, I tried to reassure myself with the thought that we were all "machines," and that one machine is as good as another so far as " mechanical " life is concerned. I don't think I quite succeeded, and certainly I had grave doubts when I listened to the never-ending chatter of some of the women, which struck me as the essence of "mechanism." I was naturally particularly interested in the doctors. There were only two. One had an expression which I can only liken to that of a solemn goat. I could not associate the idea of " waking up " or becoming more " conscious " with him at all. I am afraid that I forgot to " remember myself " in relation to him very often in later days. The other was a genial giant with a sagacious expression and Mongolian cast of features. Later, I proved both his geniality and sagacity. For the rest, there were Russians, Armenians, Poles, Georgians, and even a Syrian. Among these were a Russian baron and his wife and an alleged ex-officer of the Czar's bodyguard, who afterwards became a very successful taxi-driver in Paris. My impressions were, as I have said, mixed, like the people. But it was a case of " in for a penny, in for a pound."

In due course, Gurdjieff found and rented a suitable place for the Institute. It was a château on the outskirts of Fontainebleau, with large formal gardens and about 200 acres of wooded land. It was called " Le Prieuré des Basses Loges," and belonged to Madame Laborie, the widow of Maître Laborie, defending counsel in the Dreyfus case. Although left fully furnished except for the servants' quarters, it had not been occupied since the beginning of the war. The grounds were overgrown and neglected. Four stalwart Russians, another Englishman and myself went on an advance party with Madame Ouspensky to cook for us. Our job was to clear up and get rid of the general appearance of decay and neglect. We weeded and trimmed up the almost indistinguishable paths, washed all the glass of a large "orangerie" or vinery, which afterwards became a workshop and smithy—and, in general, worked like demons. Then came the main body and more people from England. Amongst the latter was Mr. Orage, late editor of *The New Age*, with whom I shared a room in the servants' quarters, to which those students who were going to stay for some time were relegated. The best rooms were reserved for visitors, distinguished and otherwise, in the part of the château which was called "The Ritz" by those who were not living in it.

A multitude of activities were soon set afoot by Gurdjieff. A Russian bath was improvized from a solidly built stone house in the grounds. This involved laborious excavation to a depth of ten feet. The bottom was cemented, the boiler, improvized from an old cistern, installed, and a quite luxurious and, for a time, efficient bath-house was achieved. Gurdjieff took a large part in this work, and did most of the brickwork himself. But the *pièce de résistance* was the building of the "study-house." An area of ground large enough to accommodate a grass airfield was levelled after exceedingly strenuous work with pick, shovel and barrow. The framework of an old hangar was erected on this, fortunately, as I thought, without loss of life or limb. The walls were lined within and without between the uprights with rough laths. The space between the laths was stuffed with dead leaves. The laths were then covered over inside and out with the material out of which the Hebrews made their bricks, a mixture of mud and straw, or hay chopped very small. Stoves were then put in the building and the walls dried and hardened before painting them. The roof was made of tarred felt nailed on to the joists; glass extended all the way round the upper half of the walls. This glazing was improvized from cucumber frames—a really good piece of work. After these had been fixed in position the glass was painted with various designs. The lighting effect was very pleasing. The floor, which was the naked earth pounded thoroughly and rolled, and dried by means of the stoves, was covered with matting, on which were placed handsome carpets; the walls below the windows were hung with rugs in the Oriental fashion. A stage was devised, and a kind of balcony for an orchestra; also two tiers of seats all round the walls, padded with mattresses and covered with rugs and skins, for the accommodation of visitors. A gangway ran between these two tiers of seats and a low wooden railing, which enclosed the charmed circle, reserved for the pupils.

I have described the building of this edifice to give some idea of the amount of labour that was put into it and to show how it was evolved out of the most primitive materials, with improvisation almost as guiding principle. All this was calculated to call forth ingenuity, and, above all, patience, some of the jobs being woefully monotonous. During the period before the completion of the study-house, after the strenuous day's work (from sunrise to sunset) was over, the exercises were practised in the salon of the château—usually until midnight or later. Sometimes after this evening salon, Gurdjieff would have us out to work at the building until two or three in the morning with the aid of big electric lamps hanging from the rafters. One could never be sure when one was going to get to bed. Everything was arranged, or rather disarranged, so that nobody should be allowed to fall into a routine. The multiplicity of occupations was continually being increased. Cows, goats, sheep, pigs, poultry and a mule were acquired. Those who were deputed to look after these animals had no sooner got their job going to their satisfaction than they were taken off and made to begin all over again on a new job. Verily, there was no rest for the wicked. There can be no doubt that it was an excellent training in adaptation and development of will. For a week at a time we would not have more than three or four hours sleep at night, and sometimes even only one. My hands were often so stiff in the morning from digging or pick-axeing or barrowing or sawing or felling trees that the fingers exhibited the phenomenon which is known surgically as "snap-finger"; when one had coaxed them to a certain point they suddenly straightened out with a kind of snap. Every night in the study-house people would fall asleep during the mental exercises. On one occasion this excessive sleepiness nearly resulted in a serious accident. A very strenuous Russian, who was determined to "wake up" if work would do it, was putting in bolts in the cross-pieces of the rafters in the building during an all-night séance. He was sitting in the angle between a horizontal and an upright beam, about 20 feet from the ground. Suddenly I was horrified to notice him asleep in this position, but not before Gurdjieff, who was already half-way up a ladder and got to him in time. The least movement would have resulted in what must have been a very serious fall.

Of the organized mental exercises, which were practised in the study-house, in the evening, the following is a very simple example. A series of statements was made, such as $2 \times 1 = 6$, $2 \times 2 = 12$, $2 \times 3 = 22$, $2 \times 4 = 40$, $2 \times 5 = 74$. Find the process by which these results are arrived at. In this case to the first product 4 is added, to the next 8, to the next 16, and so on. Or, again, a code (Morse, for example) was announced and had to be learnt as quickly as possible. Messages were rapped out on the piano. Everybody became moderately proficient at Morse in that way. Or, again, a list of twenty words would be read out. They had to be repeated in the same order. At first it was all one could do to remember ten, or even less, and in the wrong order. One or two of the Russians who had had much practice could remember fifty words in the right order. No great value was attached to these things in themselves. The value lay in the amount of effort expended on them.

So far, I have painted the picture of the Institute roughly and inadequately, without reference to the central figure, Gurdjieff. In spite of the fact that the whole movement had taken a direction utterly unexpected by me—the bizarre, not to say exotic, nature of the study-house, for example—I had been content for the first six months at least to repress, or keep in the background, my own criticism and frequent sense of bewilderment, partly because, theoretically, criticism from any conventional standpoint was " mechanical"; and partly, perhaps, because I was willing to let my cup of criticism gradually and naturally fill until it overflowed into action. It was also interesting to watch the ever-changing developments and frequently inconsistent changes of policy which flowed from Gurdjieff's fertile mind. At the same time I was uneasily aware at times that there was a certain amount of hypnotism involved even in my own case; otherwise I should not have been able to lay aside my critical sense so easily. This hypnotism was only too obvious in the great majority of the others. Gurdjieff was a very powerful personality—a type of man that I had never met before. There was no doubt about his capacity in manifold directions. He was a man to be reckoned with, an outstanding event in the life of a psychologist —a man whose riddle I was determined, if possible, to read.

As soon as I began to take my own criticism seriously, my former observations added fuel to the fire. A few of these observations will serve to show the degree of hypnotism to which practically the whole of the members were subject.

Gurdjieff decided to buy a car. There was a certain subdued excitement about this for many, probably because unconsciously it stood for the inclusion of something human and commonplace in a world which was rapidly becoming inhuman and outside reality. It was understood that Gurdjieff had never before driven a car, which was probably true. It was believed by many, including presumably intelligent Englishwomen, that Gurdjieff would not have to learn to drive in the ordinary way. He would be able to drive, so to speak, by inspiration. This amounted really to a superstitious belief that Gurdjieff was endowed with mysterious and exceptional powers. When there was a ghastly noise suggestive of tearing of gear-wheel cogs, the faithful insisted that it was a test of faith for sceptics such as myself. I soon discovered that it was impossible to cope with such sophistry and "will-to-believe." So, with a certain inward satisfaction and, no doubt, a sense of superiority, I hugged my belief that

Gurdjieff was as happy with that car as a child with a new toy—and, moreover, that he came as near to breaking it at the outset as a child often does. Indeed, I could not help being rather in sympathy with his evident enjoyment. It recalled my own joyful feelings when I first owned a bicycle. At the same time, I could not but be impressed by the power which accrues to a man once he has been invested with the magical attributes of the "all powerful father" or has had the "magician" archetype projected into him, as Jung would say. People in the grip of such a transference are oblivious to criticism, because they project their own unconscious power phantasies. "Himself," as masters or "gurus" are spoken of in India, can do no wrong. He is infallible. Every act of the magician has always a hidden and wonderful significance. It is never to be taken at its face value. So it was in the case of Gurdjieff.

Another example: the parents of an imbecile child got it into their heads that Gurdjieff might be able to help this child in some mysterious way, and brought it all the way from England. It had an attack of diarrhoea soon after arrival, probably due to change of diet. In this case I was really astonished to find that people who might have known better said that Gurdjieff had begun to "work" on him. They meant that by some mysterious means best known to himself he had produced the diarrhoea. As I have said, it was no use trying to cope with this kind of thing; one had simply to ignore the atmosphere of increasing sophistry in support of it. I was also assailed by another kind of sophistry by what friends I had. They said I suffered from spiritual pride, that I was opinionated, that I had never really accepted the spirit of the place, that I had never really "worked" in the true sense, etc., etc. I began to see the time of my departure rapidly approaching.

But I was still intrigued by the obscure and enigmatic factor of personality in the man which attracted such projections and held them. I came to the conclusion that that factor was intensity of purpose. I had no idea what that purpose was, but I became convinced that it had nothing in common with, and was probably antagonistic to, my own fundamental feelings. I felt that the whole business was a *personal enterprise* so far as Gurdjieff was concerned, and that that was where I " stepped off," as the Americans say. I first confided this belief to one of the many birds of passage who came to stay for shorter or longer periods at the Institute. He was a man of letters and an excellent fellow. We corresponded. I have not got my own letters of that time, but some extracts from his replies will give the gist of my own conclusions:

" Since my return, all my seething impressions gradually settled, and the one thing that survived strongly was that the place is *real*. By that I mean that Gurdjieff does possess certain knowledge, and is willing to impart it to one or two who may prove, from his point of view, worthy. It is, in other words, *a* Path of development. The question in my mind thus narrowed itself to—what Path ? Put at its briefest there are two Paths: one to what we will call ' God,' the other to Power (or what the Hindus call Siddhis). Well, everything in me, as also everything in the judgments of the friends I have talked with points to the latter. The methods, the Chief, the bullying, what I might call the brutality, and the corollary, the total lack of what one means by the term spirituality (love, compassion, heart, etc.) all point to that 'dark' Path which is taught generally in the Mongolian monasteries where, probably, Gurdjieff got his own training. It is the Path to Powers (Siddhis), and when one gets there, if ever, and has obtained the fruits of the 'will-to-power,' which . . . frankly is after, the advance of the Soul itself towards God is—nil. One arrives at the wedding feast without that essential and necessary wedding garment (as one man put it to me) which is LOVE. You know what I mean, because you said it yourself in so many words. A man I know who has studied these things *à fond*, though admittedly he has not practised them, tells me that in many of the Mongolian Schools the mental bullying, *via* anger, temper, swearing, etc., we are familiar with where you now are, is carried further into physical bullying, sticks, ropes, fists being used. Efficacious it may be, but the progress acquired is not real, not of ultimate value, that is. Old Blavatsky, also taught of Mongolia, was notorious for her rages, language, etc. The Path to which these Teachers belong is one that aims finally at power to rule the planet, and if ever you come across Ossendowski's *Beasts, Men and Gods*, you should read the final chapters about the "King of the World." It is curiously suggestive. My own intuitions and conclusions about the Institute and its chief may be quite erroneous, but my reason and intuitions are all I have to go upon, and both lead me to the same result. Nothing in me points the other way. The path there is *a* path to power and powers. The entire absence of love, compassion, spirituality in the method is a significant absence. Without these, it cannot be the Path to what I may call God . . . [another pupil] says that these virtues are useless to one 'without power'—*i.e.*, love and compassion without power are a nuisance merely—and also that if they are real in one they will survive the training. But what afflicts me is that they are not *included* in the training. I am ready to believe that Gurdjieff can teach one to develop in a certain direction, but I am convinced this teaching will be given only to those who he feels certain will use them to the end desired by himself and his own Teachers, whose emissary he probably is. The majority might spend their lives there and get nothing. I am writing, as you see, merely a general account of my own point of view, much as we used to talk together, and with frankness."

And, in answer to another letter:

" I am extremely interested in your letter. I shall read it again and again and digest it slowly. It is full of value for me. In my own mind lies no longer any faintest doubt about Gurdjieff and his Institute. Signs of hoofs and horns are all over the place, and my deep and instant distrust, which increased with every day I spent there, find confirmation now wherever I turn. Much, of course, remains inexplicable, and will always remain so. Gurdjieff, with reason, is aloof and inaccessible, and the full truth of his motive we shall never know. That it is wholly a self or selfish motive, I am convinced. Promises will ever outweigh achievement there. The note of fear, rather than love, is too conspicuous to miss. Did you meet a Russian named P., who was there recently ? I have not met him, but I hear he went to the Institute with another friend last month. I hear he had to retire to his room nightly to conceal his explosions of laughter. He reports also that what struck him so unpleasantly was that he noticed this 'fear' in the general attitude of the pupils. 'All slaves of Gurdjieff,' he described them. K's reasons for being there, I am more than ever convinced, are in the nature of 'conversion,' or as a man satiated with the world of sense, and loathing himself, yet too weak to struggle out alone, seeks the shelter and penance of a Monastery. His attitude of being determined to justify his step, of finding explanations for every blessed thing, confirm this view in me.

"To come down to our fundamental criticism: I simply cannot believe that a genuine Teacher would indulge in so much bunkum, or would produce that persistent and increasing distrust that was produced to me. Doubts one might feel, yet hardly that type of doubt which Gurdjieff's fantasy, cheapness, spectacular use of show, of megalomaniac hints of this and that to come, etc., etc., inevitably do produce in one."

These opinions will make fairly clear the state of mind which led to my departure from the Institute. I should be sorry, however, to leave the impression that the whole experience had been nothing but complete waste of an irrevocable year. So far from that, I am convinced that much that was valuable was met with on the way; and if I have failed to indicate this, it is because it is hard to communicate to others the personal gains derived from an individual experience.

Nevertheless, it was with a feeling of supreme satisfaction that I turned my back finally upon the Institute and returned once more to embrace the habits of the so-called "mechanical" life.

8

Georgette Leblanc and Maeterlinck

Georgette Leblanc died in Cannes in 1941, at the age of seventy-two. Since 1924, that is to say, since her fifty-fifth year, she had "worked" with Gurdjieff. She made her debut as a singer at the Opera Comique. She was thrilled by Maeterlinck's first works and in order to get to know him she decided to leave Paris, and signed a contract with the Théatre de la Monnaie in Brussels. In Paris she had been connected with the Sâr Péladan, the Rosicrucians, Elimir Bourges and Maurice Rollinat, who was a friend of her brother, the novelist Maurice Leblanc. In Brussels she created Massenet's *La Navarraise*. She was presented to Maeterlinck and became his companion. Their love was to last for twenty-three years and to end in a terrible parting in 1918. During these years she collaborated with the author of *The Blue Bird* and *Pelléas*, and interpreted his works. She created *Mona Vanna, Ariane* (the star of the Blue Bird) and, in

Boston, Debussy's *Mélisande*. She organized the famous presentations in the Abbey of Saint-Wandrille (*Macbeth*, translated by Maeterlinck, and *Pelléas* are important dates in the history of the open-air Theatre). After her break with Maeterlinck she sought to re-establish herself in America, and half succeeded. On her return to France she only appeared once more in public, in Marcel l'Herbier's film *L'Inhumaine*, a masterpiece of silent films, of which she had inspired the scenario.

There was quite a commotion in many circles when Georgette Leblanc and Maeterlinck parted. Had she really been Masterlinck's direct inspiration as she implied in her memoirs ? M. Bernard Grasset, in a curiously ambiguous preface to the book, contests it. Was she " guilty " when Maeterlinck decided to separate ? She denied it. He kept silent. Three years ago, I spent a day wandering round the château where they used to live, at Villennes (Seine et Oise). It is a very beautiful house, now quite dilapidated. I went there with a business man who was looking after the widow's affairs. I had gone off by myself as I wanted to dream a little, in this great ship that was about to founder. I have no very great admiration for Maeterlinck's work, but the man himself means something to me, no doubt because of our common Flemish origins. In these rooms with their broken floors and windows, and in the sound of the pick-axes and saws, I tried to find his ghost, the ghost of a man who loved silence, order, comfort and retirement, and at the same time, ostentation: a man of gross physique but given to spiritual meditations, a voluptuous Yogi, as are all the great artists of our country. I tried to reconstruct the house by dipping into my own Flemish nature, and I felt it was the last time the house would live the life that Maeterlinck had given it. There would be only *foreigners* on the wreck, after me—strangers to the art of navigation, who would be unable to detect in her sinking, even for an instant, the special manner in which she used to sail. In the stables with their rusty mangers and rotten boards, I found a trunk full of old dresses, feathers and veils. At the bottom was a packet of letters. They were written by Georgette Leblanc just before the parting and were most revealing. I read three or four and put them back in the trunk. I was certain that they would never be read again, that they would be destroyed by someone or other—by the sea that would sooner or later engulf the Maeterlinck ship on the hillside at Villennes. And so, as I have dropped them overboard, I will say nothing about what they contained. I will say only that Georgette Leblanc was not the silly and absurdly affected actress without soul or sense, that some people make out. Her letters showed unmistakable signs of *quality* and that is what matters.

She was twenty-six when she threw in her lot with Maeterlinck and forty-nine when they parted. She simply tried to continue her life—I mean to go on living with something like the same warmth and intensity that love, combined with a passion for art, had given her in her youth and dazzling maturity. She struggled for six years in New York and then met Gurdjieff. Her old age was passed in the flames of the inner life she experienced with him. This is no subject for mockery.

She wrote an astonishing book about her six years' battle in New York against despair, and spiritual and

physical death, and her subsequent conversion to the
" Teaching." This book—too little known—is called
La Machine à Courage. I realize it is written in a dis-
couraging style—a " silent-film-star style "—but I
believe one should look beyond the absurdities of her
ways of feeling and expressing herself. What is then
discovered is not a mind of great spiritual quality or
even one very far advanced in mystical experience,
but a woman prostrated by the breakdown of her love,
who is trying to rise again by embracing whole-
heartedly the inner life. Maeterlinck speaks a great
deal about the inner life, but is careful not to
experience it himself. He wanted above all to be a
" mystical poet." It was by committing herself completely to the way that he only praised from afar that
Georgette Leblanc was enabled to remain with him in
spite of everything. I take off my hat to her.

" It is impossible to think of our heroine " says Jean
Cocteau " without the legend of the Phoenix coming
to mind. She ruffles her many-coloured feathers. She
raises her crest. She cries out. She puts a light to the
funeral pyre, mounts it and is consumed. Her ashes
breathe. She re-discovers in them the strength to
invent herself again."

The next Chapter is a short extract from *La Machine
à Courage*, relating to Gurdjieff. In Part III of this
book we shall find Georgette Leblanc in Paris amongst
the disciples of Gurdjieff's last years.

9

Extract from " La Machine à Courage "
by Georgette Leblanc

" Here I am, at the point that we all reach, and that seems to be the negative point of existence. Women produce no more children and men do no more business. We rest, and imagine we are slipping down the hill (as though we had ever mounted it). We declare—with an incomprehensible tone of satisfaction —that we are getting old, that the task is done, that we are no longer what we were, that it is other people's turn to live . . . and this life that they talk so much about, extends, roughly, from the ages of twenty to fifty—and that is stretching it a bit, as the period of women's youth is more elastic now than it used to be in Balzac's time. It is judged to be over, when I consider that it has hardly begun. Life is held to be an arc, when it can and should be looked upon as an ascending straight line. According to me, life begins at fifty, and afterwards rises all the time. Everything worth while begins at that age. It is the time for " something else."

I have the feeling that I have lived the whole of my life for this particular present. I must admit that I have not yet finished with art and moonlight, with music and spring, and that I shall never be insensitive to all the delights that are the delicious froth of the earth. But in order to learn to live one must be prepared to abdicate, to make way for changes of plan and level. There is a way of looking at things that is eternal and that accords to happiness the place it deserves.

In 19... Colette wrote to me about my first book *Le Choix de la Vie:* " But I shall never dare to speak to you again ! You say: ' We lose nothing when a sad truth takes the place of a beautiful dream.' Shall I ever think in so noble a way ? No, I am quite sure I should regret. Forgive me—I know that amongst many other things, the ' need for knowledge ' is lacking in me. To half ignore, to fear, despise, desire passionately and passively, to hate and curse, and even come to blows, this is my lot. I was astonished (forgive me)—really astonished—at the inexhaustible strength one divines in you. I could wish you Queen of something or somewhere, and your subjects would be overjoyed."

But I am not one of those impatient people who throw themselves, from the very beginning, on something they have only caught a glimpse of; I search, and doubt, and wait, and search again, and wait again. This cycle has repeated itself all my life until 1924. Since then my search has been slowing down—until it finally came to rest in 1934.

It was in New York in 1924 that I met someone and something. I began to think: " There is a truth here."

Since then I have never left this truth. I have studied it, sometimes looked at it askance, trying almost to betray it, but it triumphed over my schemes, and continued—getting stronger and stronger. And now—fifteen years later—it has become for me the Truth.

To say it in a word, in many words—in countless words—would be to annihilate it. A truth that can be contained in a formula is nothing. I shall only tell what I have felt and understood, what it has done for me by transforming my aspirations into one united force. I will not say what I hope for, but what I have learnt to will. I shall proceed by an elimination of systems, beliefs and methods. I will quote a few pages from my notes and my impressions. I will do it without pride or false modesty. I am not unaware of the danger of speaking about ideas unless it is to deny them. Negation is always well received, and thinkers who only put forward hypotheses are always seemingly respectable. Hypothesis is a kind of lifebelt for the mind, which, by clinging on, can float a little further before sinking. I am not unaware of all that can be said against the word "search"—it's stupid, useless, incomplete, mistaken, limited, excessive, feverish, hysterical, pretentious and vain. If searching seems vain, it is less so than living comfortably with one's eyes shut, living a life one no longer believes in.

At first it seemed to me terrible to be approaching the truth when no longer young. I sank into deep despair. But the very fact of working on a new and unawakened part of myself has restored to me my youth. A fresh start is ahead of me and barring all accidents I shall know how to use it. The future seems to me like the mould of a honey-comb, each cell of which is waiting to be filled.

Someone and Something

And so, in New York in 1924, I met someone and something.

I was asked: " Is he the man Katherine Mansfield knew?" I answered, seemingly yes, but in reality no. She understood him " religiously "—I am tempted to say " ordinarily." He was misunderstood by her, her husband and her friends. The greater a man is, the less likely one is to see the whole of him. If I succeed in understanding him a little, it is because I have studied him for a long time.

I am convinced that Katherine Mansfield was seeking a spiritual life. She was not pious, but she needed some prop. She, who was already " pure," was preoccupied with the idea of a system of purity. She was pure and did not know it. Knowing is everything. That is what was wrong with her seeking, for naturally she found what she was looking for. She was seeking a spiritual life—but a spiritual life without religion. That is nothing much. It is the first stage after that of religion. It is not worth it.

Her greatness was to wish for truth; she did not see that Gurdjieff offered her more—that is to say knowledge. Of course knowledge is spiritual life, but it is not that only. Spiritual life is still ourselves. Knowledge is beyond ourselves. The Truth, of which she had such a splendid need, was still too much tied to life—human life. In life, the true and the false have no great importance as they are both, after all, more or less nonsense. It is beyond, where there is no boundary between physical, mental and emotional life, that everything begins. These lives were meant to function together—that is why they were created. We have divided them by our inability to use them properly. When we feel, we live badly; when we think, we no longer feel; when we live, we neither feel nor think.

I believe that Katherine's subconscious, aware of her approaching death, impelled her towards an idea that was both consoling and without the religious trappings that would have put her off; but, in fact, what she absorbed from Gurdjieff was a religious force that enabled her to say: "All is well" and gave her resignation. Now, Gurdjieff is not consoling. He is something better. What he brings us is as tough as Jesus is, if one goes back to the source. There is no question of soothing truth. I think the primary condition for approaching Gurdjieff is to be in good health. One must be in a state to withstand the first shocks. Above all there is the unbelievable torture of feeling something beginning to work in one. Suddenly all one's strength is engaged on a work that is unknown—impossible. The more one sees of it the more one thinks: "I shall never be able to." But is it really our own strength that is being called on? No—we have never used it, we know nothing about it. It is an energy awakened by a new need and directed towards a new end.

The Priory, Fontainebleau

It was in June 1924 that I settled for the first time at Fontainebleau-Avon in order to get to know Gurdjieff. I had the impression of a giant who had chosen the smallest doorway to the world and had to bend double to pass through. The earth seemed like a coat too tight for him, bursting at the seams. Where was he, himself? A great deal in his writings, a great deal in his words, but not at all in social life—a huge joke that he treated roughly and with impatience.

I was not surprised that he should be little known or recognized. Neither money nor "friends" could open the door of the fortress he had built around him.

At the Priory I have seen sweet smiles and outstretched hands brushed aside and Gurdjieff himself turn away, mumbling "Dirty money" between his teeth. He created all sorts of difficulties to discourage at once the lazy-minded.

I have never been able to accept ordinary polite behaviour. I don't believe in it and I always turned away. But the atmosphere at Gurdjieff's, on the contrary, held me—a difficult atmosphere, almost despairing. To remain there one had to have an invincible need of "something else."

During my last weeks at the Priory, every day, even every hour strengthened my wish to remain. In listening to the reading of his manuscript—a huge volume in nine parts—I felt for the first time satisfied by a revision of human values. My silence slightly disappointed everyone, but I was entirely preoccupied in absorbing his life, as a plant absorbs water. "I cannot develop you" Gurdjieff used to say, "I can only create the conditions in which you can develop yourself."

The conditions were hard; however, my greatest concern was not having known sooner about this work, which would have taught me how I might have lived. I felt a growing despair, as every moment I became more aware of the soul I had not yet acquired. There are two histories for every individual, his own history and that of his shadow (that is to say, his soul). The visible self comes and goes with a force, a name and a position. The shadow—a reality that only exists through light—awaits its hour, and makes its appearance only at the end. I saw myself as we all are, a repeating machine; I, who had always aspired to some different state . . . oh to finish with this life, so sweet but so empty—human life that leads to nothing unless it leads to all. I had rested too long in the illusory "me" that perpetually approves of us. It says "yes" to all our stupidities, like a nodding china mandarin—that is its only gesture.

Now I was working at changing my direction and I felt great upheavals. How was it that I could go on clinging to what I did not want and had never wanted? I did not realize the strength of the ties that bound me to nothing—all the ties of my heredity. I thought myself different from my parents because I spent my time differently, but what of that? It was only the bill of fare for the day like the bill of fare for a meal.

I had to reduce every question even further in order to find the answer—reduce it to a point, the worst, perhaps. . . The question is the stone thrown into the water. One sees only the rings on the surface; one responds to the rings, not to the question. One ignores the stone that has fallen to the bottom.

While joining in all the activities at the Priory, the exercises, the readings, the rhythmical movements, I also worked in the garden. I used then to try to distinguish the different phases of my development, and I laughed at myself—this poor human creature that dared to write: "I want to be—to devote my whole life to this end." It was as monstrous as though I had said: "I am working so as to be able to fly like the birds." The road leads from tadpole to bird, and I could not even imagine the number of stages on the way. I knew only that each step creates the next one and that nothing in the world—no book, saying or prophecy—could give me any inkling of what the next step would be. It depended entirely on my own make-up, only my own " me " could tell me, this " me " that I was getting to know better every day.

What astonished me was not that I should understand—a little—but to see so many not understanding. Sometimes my conscience shook me so violently that I became hot all over. My pulse beat in my temples, my breathing stopped and I was afraid—afraid of what ? Of no longer recognizing myself. Between the non-existent picture of myself that had been my constant companion, and the new picture that I sometimes caught a glimpse of, there stretched a mist. Everything disappeared, and I pursued myself, panting and despairing, with the terrible fear of never finding myself again.

I often felt I was falling into an abyss, and a kind of dizziness came over me. I longed to fly, to escape from this science that asked too much of me. Why did that seem to me both criminal and impossible ? Because once one has caught even a glimpse of the truth it never leaves one but will make itself felt at whatever cost. And if one really wants to live this truth one is bound to have given oneself to it, and it is impossible that all the events of one's life should not always have been conspiring towards it. I felt I was like a chick beating on its shell to get out. All that is beyond, is, for us, quite as different as the outside world is for the chick. I believe that any preparation " before " is equally impossible for everyone, as that would be a negation of the new life that comes " after."

The Other Life

Many people have surely come across some science similar to the one I am describing, but there is nothing in it that can be of any use in a worldly life. Even intelligence takes second place. Why should anyone who is satisfied go in for it?

I lived for two years on end at the Priory. Later on, in Paris, I met Gurdjieff less often but I continued to live according to his principles and incorporated his teaching more and more deeply. "Why do you want knowledge?" I was asked. A strange question! One does not ask: "Why do you want happiness?" Knowledge for me is synonymous with happiness, a sure happiness.

My friends inundated me with questions and advice. "Never look into yourself—it's fatal." Or: "What can one do with life when one has lost all illusion?" I answered: "It is as though a peasant said: they have removed all the weeds from my field—what can I do with it now?"

Another time I used to think: "Our natures must be ploughed, like the land. But where is the plough, and who guides it? Alone we can do nothing. The labourer is as necessary as the seed."

In Gurdjieff's work the way was indicated, the plough and the labourer were ready. It was up to me to be ready. Desire, need, preparation, realization—this is where the other life begins, with its special efforts, new laws, and essential evolution which even tends to change one's chemical constitution. It is hard. I have seen people stop half-way, renounce the work or diverge from it, or even turn against it and embark on a different system that promised for certain a paradise at the end of their lives. Sometimes they went back to some religion, declaring themselves suddenly touched by grace—a grace that usually corresponded to their most material needs and in which they settled down comfortably with every convenience, as though for a long journey. They took a single ticket to paradise, which, more often than not, proved to be a return.

I think the place for religion is in a monastery, where self-centred egoism can be unbounded. In real life, religion limps, in society it poisons—and what a mistake to imagine that suffering is sufficient for growth. If that were the case our planet would be full of saints and angels. Suffering kills some, spoils or maddens others; very few are improved or able to progress through grief. That requires a special technique, the hardest of all, perhaps. I was always a believer by instinct, but I could not accept the God offered me by religion—God as a refuge, when He should be the divine goal of a soul that contains him. He is neither a refuge nor a hope. But everyone is the mirror of the God he conceives, and many are pocket mirrors.

My only hope was in the efficacy of effort.

At the Priory I knew hours of happiness such as I had never known before, but, in reality, I lived from one despair to another. What was my anxiety ? It was total. I was living the meaning of the word " distraught." I had the feeling of being driven out of myself.

10

The Little Review

Margaret Anderson, a friend of Georgette Leblanc's in New York, was no doubt one of the most intelligent of Gurdjieff's disciples. Here is a short *résumé* of this remarkable woman's intellectual career.

In 1914 Margaret Anderson started *The Little Review*, one of the most advanced American reviews of literature, music, criticism, the theatre, cinema, painting, sculpture, architecture and science. Her slogan was: "A magazine that makes no concessions to the public taste." It was not meant for "middlebrow" writers like Sinclair Lewis, nor for a small clique. Created by and for the *élite* of all countries, it presented Rimbaud, Apollinaire, Max Jacob, Cocteau, Paul Eluard, Reverdy, Louis Aragon, André Breton, Delteil, Radiguet, Jules Romain, Gide, Tzara, Philippe Soupault . . . Stravinsky, the "Six," Sartre, Schoenberg, Bartok . . . Picasso, Modigliani, Derain, Matisse, Braque, Leger, Juan Gris, Picabia, Marc Chagall . . .

Brancusi, Zadkine, Lipschitz, and the astonishing Gaudier Brzeska, the young Polish sculptor who was killed in the war, fighting with the French army. Among the English writers published by *The Little Review* were Ernest Hemingway, Aldous Huxley, T. S. Eliot, Ezra Pound, Gertrude Stein, and Margaret Anderson was the first to print, in serial form, that masterpiece of contemporary English writing, *Ulysses* by James Joyce. In Puritan America this publication caused a scandal. Margaret Anderson and her collaborator were accused of publishing obscene literature. There was a law-suit which they lost brilliantly. All the numbers of *The Little Review* in which *Ulysses* appeared were burnt, and the two women had their finger-prints taken, as though they were criminals. It was an historic case.

In Paris, in May 1929, Margaret Anderson brought out the last number of *The Little Review* with the following announcement: "We have presented twenty-three modern-art movements representing nineteen countries. For more than a decade we have discovered, glorified and killed. We have battled, suffered from hunger and risked prison. We have kept a record of all the most energetic manifestations of contemporary art. The archives of *The Little Review* constitute a film of the modern art world. Our mission is over. Contemporary art has "arrived" and, for the next hundred years, perhaps, there will be nothing but repetition."

Here is her testimony on Gurdjieff and the life at the Priory.

11

Margaret Anderson's Article

... It was announced that the Gurdjieff group would give its special " dances " in the Neighbourhood Playhouse, and all New York gathered again. Orage read explanatory notes for each dance, and everyone in the audience (except the genus intellectual) realized that he was in the presence of a manifestation which had its roots in a source of which we know nothing. Our sense of this phenomenon was so sharp that we almost forgot about the man Gurdjieff, who was supposed to be somewhere behind the scenes directing the dances. From my seat down front I saw him for a moment in the wings, commanding his pupils, exhorting them to greater, and ever greater, precision. When we went back later to find Orage I had just time to look carefully at a dark man with an oriental face, whose life seemed to reside in his eyes. He had a presence impossible to describe because I had never encountered another with which to compare it. In other words, as one would immediately recognize Einstein as a " great man," we immediately recognized Gurdjieff as the kind of man we had never seen — a seer, a prophet, a messiah ? We had been prepared from the first to regard him as a man different from other men, in the sense that he possessed what was called " higher knowledge ". or " permanent knowledge." He was known as a great teacher and the knowledge he had to offer was that which, in occult books and in the schools of the East, is given through allegory, dialogue, parable, oracle, scripture, or direct esoteric teaching. From what Orage had told us we knew that Gurdjieff presented his knowledge in a terminology which would not alienate the factual minds of Western thinkers. We had never been ranged among the factual; but neither had we ever been, nor could we ever be, satisfied with the purely mystical or metaphysical.

We looked upon this man standing in the wings of the Neighbourhood Playhouse in New York City as a messenger between two worlds, a man who could clarify for us a world we had hoped to fathom — the world which the natural scientists had revealed but not interpreted.

I think I really thought of Gurdjieff, at first, as a sort of Hermes, teaching his son Tat. But while it was impossible to understand the Hermetic dialogue, merely by reading it or speculating about it, I felt that the essence of the Emerald Tablet itself might be made understandable to us through Gurdjieff's method of teaching. What I mean exactly is this: that what philosophers have taught as " wisdom," what scholars have taught in texts and tracts, what mystics have taught through ecstatic revelation, Gurdjieff would teach as a science — an exact science of man and human behaviour — a supreme science of God, world, man — based on sources outside the scope, reach, knowledge or conception of modern scientists and psychologists.

Later, at Carnegie Hall, another series of dances was given. Plans had been made for an accompaniment of four pianos but as it turned out there was only one, played by M. de Hartmann with the percussive splendour demanded by Gurdjieff. These dances were taken from, or based upon, sacred temple dances which Gurdjieff had seen in the monasteries of Tibet, and their mathematics were said to contain exact esoteric knowledge. New York was still interested, but the intellectuals had begun to complain that the performers' faces didn't register "joy" as they danced. I suppose these critics would have been pleased by an Isadora Duncan expressiveness over the movements of the planets in space.

We spent all the time we could with Orage, listening to the ideas of Gurdjieff. And then one night Gurdjieff himself talked. He presented his ideas as not new but as facts always known and always hidden — that is, never written down but passed from age to age through the teachings of the great initiates. "Initiate" had always been a word that left us cold, if not hotly antagonized, because of the nebulous thinking of the people who used it. But now we had no time to waste in revolt over words. The substance of Gurdjieff's doctrine was, for all of us, for the first time, an answer to questions.

All our lives our questions had been, we thought, everyman's questions; but everyman seemed satisfied with answers which didn't satisfy us. If a great scientist said, " We can erect a coherent system dealing with all aspects of human knowledge and behaviour by the refinement, extension and continued application of the methods which have been so successful in the exact sciences," we said, " No, you can't, there's something you won't be able to get at with those methods." If a great doctor said, " Prayer is power," we said, " Yes, it must be, but why ? " If a great philosopher based his doctrine on the " incalculable forces of the spirit," we knew what he was talking about, but the phrase was vague. What *are* those forces ? What more, if anything can be learned about them ? We found more meat in Hermes: " For the Lord appeareth through the whole world. Thou mayest see the intelligence, and take it in thy hands, and contemplate the image of God. But if that which is in thee be not known or apparent to thee, how shall He in thee be seen, and appear unto thee by the eyes ? But if thou wilt see Him, consider and understand the sun, consider the course of the moon, consider the order of the stars."

But since astronomers had no revelations to make (except physical ones), and since no philosopher had ever spoken clearly about what it is to " know thyself." we were left stranded. All we could do was to reiterate: in that region between physics and philosophy is there no firm ground for the mind's construction of a faith ?

Gurdjieff's statement was that there does exist a super-knowledge, a super-science; and what he had to say about it convinced us that we would never hear anything else to compare with it, never find anything else which could illuminate the great texts to which we had always wanted to give a reverent investigation.

When he spoke of the " way " in which this knowledge could be acquired — a way which brought you gradually into a "condition of knowledge" — we were ready to believe that it might indeed be a way for us. But though we suspected the magnitude of the knowledge, we didn't realize how different its development and application would appear to us fifteen years after our first encounter with it. And we certainly hadn't the faintest idea how difficult this particular "way" would sometimes be . . .

Even now I cannot attempt to describe Gurdjieff. I would feel as if I had been asked to write a description of Nature in all her moods. And I cannot talk of the material of his teaching, of its method or its meaning. I can tell what it did to me, that is all. It is adjusted differently to every individual, and everyone would tell of it differently. It is completely different from what I imagined it would be, from what I understood it to be, stage by stage. It is not a story of learning something through the mind, or of assimilating something that is told to you. It is a story of a new education, of taking whatever degree your heredity and upbringing, your wish and your will, make possible. It has no relation to psychoanalysis or any of the other modern introspections. Introspections into what? Into what non-existence? It is a cleansing and a filling. Its science consists in the precision with which you are charted, by which you are aided — slowly enough not to break you, fast enough to keep you in that state of wonder, surprise, shock, torment, remorse, reward, which alone taps your potential forces. The first statement I heard Gurdjieff make about his teaching was: "I cannot develop you; I can create conditions in which you can develop yourself." . . .

Of all the people who came to the Prieuré while I

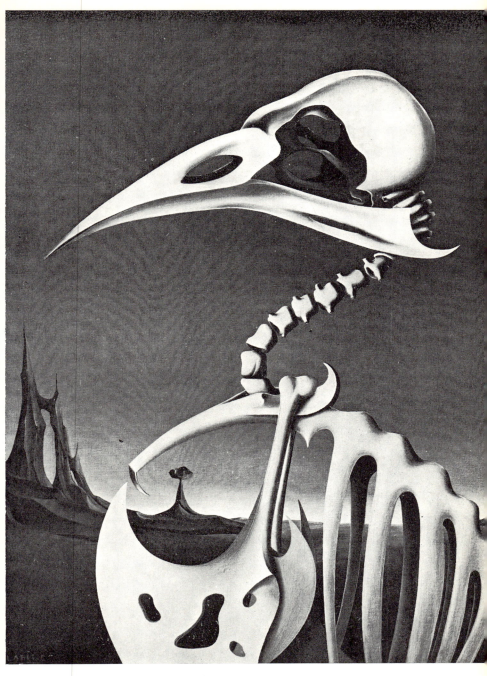

Felix Labisse: Le grand Fulgurateur, 1954

(above) Felix Labisse: La matinée poétique, 1944

"Le lit," 1952 by Georges Rohner

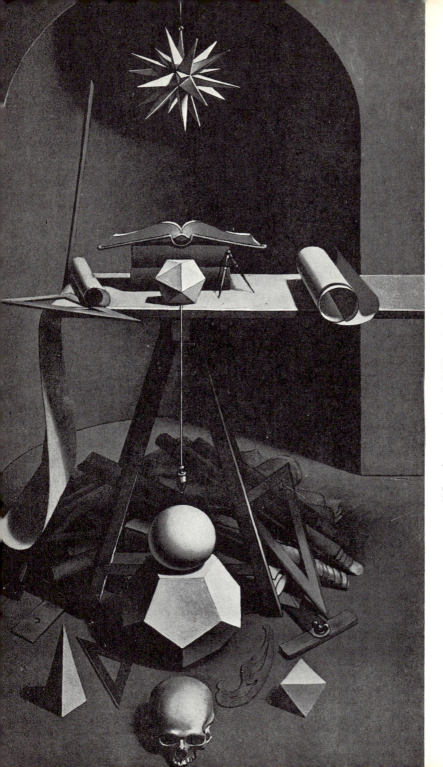

"Les formes reines," 1953 — by Georges Rohner

La bataille perdue, 1957 — by Georges Rohner

Le football, 1962 — by Georges Rohner (above) *La femme couchée dans une draperie*, 1958 — by Georges Rohner

Femme et guitare, 1960 — by Georges Rohner

was there, no one was ever asked to stay if he wanted to leave, and no one was asked to leave if he really wished to stay. Some were not received at all. One well-known woman came out from Paris expecting to be received as a celebrity. Gurdjieff didn't know who she was but he saw her from a window when she arrived. She was told he wasn't there. The story of his brief explanation of course went the rounds — at least to the three of us who always had our ears at the psychological keyhole: her vanity was too fixed, it would take years to break it up; she was not young, the chances were against success, his effort would be disproportionate since hers would probably be non-existent.

Another quick flight was made by an American woman who stayed only three days. She reacted to new situations as if they were old ones. This made her angry and she left in disdain. One of the most touching people who fled was the man who said he hadn't the courage to start on what might be only another wild-goose chase after knowledge. He left sadly. There was an Englishwoman who identified everything she heard with her own idea of Buddha, and then left to continue a life devoted to her own nebulous conception of "know thyself"; and there was another woman who announced that you could find a hundred such teachers in the world, that this doctrine was no more interesting than any other. If we hadn't already heard enough to know its uniqueness (at least for our time and place in the world) we might have been influenced by all the cross-currents — the people who called it and us too material, those who said we were hypnotized, those who predicted our decline into mysticism or a sort of super-metaphysics. But it would have taken a lot of effort to be influenced by people who discovered only mysticism in the most lucid formulations, and who sensed neither mystery nor knowledge in the most paradoxical. So we simply got to work on the doctrine, and on ourselves. And there was nothing simple about either activity.

Outwardly, at the Prieuré, we felt that our days were numbered. Inwardly we felt that we had been given a key to a new model of the universe.

Outwardly we didn't go through any of the training that the older pupils had demonstrated in New York. That was over for the moment, Gurdjieff was finishing the last chapters of his book, and everyone was absorbed in translation from Russian into English, French, German. Besides this we worked in the kitchen gardens, we straightened garden paths ("Too slow," Gurdjieff said, walking by, "must find way to do in half time."). We cut grass and helped to cut down trees. I had a small silent portable piano which I sometimes took out under the yew trees to practise on. "Waste of time," Gurdjieff said, walking by with the musician, M. de Hartmann; "must find short cut." I sought out the musician later, hoping for interpretation. He began: "Arensky had only four fingers on one hand but he could play anything and play it as he wanted to. Question of engineering." Then he gave me so much new information about techniques and the mechanics of bodies in relation to instruments that I was tempted to return to Art.

But I had not gone to Gurdjieff to learn more about Art; I wanted to learn more about the universe. If anyone had asked me exactly what I wanted to find out, and if I could have answered as simply as a child, I would have said, "I want to know what is God." When I realize now how I might have related this wish to an essential conduct, and how I couldn't, I am appalled. If I had known how to ask a question, if I could have been simple (I who have always been so sure of simplicity), I could have asked " What does it mean — ' in My Father's house there are many mansions ' ? What does it really mean ? Or " Will you tell me something about the Last Supper ? — why does religion seem to offer no real interpretation of this sacrament ? " I wouldn't have received answers that could be regarded as answers, since "what" and "why" were always discouraged at the Prieuré and only "how" was sometimes rewarded; but I might have started ten years earlier on that break up of my own image which precedes any *study* of man created in the image of God. As it was, " God " was not mentioned in this place after the day when someone at the table succeeded in a direct question and Gurdjieff answered " You go too high." I never found a way to overleap these barriers, made for leaping. I had so much awe of all that I heard, I was so convinced that I would learn what it meant through some extension of the mind, that I could think only of studying it, discussing it with everyone — that is, continuing to live as I had always lived, by imagining what I could of the ideas involved, hoping that everyone else's imagination would work too, and believing that if we thought and discussed long enough we would come upon revelation.

I don't regret the endless discussions — these first years of the Gurdjieff abstractions were a golden age to me. But if you linger on in it you never arrive at essentials. When you get beyond it you realise why all the stories told about Gurdjieff's presentation of the Hermetic wisdom are surface stories. I have yet to see in print, even in the two respectable articles written by men who have worked with him, a single indication of the concrete substance of his mentation. Someone writing anonymously said: "For me the most sensational aspect of Gurdjieff's work was a sort of sublime common sense. I mean that my experience resembled many times those of the initiate in antiquity who was asked by his friends how he felt when he was told the secrets of an occult brotherhood. 'Like a fool,' he said, 'for not having seen for myself the truths they taught.'"

KATHERINE MANSFIELD'S LAST HOPE

12

D. H. Lawrence, Middleton Murry, Ouspensky

D. H. Lawrence refused to embark on the Gurdjieff adventure. He was on the point of believing that the "Teaching" might be the answer to his profound anxiety, possibly he did believe it, but he could never make up his mind to take the plunge. He feared that in adopting the mental disciplines required by Gurdjieff he would lose his creative freedom. He feared above all having to question his blind faith in the kindness of Fate towards him, which stood for him in lieu of religion. He believed that he felt a beneficent force that guided him, D. H. Lawrence, whatever he might do, towards the Light, and guided him all the more surely the more he gave himself up to the disorders of human passions, on condition that he abandoned himself with heart and soul opened *from above*. I say " on condition," but he never for a moment doubted that it was in this way that he abandoned himself; it was all part of his vocation. In following Gurdjieff he would have had to renounce this belief, which afforded him much self-satisfaction, and, indeed, admiration.

Katherine Mansfield guessed what the obstacles would be for her old friend. "Lawrence and E. M. Forster would both be capable of understanding this place if they wanted to," she wrote to her husband, "but I think Lawrence's pride would prevent him." And, in fact, pride did prevent him. However, there was nothing in the long run to make one think him wrong to act as he did.

He was much put out by the excesses of enthusiasm of his initiator, Mrs. Mabel Dodge, a devoted follower of Gurdjieff. In April, 1926, he wrote to her: "My Self, my fourth centre, will look after me much better than I could" — thus reaffirming his belief in a guardian angel. And again, the following month: "As for Gurdjieff, and Orage, and the awakening of the various centres of being, the Self, and all that, to tell you the truth, I don't know . . . There is no clear path; there never will be . . ." Finally when pressed to reach a decision by Mrs. Dodge, he flew into one of his habitual great rages and definitely broke away: "I think that I don't want to go and see Gurdjieff. You can't imagine how little interest I feel in his methods of salvation . . . I don't like squibs like Gurdjieff and Orage."

Katherine Mansfield thought that Lawrence, because he *loved himself,* would never come to the "teaching." She herself came to it because she *loved.* This will be understood better further on.

As far as I know there has been no exact account written of the last months of Katherine Mansfield's life. In the course of these months, however, she herself and the whole of her work were illuminated from all sides. Rarely can a mind and body have been so radiant in the face of death. Rarely can work, at the moment of its interruption, have yielded up more completely its secret springs. Katherine Mansfield's devotees who come to Paris to stay for one night in hotel bedrooms that she has occupied, and who make the pilgrimage every year to the cemetery at Avon-Fontainebleau, have had to be content, till now, with very vague accounts of her time with Gurdjieff, of her reasons for going to the Priory, and of the nature of her questing and hope in this colony, founded by the man she used to call "The Great Lama of Tibet." Her biographers say that she took refuge in a "theosophical Society" which shows their complete ignorance. There is only one book that attempts to describe her last adventure, M. Roland Merlin's *The Secret Drama of Katherine Mansfield*. Unfortunately, M. Roland Merlin does not appear to have had at his disposal Katherine Mansfield's own testimonies about her life at the Priory; worse still, he seems to know very little about Gurdjieff.

I have included, further on, Katherine Mansfield's letters to her husband, John Middleton Murry, in which she explains her decision to take the plunge; tries to assess her past life; defines the objects of her search; tells what goes on from day to day in her head, heart and body, at grips with the first elements of the "Teaching," and describes the spectacle of this curious society of "Forest Philosophers," as seen through the eyes of a novice.

Most of these letters are not yet published in French. They are taken from the important collection that has just been published in London by Middleton Murry.

I feel it would be impossible to understand them fully without knowing something about Gurdjieff, his influence and his relations with others — that it would be difficult to feel the "secret drama" they express without certain clues. These clues are, I hope, given in this book.

In August, 1922, Katherine Mansfield was in Switzerland for the benefit of her heart and her lungs. Tuberculosis had already for some time been undermining her creative energy, spoiling her physically and destroying the love that united her to Middleton Murry. A certain disposition to nervous distress, which most of those endowed with religious sensibility are apt to feel in the modern world, as it becomes less and less habitable for them, increased in her until she felt that her heart and nerves were being slowly crushed. She suffered, of course, from the disease of the lungs which might prove to be curable by doctors; but she also had, as she thought, another, more serious illness that doctors were powerless against — that could not even be described; the illness of the constant question — do I really exist? Where is the true and permanent Me behind the endless waves of moods, feelings, anxieties, pleasures and pains? How can I at last feel safely attached to something solid? Where is the firm ground in myself? Everything, in fact, encouraged Katherine Mansfield to believe that tuberculosis was only one of the visible signs of this other illness, or rather that her destiny had decreed this weakness of her flesh in order that her sensitivity to such problems should be pushed to the limit. She had to find an answer, and, having found it, she would be restored; but not to "normal life" as people say who do not know that "normal life" is no more worth living than the life of a consumptive; it would be the beginning of a new life, of real life.

In Switzerland she had just received Ouspensky's essay *The Cosmic Anatomy*. Many English intellectuals and artists were attending Ouspensky's lectures, and an active circle was formed around him and his friend Orage. She considered going to see Orage; it was from him that she hoped for answers, or beginnings of answers, to her questions. No doubt she said little about this to her husband; what could she say? " By keeping quiet, they managed to get on." They avoided all dangerous topics: she was afraid of dying and hid her fear so that their life together might at least have some happiness; he wished to detach himself from her and redoubled his care and attentions in an attempt to compensate her for the loss of physical love. They talked with enthusiasm of the past and dreamt of a similar future, but were both careful not to mention the sad present — their ruined love, desire gone, the fear of death and their marriage become merely a matter of habit and care, without hope. He thought only of his suffering at seeing her suffer. She worked ceaselessly and alone to retain her dwindling energies so as not to fall into total despair. They were both shut up in themselves and the smallest real exchange would have precipitated the end. They smiled at each other discreetly, from afar, in order not to upset their precarious balance. They held their breath.

She told him only that she wanted to go to London to consult Dr. Sorapure, the heart specialist. This kind of suggestion was not dangerous as it concerned her recovery. When she was better, everything would look rosy again. But she knew well that there was far more the matter with her than her physical illness, and that more was needed to save them and their marriage than pills, diets, injections and X-rays. He knew it too. They both pretended to be going to London to consult a doctor, but in fact they were making the journey to play their last card. " *I say that ' ostensibly' the purpose of her visit was to get Dr. Sorapure's opinion,*" wrote Middleton Murry, "*but I believe the real purpose was to see Orage . . . At any rate, I was surprised at the swiftness with which she joined the circle formed about M. Ouspensky, to which Orage and J. D. Beresford belonged. We sometimes talked of the matter which most deeply concerned us*" (that is to say, her recovery, the only " safe " subject, and of the happy days ahead for them after her cure), "*but now our love spoke across a vast; and my memory of these days is one of despair and anguish. It was evident to me as it was to Katherine that re-birth was the only remedy. But how to be born again? It was impossible for me to follow her into the Ouspensky circle; or at least it seemed impossible without violating my own integrity. Thus, I had no part in what had come to be Katherine's absorbing interest. I had to acknowledge that I was becoming useless to her — even worse, a positive hindrance to her effort towards liberation.*"

And so, having crossed the Channel, they gambled. They agreed to face the present, and everything collapsed. It was either re-birth or a continuation of a false life, a falsified love. She took the decision: she would leave him, she would break away from the pious lies of their life together. She would try to get better alone, that is to say, to find the way to her Me, to a permanent *me* without fear or hope, to some place in herself from which she would no longer fear death and from which love could radiate without having to be submitted to the sad contingencies of their life together. Katherine left. She went to a place wherefrom she was able to see John in all his weakness, but a place where, on the other hand, she could revive her love and keep it at its highest pitch.

In August, 1920, she wrote in her Journal: " I cough and cough . . . Life consists in getting back my breath. And he remains silent, head bent and his face hidden in his hands, as though it were unbearable. ' This is what she does to me ! Every sound gets on my nerves ! ' I know these feelings are involuntary, but oh God how bad they are ! If he could only help me for one instant, *forget himself*. What a destiny — to be one's own prisoner ! "

It is true that Middleton Murry was his own prisoner, as Katherine Mansfield says, and could never turn his eyes outwards from himself. He lived in the constant pain of being the husband of a woman who, though remarkable, was damaged in body, heart and soul by her illness, and who, moreover, now questioned the whole of existence, whereas he himself had no metaphysical anxiety, or rather, could only grasp it intellectually.

" Stop being emotional, stop writhing, stop feeling anything at all. It's brains that one needs and not sentimental introspection " as D. H. Lawrence said to him. " That is your vice, and with it you rot your manhood to its very core, but one is forced to believe that that is what you need." Admirable advice ! Lawrence says: " Change yourself." But how to change ? And is it really a question of changing ? Is it not, rather, a question of assuming one's own nature, whatever the cost? Middleton Murry knew very well what his "vice" was, according to Lawrence. He knew that, however he might wish otherwise, the look that he cast on life was at once bent back upon himself. But from the depths of this self that was for ever examining, judging, pitying or congratulating itself, there flowed a real grief, a great cry of wounded love for the dying Katherine, who, with the lucidity of the dying passed judgment on his inability to escape from himself, that was for her husband the special cross he had to bear. He loved her, but turned towards her in vain, bound to the cross that he called his "integrity," not being able to escape from it.

How difficult everything was becoming! "She would have liked me not to notice her illness" wrote Middleton Murry, "but that was impossible. My nerves were exasperated to such a point that at night when we were lying side by side, her spasms of coughing made me shudder through and through. To see her thus, emaciated, with glittering eyes, and a mere shadow of her former self, broke my heart. I used to queue up and fight to find suitable food for her, but my desperate eagerness seemed to her out of place. Why could I not forget this sickness, that was not herself? I had really terrible moments of exasperation when I felt caught in a trap. That she should interpret my anguish as a desire to get rid of her seemed too much."

Katherine realized that she was unjust; the fear of dying was the cause of her injustice. John found himself unable to overcome his day-to-day anxieties; she watched his ineffectual struggles and sufferings and under her gaze he lost countenance. But already she was dreaming of passing beyond her illness and beyond the quicksand of their relationship and of reaching firm ground. To do this meant breaking away from the sickening insincerities of the couple Katherine - John. It meant dying as John's wife, made up of injustices, hidden fears, passing tenderness and uncertainties; in a word, it meant dying as the person John loved, with a sincere though trembling love, and becoming another, being re-born. But John for his part was unwilling to die to himself, he did not wish to launch himself on this adventure. She, yet again, found him faint-hearted. She thought that to revive their love it would have to be enough for her alone to be re-born, but she also felt that, as usual, he was showing too much attachment to his own little " me ", that he preferred their present mediocrity to a real union, and that she must leave him in order the better to help him to attain to a deeper life with her, and to a truer love.

I do not think that even Lawrence, strong as he was, could have found any solution except, perhaps, in one of his great rages, which might have retained Katherine in "ordinary life" but would have led, in the end, to her dying in despair in a sanatorium at more or less the same time that she died, full of hope, in her room at the Priory. It is easy to condemn those we passionately disagree with, this is just part of the ferocious and absurd game of terrestrial life; but we cannot really judge. God is the sole judge, as the pious say. I shall try not to judge Murry as I have tried, in this book, not to judge Gurdjieff. Murry could do nothing for Katherine, and Katherine could only do for herself exactly what she did do. I want to consider the chain of events, material and non-material, that made it possible for Katherine to die on the very day that her husband came to the Priory to see her — a miraculous chain of events. I believe there is a sign here. I cannot decipher it, but I do not doubt that Gurdjieff is connected with the chain, or rather that it is no mere chance that the sign was made under his roof, gifted as he was with second sight.

13

Orage

As arranged, Katherine Mansfield consulted Dr. Sorapure in London. He reassured her about the state of her heart. John was overjoyed, but she was already indifferent to what the doctors had to say. That he should be willing to trust solely to them to change their lives was yet another proof of his weakness and inability to face the real problem. Everything had become heartbreaking for them and exposed their profound disunity. She went to stay with a friend, and he to Selsfield. Henceforth she needed to be alone, he would only distress her. He believed she was destroying herself and might destroy them both. She, when she saw him, was afraid of this too, and weakened, hesitated, and begged him to go. He secretly, perhaps, preferred to see and know no more — to bury his head in the sand. In theory she was staying in London to undergo treatment from a radiologist; this she did out of pity for him, to please him and enable him to go on believing a little longer in the old life. Her real reason for being there was in order to attend Ouspensky's group, to try to find the key to a real " change "

This is what she says in her Journal:

" My first conversation with Orage took place on August 30th, 1922.

" On that occasion I began by telling him how dissatisfied I was with the idea that Life must be a lesser thing than we were capable of " imagining " it to be. I had the feeling that the same thing happened to nearly everybody whom I knew and whom I did not know. No sooner was their youth, with the little force and impetus characteristic of youth, done, than they stopped growing. At the very moment that one felt that now was the time to gather oneself together, to use one's whole strength, to take control, to be an adult, in fact, they seemed content to swop the darling wish of their hearts for innumerable little wishes. Or the image that suggested itself to me was that of a river flowing away in countless little trickles over a dark swamp.

" They deceived themselves, of course. They called this trickling away — greater tolerance — wider interests — a sense of proportion — so that work did not rule out the possibility of " life ". Or they called it an escape from all this mind-probing and self-consciousness—a simpler and therefore a better way of life. But sooner or later, in literature at any rate, there sounded an undertone of deep regret. There was an uneasiness, a sense of frustration. One heard, one thought one heard, the cry that began to echo in one's own being: " I have missed it, I have given up. This is not what I want. If this is all, then Life is not worth living."

"But I *know* it is not all. How does one know that? Let me take the case of Katherine Mansfield. She has led, ever since she can remember, a very typically false life. Yet, through it all, there have been moments, instants, gleams, when she has felt the possibility of something quite other . . . September 30. " Do you know what individuality is ? "

" No."

" Consciousness of will. To be conscious that you have a will and can act;" Yes, it is. It's a glorious saying."

These notes contain the first themes of the " Teaching ". From now on, it was, for Katherine, a question of acquiring this " conscious will," this " will to will " as they still say in the groups. Having acquired it, it becomes really possible to work on oneself, to develop a centre of gravity, to make something of life, instead of for ever being " re-made " by life, to rule oneself in actual fact, and to link oneself firmly to the energy of the Universe. It becomes possible, too, to love effectively, which means entering, together with the loved one, into a kind of eternal fulfilment. Was this possible? Intelligent people said it was, and offered to prove it; their master Gurdjieff held the proof. In any case, Katherine felt herself drawn that way. Her biographers often infer that she was only searching for a way to regain her health. They draw on certain phrases where she, in fact, explains to her husband that Gurdjieff will help her to recover more surely than doctors, who only take the body into account. But I believe she was looking beyond her own recovery to a great recovery of human love, and that, in his heart of hearts, Middleton Murry would agree with me. She was not able to tell him the basis of her hope; that would have meant re-opening the whole question of their relationship, of the trouble between them and between all other married couples. It was safer to go gently; their separation, and her decision to join Gurdjieff were already quite dramatic enough. Having almost taken this plunge, she felt she must again keep silent, or at least say as little as possible.

A month after her meeting with Orage she decided to go to Paris. She told her husband that the radiologist was not good enough. " I am not at all satisfied by the purely experimental way he applies the treatment. You see Dr. Webster is only a radiologist. He doesn't examine one or weigh one, and only look after one's case as one does in a clinic." She says she needs to see a better doctor, the inventor of the treatment, Dr. Manoukhin, who lives in Paris. " I would put up with any hotel in any suburb for Manoukhin." Thus she forestalls any objections Middleton Murry may wish to make; the undertaking of a journey in her state of physical weakness, the inconveniences of life in a hotel for a very sick woman, etc. She also disguises the real object of her journey — a visit to Fontainebleau to see Gurdjieff.

She arrives in Paris. Her first letter ends thus: " I hope to see Manoukhin to-morrow. I'll tell you what he says." The letter of the following day says nothing about this visit but begins with the words: " No, I don't *feel* influenced by Ouspensky. I merely feel I've heard ideas like my ideas, but bigger ones, far more definite ones. And that there really is Hope, real Hope, not half-Hope."

M. Merlin, who was able to talk to Dr. Manoukhin, tells us that the latter assured her that she could probably be cured if she followed scrupulously his treatment. She pretended to follow it, but announced two weeks later, that she had decided to go and live at the Priory amongst Gurdjieff's disciples. Dr. Manoukhin begged her to do nothing of the kind; he told her she was risking death by putting herself in the hands of this Caucasian he had heard about vaguely, and refusing orthodox medical care. Further, he wrote to Gurdjieff telling him that his patient was in no fit state to dispense with her doctor's help and begging him to dissuade her from living at the Priory for the time being. Gurdjieff never answered and a few days later Katherine Mansfield was ringing at the gate of the " Forest Philosophers ' " château.

She had hesitated for another whole day and night. By the morning of the second day she had finally decided.

" October 14th. I have been thinking this morning until it seems I may get things straightened out if I try to write . . . where I am.

Ever since I came to Paris I have been as ill as ever. In fact yesterday I thought I was dying. It is not imagination. My heart is so exhausted and so tied up that I can only walk to the taxi and back. I get up at *midi* and go to bed at 5.30. I try to " work " by fits and starts, but the time has gone by. I cannot work. Ever since April I have done practically nothing. But why ? Because, although Manoukhin's treatment improved my blood and made me look well and did have a good effect on my lungs, it made my heart not one scrap better, and I only won that improvement by living the life of a corpse in the Victoria Palace Hotel.

My spirit is nearly dead. My spring of life is so starved that it's just not dry. Nearly all my improved health is pretence — acting. What does it amount to ? Can I walk ? Only creep. Can I do anything with my hands or body ? Nothing at all. I am an absolutely hopeless invalid. What is my life ? It is the existence of a parasite. And five years have passed now, and I am in straiter bonds than ever.

Ah, I feel a little calmer already to be writing ! I am so terrified of what I am going to do. All the voices out of the "Past" say "Don't do it." Bogey says "Manhoukhin is a scientist. He does his part. It's up to you to do yours." But that is no good at all. I can no more cure my psyche than my body. Less, it seems to me. Isn't Bogey himself, perfectly fresh and well, utterly depressed by boils on his neck ? Think of five years' imprisonment. Someone has got to help me to get out. If that is a confession of weakness — it is. But it's only lack of imagination that calls it so. And who is going to help me ? Remember Switzerland: "I am helpless." Of course, he is. One prisoner cannot help another. Do I believe in medicine alone ? No, never. In science alone ? No, never. It seems to me childish and ridiculous to suppose one can be cured like a cow *if one is not a cow*. And here, all these years, I have been looking for someone who agreed with me. I have heard of Gurdjieff who seems not only to agree but to know infinitely more about it. Why hesitate ?

Fear, Fear of what ? Doesn't it come down to fear of losing Bogey ? I believe it does. But, Good Heavens ! Face things. What have you of him now ? What is your relationship ? He talks to you — sometimes — and then goes off. He thinks of you tenderly. He dreams of a life with you *some day*, when the miracle has happened. You are important to him as a dream. Not as a living reality. For you are not one. What do you share ? Almost nothing. Yet there is a deep, sweet, tender flooding of feeling in my heart which is love for him and longing for him. But what is the good of it as things stand ? Life together, with me ill, is simply torture with happy moments. But it's not life. I have tried, through my illness (with one or two disastrous exceptions) to prevent him facing wholly what was happening. I ought to have tried to get him to face them. But I couldn't. The result is he doesn't know me. He only knows Wig-who-is-going-to-be-better-some-day. No. You do know that Bogey and you are only a kind of dream of what might be. And that might-be never, never can be true unless you are well. And you won't get well by " imagining " or " waiting " or trying to bring off that miracle yourself.

Therefore, if the Grand Lama of Tibet promised to help you — how can you hesitate ? Risk ! Risk anything ! Care no more for the opinions of others, for those voices. Do the hardest thing on earth for you. Act for yourself. Face the truth.

True. Tchekov didn't. Yes, but Tchekov died. And let us be honest. How much do we know of Tchekov from his letters ? Was that all ? Of course not. Don't you suppose he had a whole longing life of which there is hardly a word ? Then read the final letters, they are terrible. There is no more Tchekov. Illness has swallowed him.

But perhaps to people who are not ill, all this is nonsense. They have never travelled this road. How can they see where I am ? All the more reason to go boldly forward alone. Life is not simple. In spite of all we say about the mystery of Life, when we get down to it we want to treat it as though it were a child's tale. . . .

Now, Katherine, what do you mean by health ? And what do you want it for ? Answer: By health I mean the power to live a full, adult, living, breathing life in close contact with what I love—the earth and the wonders thereof—the sea—the sun. All that we mean when we speak of the external world. I want to enter into it, to be part of it, to live in it, to learn from it, to lose all that is superficial and acquired in me and to become a conscious and direct human being. I want, by understanding myself, to understand others. I want to be all that I am capable of becoming so that I may be (and here I have stopped, and waited and waited and it's no good--there's only one phrase that will do) *a child of the sun*. About helping others, about carrying a light and so on, it seems false to say a single word. Let it be that. *A child of the sun.*

Then I want to *work*. At what ? I want so to live that I work with my hands and my feeling and my brain. I want a garden, a small house, grass, animals, books, pictures, music. And out of this, the expression of this, I want to be writing. (Though I may write about cab-men. That's no matter.)

But warm, eager, living life—to be rooted in life—to learn, to desire, to know, to feel, to think, to act. That is what I want. And nothing less. That is what I must try for. I wrote this for myself. I shall now risk sending it to Bogey. He may do with it what he likes. He must see how much I love him.

And when I say " I fear "—don't let it disturb you, dearest heart. We all fear when we are in waiting-rooms. Yet we must pass beyond them, and if the other can keep calm, it is all the help we can give each other. . . .

And this all sounds very strenuous and serious. But now that I have wrestled with it, it's no longer so. I feel happy—deep down . . . *All is well.*"

These pages must, I think, be understood simultaneously on two levels, the level of physical illness and the level of spiritual anguish. It will then easily be realized that Katherine was not dreaming only of renewing the contact with earthly things that healthy people naturally enjoy; her dream was on a quite different scale. Restrained as her writing is, she would certainly not have spoken of a " child of the sun " for so slight a reason. It was, for her, a question of entering, body and soul into the light, where stones, animals, plants and humans have a living presence that we scarcely suspect because we are not really alive ourselves. Why are we not really alive ? Because we have lost the sense of unity. For centuries humanity has been wasting itself in Christian dualism, God and creation, body and soul, just as nowadays it wastes itself over Marxist dualism, matter and spirit. The problem is to rediscover the key to the immediate renewal of contact between body and soul, matter and spirit, the key to the unity of physical and spiritual forces and of human and universal energy. The problem is to return to the source, to re-establish this lost unity in ourselves. This would be real recovery. Until this is achieved, whether we are well or ill matters little; we are only half alive, we cannot really communicate with things, we only imagine that we are linked with other beings, a veil separates us from Nature, and as for our love affairs, they are short, feeble and without magic.

This is Katherine Mansfield's dream and it is not merely the dream of an invalid. Illness has revealed this state of being "half-alive" in a clear light and made it a hundred times more uncomfortable for her than for a healthy person. But Katherine Mansfield is not only wanting to recover, she is wanting to change. She is not only wanting to renew her contacts with the external world, but wishing the world itself to take on again the colours of an earthly paradise. She is not only hoping to be able once more to inspire love in her husband, she wants love itself to rediscover its grandeur and magic, its innocence and infinite power, to become again as it was in the Golden Age.

It is well worth while to compare these pages of hers with those written by Lawrence a little while before his death. Lawrence would not accept Gurdjieff, but his dream was identical with Katherine's on the morning that she decided to go to the Priory. His book *The Man Who Died*, probably one of the greatest works of the century, magnificently develops the theme of the " child of the sun."

The Man Who Died is resurrected, but he is still in that intermediate state between life and death that we are nearly all in, the state known to Katherine Mansfield, not solely through her illness, the state from which she longed to escape. " He went on, on scarred feet, neither of this world nor of the next. Neither here nor there, neither seeing nor yet sightless, he passed dimly on, away from the city and its precincts, wondering why he should be travelling, yet driven by a dim, deep nausea of disillusion, and a resolution of which he was not even aware."

Thus was Katherine Mansfield at the moment of her departure for Fontainebleau. *The Man Who Died* was searching in himself and in the world for a lost unity. He has just experienced death and knows now that in order truly to triumph over it he must establish full connection between soul and body, between his unified self and the world, which will then appear radiant to him. But how to achieve this harmony ? *The Man Who Died* knew only two things, but he knew them well: the horror of a divided life, which is worse than death, and the absolute necessity to escape from it. This is enough. If this is fully known, the keys will be given.

Thus thought Katherine Mansfield, and went off to Gurdjieff, not knowing if it was the right place to go to, but knowing that she must go somewhere, and that she must risk all and leave everything in order to go. No doubt the way to harmony is through love, and *The Man Who Died* goes up to the temple of Isis, towards a human but solemn and innocent love, a magic and powerful love belonging to a Golden Age that we can, if we will, ceaselessly recreate. Those who make this attempt doubtless incur grave danger from defying the laws of the false world, which are upheld by the falsely living, by those who are for ever anxious to protect their slumbers and their inner slackness. They must abandon all caution and risk reprisals, and it is here that one finds in Lawrence as well as in Katherine Mansfield the will to believe that those *on the move* are under semi-divine protection, and enjoy a mysterious invulnerability. "I want to be a child of the sun," and from Lawrence, this splendid counterpart to Katherine Mansfield's notes, which I quoted above:

' " If they can, they will kill us," he said to himself. " But there is a law of the sun which protects us."

And again he said to himself: " I have risen naked and branded. But if I am naked enough for this contact, I have not died in vain. Before I was clogged."

He rose and went out. The night was chill and starry, and of a great wintry splendour. " There are destinies of splendour," he said to the night, " after all our doom of littleness and meanness and pain."

So he went up silently to the temple, and waited in darkness against the inner wall, looking out on a grey darkness, stars, and rims of trees. And he said again to himself: " There are destinies of splendour, and there is a greater power." '

And so Katherine Mansfield wrote in her Journal that the die is cast, that she has decided to risk all and to leave all in the hope of changing her life and her love. I do not know if the way she took was the right way. The reader will perhaps be able to decide for himself at a later stage in this book, when we have examined Gurdjieff's thought and method, which have never seemed to me to bear the fruits of love. However, it was rather of Orage than of Gurdjieff that she was thinking that morning, and if one wishes to understand what was going on in her mind as she prepared to catch the train to her last strange abode, one should refer to the following extracts from an essay by Orage. It is this solemn and magnificent discourse that she hears as a pure echo of her own personal drama, this and no other, and it is because of this that she sets out.

" . . . The conscious love motive, in its developed state, is the wish that the object should arrive at its own native perfection, regardless of the consequences to the lover. ' So she become perfectly herself, what matter I ? ' says the conscious lover. ' I will go to hell if only she may go to heaven '. And the paradox of the attitude is that such love always evokes a similar attitude in its object. Conscious love begets conscious love. It is rare among humans because, in the first place, the vast majority are children who look to be loved but not to love; secondly, because perfection is seldom conceived as the proper end of human love—though it alone distinguishes adult human from infantile and animal love; thirdly, because humans do not know, even if they wish, what is good for those they love; and fourthly, because it never occurs by chance, but must be the subject of resolve, effort, self-conscious choice. As little as Bushido or the Order of Chivalry grew up accidentally does conscious love arise by nature. As these were works of art, so must conscious love be a work of art. Such a lover enrols himself, goes through his apprenticeship, and perhaps one day attains to mastery. He perfects himself in order that he may purely wish and aid the perfection of his beloved.

Would one enrol in this service of conscious love? Let him forswear personal desire and preconception. He contemplates his beloved. What manner of woman (or man) is she (or he)? A mystery is here: a scent of perfection the nascent air of which is adorable. How may this perfection be actualized—to the glory of the beloved and of God her Creator? Let him think, is he fit? He can only conclude that he is not. Who cannot cultivate flowers, or properly treat dogs and horses, how shall he learn to reveal the perfection still seedling in the beloved? Humility is necessary, and then deliberate tolerance. If I am not sure what is proper to her perfection, let her at least have free way to follow her own bent. Meanwhile to study—what she is, and may become; what she needs, what her soul craves and cannot find a name, still less a thing, for. To anticipate today her needs of tomorrow. And without a thought all the while of what her needs may mean to me.

You will see, sons and daughters, what self-discipline and self-education are demanded here. Enter these enchanted woods, ye who dare. The gods love each other consciously. Conscious lovers become gods.

Without shame people will boast that they have loved, do love or hope to love. As if love were enough, or could cover any multitude of sins. But love, as we have seen, when it is not conscious love—that is to say, love that aims to be both wise and able in the service of its object—is either an affinity or a dis-affinity, and in both cases equally unconscious, that is, uncontrolled. To be in such a state of love is to be dangerous either to oneself or to the other or to both. We are then polarized to a natural force (which has its own objects to serve regardless of ours) and charged with its force; and events are fortunate if we do not damage somebody in consequence of carrying dynamite carelessly. Love without knowledge and power is demoniac. Without knowledge it may destroy the beloved. Who has not seen many a beloved made wretched and ill by her or his 'lover'? Without power the lover must become wretched, since he cannot do for his beloved what he wishes and knows to be for her delight. Men should pray to be spared the experience of love without wisdom and strength. Or, finding themselves in love, they should pray for knowledge and power to guide their love. Love is *not* enough.

'I love', said the man. 'Strange that I feel none the better for it', said the woman. . . .

Until you have wisdom and power equal to your love, be ashamed, my sons and daughters, to avow that you are in love. Or, since you cannot conceal it, love humbly and study to be wise and strong. Aim to be worthy to be in love.

All true lovers are invulnerable to everybody but their beloved. This comes about not by wish or effort but by the fact of true, i.e., whole, love alone. Temptation has not to be overcome: it is not experienced. The invulnerability is magical. Moreover, it occurs more often than is usually supposed. Because 'unfaithfulness' is manifested, the conclusion is drawn that invulnerability does not exist. But 'infidelity' is not necessarily due to temptation, but possibly and often to indifference; and there is no Fall where there is no Temptation.

. . . The state of being in love is not always defined in relation to one object. One person has the talisman of raising another to the plane of love (that is, of polarizing him or her with the natural energy of love); but he or she may not be then either the sole beloved or, indeed, the beloved at all. There are, among people as among chemical substances, agents of catalysis which make possible interchanges and combinations into which the catalysts themselves do not enter. Frequently they are unrecognized by the parties affected, and usually by themselves as well. In the village of Bor-na, not far from Lhasa, there once lived a man who was such a catalyst. People who spoke to him instantly fell in love, but not with him, or indeed, immediately with anybody in particular. All that they were aware of was that they had, after conversation with him, an active spirit of love which was ready to pour itself out in loving service. The European troubadours were perhaps such people. . . .

. . . Take it as the fundamental truth about Love:

that it always creates. Love created the world: and not all its works are beautiful ! ... The aim of conscious love is to bring about rebirth, or spiritual childhood. Everybody with perceptions beyond those of male and female must be aware of the change that comes over the man or woman, however old in years, who loves. It is usually instinctive; yet it symbolizes the still more marvellous change occurring when a man or woman loves consciously or is aware of being consciously loved. The youth in such cases has all the air of eternity; and it is, indeed, the divine youth. The creations of such a spiritual child in each of the two lovers is the peculiar function of conscious love; and it depends neither upon marriage nor upon children . . .

We are not one but three in one. . . . Three quite different people, each with his own ideas of how his organism should act, exist in us at once: and usually they refuse to co-operate with each other, and in fact, get in each other's way. Now imagine such an organism, tenanted by three squabbling persons, to 'fall in love', *What* has fallen in love; or, rather, which of the three ? It seldom happens that all three are in love at the same time or with the same object. . . .

You imagine that you are continent because you have refrained from sex-relations; but continence is of the senses as well as of the organs, and of the eyes chiefly. . .

The chastity of the senses is natural in a few people; but by the many it must be acquired if it is to become common. Under the greatest civilization human history has yet known, the capital of which was the city whose poor remains are Baghdad, the chastity of the senses was taught from early childhood. Each sense was carefully trained; and exercises were devised to enable pupils to discriminate the different emanations arriving from the sense perceptions intellectually, emotionally, instinctively or erotically motived. From this education people acquired the power of directing their senses, with the result that chastity was at least possible, since it was under control. Eroticism thereby became an art, in the highest form the world has seen. Its faint echoes are to be found in Persian and Sufi literature today. . . .

Love without divination is elementary. To be in love demands that the lover shall divine the wishes of the beloved long before they have come into the beloved's own consciousness. He knows her better than she knows herself; and loves her more than she loves herself; so that she becomes her perfect self without her own conscious effort. *Her* conscious effort, when the love is mutual, is for him. Thus each delightfully works perfection in the other.

But this state is not ordinarily attained in nature: it is the fruit of art, of self-training. All people desire it, even the most cynical; but since it seldom occurs by chance, and nobody has published the key to its creation, the vast majority doubt even its possibility. Nevertheless it is possible, provided that the parties can learn and teach humbly. How to begin ? Let the lover when he is about to see his beloved think what he should take, do or say so as to give her a delightful surprise. At first it will probably be a surprise that is not a complete surprise: that is to say, she will have been aware of her wish, and only delighted that her lover had guessed it. Later the delightful surprise may really surprise her ; and her remark will be: 'How did you know I should be pleased, since I should never have guessed it myself ?' Constant efforts to anticipate the nascent wishes of the beloved while they are still unconscious are the means to conscious love.

Take hold tightly; let go lightly. This is one of the great secrets of felicity in love. For every Romeo and Juliet tragedy arising from the external circumstances of the two parties, a thousand tragedies arise from the circumstances created by the lovers themselves. As they seldom know the moment or the way to 'take hold' of each other, so they even more rarely know the way or the moment to let go. The ravines of Mount Meru (i.e. Venusberg) are filled with lovers who cannot leave each other. Each wishes to let go, but the other will not permit it. There are various explanations of this unhappy state of affairs. In most instances the approach has been wrong: that is to say, the parties have leapt into union without thought of the way out. Often the first five minutes of the lovers' *first* meeting are decisive of the whole future of the relations . . . When one of the parties desires to separate, the other's love-duty is to 'let go.' Great love can both let go and take hold.

Jealousy is the dragon in paradise; the hell of heaven; and the most bitter of the emotions, because associated with the sweetest. There is a specific against jealousy, namely conscious love; but this remedy is harder to find than the disease is to endure . . . "

This is what Katherine Mansfield was searching for at the Priory — a knowledge and a power of the same degree as her love of loving and being truly loved. It was a woman, with a woman's body and heart, and desire to enjoy completely this terrestial life, who closed her bedroom door and set out on the last adventure. There was no mysticism in all this, as Lawrence would have said, Lawrence who was furious if anyone called him a mystic. There was only a natural need to reach a life at last that was full and free and to reach it at once. A cab left Fontainebleau station, crossed a bridge, took the road to Valvins and stopped before an iron gate on the edge of a wood. M. Dimitri Gurdjieff, the brother of the "Grand Lama of Tibet," came to open the gate, with great kindness and consideration. Katherine Mansfield entered the damp and dilapidated chateau. She was breathless, worn out by her journey and by much else besides. Through the uncurtained windows could be seen the huge, neglected park. It was a fine October afternoon, and the leaves were falling.

14

Katherine Mansfield's Letters to Her Husband

Written from the Priory

Le Prieuré,
Fontainebleau-Avon,
(Seine-et-Marne).
October 18, 1922

My dear, darling Bogey,

I have been through a little revolution since my last letter. I suddenly made up my mind (for it was sudden, at the last) to try and learn to live by what I believed in, no less, and not as in all my life up till now to live one way and think another ... I don't mean superficially, of course, but in the deepest sense I've always been disunited. And this which has been my 'secret sorrow' for years, has become everything to me just now. I really can't go on pretending to be one person and being another any more, Boge. It is a living death. So I have decided to make a clean sweep of all that was 'superficial' in my past life and start again to see if I can get into that real living, simple, truthful, *full* life I dream of. I have been through a horrible deadly time coming to this. You know the kind of time. It doesn't show much, outwardly, but one is simply chaos within !

So my first Leap into the Dark was when I came here and decided to ask Mr. Gurdjieff if he would let me stay for a time. 'Here' is a very beautiful old château in glorious grounds. It was a Carmelite monastery, then one of Madame de Maintenon's ' seats.' Now it is modernised inside — I mean, *chauffage centrale,* electric light and so on. But it's a most wonderful old place in an amazingly lovely park. About 40 people— chiefly Russians — are here working, at every possible kind of thing. I mean, outdoor work, looking after animals, gardening, indoor work, music, dancing — it seems a bit of everything. Here the philosophy of the ' system ' takes second place. Practice is first. You simply *have* to wake up instead of talking about it, in fact. You *have* to learn to do all the things you say you want to do.

I don't know whether Mr. Gurdjieff will let me stay. I am ' under observation ' for a fortnight first. But if he does, I'll stay here for the time I should have been abroad and get really cured — not half cured, not cured in my body only and all the rest still as ill as ever. I have a most lovely sumptuous room — a kind of glorified Garsington — for the fortnight. As for the food, it is like a Gogol feast. Cream, butter — but what nonsense to talk about food ! Still, it's very important, and I want you to know that one is terribly well looked after, in every way. There are three doctors here — real ones. But these, too, seem details. The chief thing is that this is my Selsfield for the time, the house of *my dreams.* If Mr. Gurdjieff won't let me stay, I shall go to the South, take a little villa and try and learn to live on my own, growing things and looking after rabbits and so on, getting into touch with *Life* again.

No treatment on earth is any good to me, really. It's all pretence. Manoukhin did make me heavier and a little stronger. But that was all if I really face the facts. The miracle never came near happening. It couldn't, Boge. And as for my spirit — well, as a result of that life at the Victoria Palace I stopped being a writer. I have only written long or short scraps since *The Fly*. If I had gone on with my old life I never would have written again, for I was dying of poverty of life.

I wish, when one writes about things, one didn't dramatize them so. I feel awfully happy about all this, and it's all as simple as can be. It's just the same for us, darling, as though I had stayed on in Paris, *except* that I hope I shall be well when you see me again, instead of knowing it would be a variation on the old theme.

Will you send me letters here for a fortnight ? Ida will be at the Select Hotel for that time, so, if you prefer to send them there, she'll post them on. At the end of that time, I'll either stay on here or, as I say, go off to some warm place where I can turn into a worker. But I hope it will be here.

Mr. Gurdjieff is not in the least like what I expected. He's what one wants to find him, really. But I do feel *absolutely confident* he can put me on the right track in every way, bodily and t'other governor.

I haven't talked money to Mr. Gurdjieff yet. But in any case I shan't write any stories for three months, and I'll not have a book ready before the spring. It doesn't matter.

When we have discussed finances I'll tell you. The fact is I've hardly talked with him at all. He's terribly busy just now and he only speaks a few words of English — all is through an interpreter. I can't say how ' good ' some of the people seem to me here — it's just like another life.

I start Russian today, and my first jobs: which are, eat, walk in the garden, pick the flowers and rest *much*. That's a nice calm beginning, isn't it ? But it's the eat much which is the job when it's Gurdjieff who serves the dish.

I must stop this letter, dearest. I'm awfully glad Delamare is a real person: I know just what you mean about Sullivan and Waterlow. It seems ' right ', somehow, in a queer way.

I take back my words, Betsy, about your quarrying. It sounded very different when you told me about the sand.

Goodbye for now, darling heart,
Ever your own,
Wig.

. . . .

(October 20, 1922)

My darling Bogey,

I'll tell you what this life is more like than anything; it is like Gulliver's Travellers *(sic)*. One has, all the time, the feeling of having been in a wreck and by the mercy of Providence got ashore ... somewhere. Simply everything is different. Not only language, but food, ways, people, music, methods, hours — *all*. It's a real new life.

At present this is my day. I get up 7.30 — light the

fire, with kindling drying overnight, wash in ice-cold water (I'd quite forgotten how good water is to wash in and to drink) and go down to breakfast — which is coffee, butter, bread, gorgonzola cheese and quince jam and eggs. After breakfast, make my bed, do my room, rest, and then go into the garden till dinner, which is 11 a.m. Which is a very large meal with things like — beans mixed with raw onions, vermicelli with icing sugar and butter, veal wrapped in lettuce leaves and cooked in cream. After dinner, in the garden again till 3 o'clock, tea-time. After tea, any light job that is going until dark — when all knock off work, wash, dress and make ready for dinner again at 7. After dinner most of the people gather in the salon round an enormous fire, and there is music — tambourine, drums and piano — dancing and perhaps a display of all kinds of queer dance exercises. At ten we go to bed. Doctor Young, a real friend of mine, comes up and makes me up a good fire. In ' return ' I am patching the knee of his trousers today.

But it's all ' stranger ' than that. For instance, I was looking for wood the other evening. All the boxes were empty. I found a door at the end of the passage, went through and down some stone steps. Presently steps came up and a woman appeared, very simply dressed, with her head bound in a white handkerchief.* She had her arms full of logs. I spoke in French, but she didn't understand. English — no good. But her glance was so lovely — laughing and gentle, absolutely unlike people as I have known people. Then I patted a log and she gave it to me and we went our ways . . .

At present the entire Institute is devoted to manual

* This was the Olga Ivanovna mentioned later.

work, getting this place in order, out and inside. It's not, of course, work for the sake of work. Every single thing one does has a purpose, is part of a system. Some of the English, ' arty ' and theosophical people are very trying, too. But one can learn to use them, I am sure —though I'm not much good at it yet. On the other hand, some of the advanced men and women are truly wonderful. I am still on my fortnight's probation, simply spending a fortnight here. Mr. Gurdjieff hardly speaks a word to me. He must know me pretty well.

But even if he won't let me stay here, I am finished for the time being with *old circumstances*. They have just not killed me, and that's all there is to be said for them. All the people I have known don't really matter to me. Only you matter — more and more, if that is possible, for now that I am not so ' identified ' with you I can see the real tie which holds us.

Ida, of course, was very tragic. She had got to the pitch of looking after me when she gave me a handkerchief without my asking for it. She *was* me.

However, I am sure Ida will recover. There is something rock-like in her under all the passion for helplessness.

Jeanne's wedding made me feel sad, Bogey. I think the fat, purple fellow was McGavin, for some reason. Thank you for telling me about it. I must write to Marie in a day or two. Forgive this hasty writing. Do send *Lit. Sups*. They are so good for lighting fires. I wish you were here. It's such happiness.

    Ever, my darling,
      Your
       Wig Voyageuse.

Tuesday,
(October 24, 1922)

My darling Bogey,

I was so glad to get your second letter today. Don't feel we are silently and swiftly moving away from each other ! *Do you really ?* And what do you mean by us meeting ' on the other side ' ? Where — Boge ? You are much more mysterious than I !

I have managed this badly for this reason. I never let you know how much I have suffered in these five years. But that wasn't my fault. I could not. You would not receive it, either. And all I am doing now is trying to put into practice the ' ideas ' I have had for so long of another, and a *far more truthful* existence. I want to learn something that no books can teach me, and I want to try and escape from my terrible illness. That again you can't be expected to understand. You think I am like other people — I mean: *normal*. I'm not. I don't know which is the ill me or the well me. I am simply one pretence after another. Only now I recognise it.

I believe Mr. Gurdjieff is the only person who can help me. It is great happiness to be here. Some people are stranger than ever, but the strangers I am at last feeling near, and they are my own people at last. So I feel. Such beautiful understanding and sympathy I have never known in the outside world.

As for writing stories and being true to one's gift— I wouldn't write them if I were not here, even. I am at an end of my source for the time. Life has brought me no FLOW. I want to write — but differently — far more steadily. I am writing this on a corner of the table against orders, for the sun shines and I am supposed to be in the garden. I'll write again, my darling precious.

Ever your own
Wig.

. . . .

(October 27, 1922)

Darling Bogey,

I was so glad to hear of your Sullivan excursion. But doesn't his chess obsession bore you dreadfully? It did me. But Beethoven and the stars and the baby all sounded nice.

What are you going to do to the fruit trees? Please tell me. We have masses of quinces here. They are no joke when they fall *exprès* on your head.

I do hope you are having this glorious weather. Day after day of perfect sunshine. It's like Switzerland. An *intense* blue sky, a chill in the air, a wonderful clarity so that you see people far away, all sharp-cut and vivid.

I spend all the sunny time in the garden. Visit the carpenters, the trench diggers. (We are digging for a Turkish Bath — not to discover one, but to lay the pipes). The soil is very nice here, like sand, with small whitey pinky pebbles in it. Then there are the sheep to inspect and the new pigs that have long golden hair — very mystical pigs. A mass of cosmic rabbits and hens —and goats are on the way, likewise horses and mules to ride and drive. The Institute is not really started yet for another fortnight. A dancing hall is being built and the house is still being organized. But it has started really. If all this were to end in smoke tomorrow I should have had the very great wonderful adventure of my life. I've learnt more in a week than in years *là-bas*. As to habits. My wretched sense of order, for instance, which rode me like a witch. It did not take long to cure that. Mr. Gurdjieff likes me to go into the kitchen in the late afternoon and 'watch'. I have a chair in a corner. It's a large kitchen with six helpers. Madame Ostrovsky, the head, walks about like a queen exactly. She is extremely beautiful. She wears an old raincoat. Nina, a big girl in a black apron — lovely, too—pounds things in mortars. The second cook chops at the table, bangs the saucepans, sings; another runs in and out with plates and pots, a man in the scullery cleans pots — the dog barks and lies on the floor, worrying a hearthbrush. A little girl comes in with a bouquet of leaves for Olga Ivanovna. Mr. Gurdjieff strides in, takes up a handful of shredded cabbage and eats it . . . there are at least 20 pots on the stove. And it's so full of life and humour and ease that one wouldn't be anywhere else. It's just the same all through — *ease* after *rigidity* expresses it more than anything I know. And yet I realise that as I write this, it's no use. An old personality is trying to get back to the outside and observe, and it's not true to the present facts at all. What I write sounds so petty. In fact, I cannot express myself in writing just now. The old mechanism isn't mine any longer and I can't control the new. I just have to talk this baby talk.

I would like you to see the dancing here. There again you see it's not to be described. One person sees one thing; one another. I have never really cared for dancing before, but *this* — seems to be the key to the new world within me. To think that later I shall do it is great happiness. There may be a demonstration in Paris in a month or two. If so, I wish you could see it. But would it just look like dancing? I wonder. It's so hard to tell.

Oh, about money. I don't need any, thank you, Bogey. If ever I do need money I shall ask you first, but at present I don't.

I wish you'd ask Ouspensky out to dinner when you are in London. His address is 28 Warwick Gardens. He is an extraordinarily sympathetic person.

There are masses of work going on in this garden — uprooting and digging and so on. I don't see why there isn't in yours. Or perhaps you are more forward.

Won't you send Ida a card to Paris 'Select Hotel' and ask her to spend a week-end with you if she returns to England? I don't know her plans.

Still got cramp in my thumb. Oh, I wish I could write to you from this self, not the other.

Suppose you throw up every single job in England, realize your capital, and come over here to work for Gurdjieff. Burn every single boat for once! Do you like the idea? That's why I thought you might care to see Ouspensky. Do you like that old mechanical life at the mercy of everything? And just living with a little tiny corner of yourself?

You could learn the banjo here and if the worst came to the worst always make enough to keep you with playing it — or anything. But perhaps this sounds very wild talk. We are not really wild here, at all. Very serious, in fact.

    My darling precious Bogey,
       Yours ever
         Wig.

   . . . . .

        Saturday,
      (October 28, 1922)

Darling Bogey,
 Forgive me if I don't write just now. I am so glad

you are happy. I am happy, too. And our happiness does not depend on letters. I feel certain we shall move towards each other. But we shall do it in our several ways. If I write at present I 'falsify' my position and I don't in any way help yours. It's absurd to give you the news here. News there is none that can be so expressed. As to the people I have known I know nothing of them and they are out of sight just now. If I am sincere, I can only say we *live* here — every moment of the day seems full of life. And yet I feel I can't enter into it as I shall be able to; I am only on the fringe. But write about it I can't.

Dunning's phrase is half good, I feel — no more. He always seems to me half way in everything. He has insight but not direction. Can he really help?

There is always this danger of deceiving oneself. I feel it, too. I only begin to get rid of it by trying and trying to relax — to give way. Here one *learns* how to do it. Life never would have taught me.

But I am sure you will understand why it is so hard to write. We don't move in our letters. We say the same things over and over.

As I tried to explain, I'm in such a state of transition. I could not if I would get back to the old life, and I can't deal with the new.

But *anxiety* I never feel. Perhaps I shall; I cannot tell. But I am so busy and so many people are here — so much is happening.

Goodbye for now, darling
Wig.

Let us speak the new truth. What present relationship have we? None. We feel there is the possibility of one.

that is deep-down truth, don't you feel? But no more. It doesn't mean we are moving away, though! It's a thousand times more subtle.

. . . .

(November 2, 1922)

My own Bogey,

Ever since my last letter to you I have been so enraged with myself. It's so like me. I am ashamed of it. But you who know me will perhaps understand. I always try to go too fast. I always think all can be changed and renewed in the twinkling of an eye. It is most fearfully hard for me, as it is for you, not to be 'intense'. And whenever I am intense (really, this is so) I am a little bit false. Take my last letter and the one before. The tone was all wrong. As to any new truth — oh, darling, I am really ashamed of myself. It's so very wrong. Now I have to go back to the beginning and start again and again tell you that I have been 'over-fanciful' and I seem to have tried to force the strangeness. Do you know what I mean? Let me try now to *face facts*. Of course, it is true that life here is quite different, but violent changes to one's individuality — of course, they do not occur. I have come here for a 'cure'. I know I shall never grow strong anywhere in the world except here. This *is* the place, and here at least one is understood entirely, mentally and physically. I could never have regained my health by any other treatment. And all my friends accepted me as a frail half-creature who migrated towards sofas. Oh my dearest Bogey, just wait and see how you and I will live one day — so happily, so splendidly. But in the meantime, love, please never take what I say for 'absolute'. I do not take what you say for 'final'. I try to see it as relative. Essentially, you and I are together.

I love you and feel you are my man. It's that I want to build on and realise and live in, one of these days.

So I shall write at least twice a week and tell you any odd things that are happening. Will you tell me, too?

Last night, for instance, in the salon we learnt to make rugs from long pieces of corn. Very nice ones. Very easy to make, too. I have been in the carpenter's shop all the morning. The small forge is alight; Mr. Gurdjieff is planing, a Mr. Salzmann is making wheels. Later on I shall learn carpentry. We are going to learn as many trades as possible, also all kinds of farm work. The cows are being bought today. Gurdjieff is going to build a high couch in the stable where I can sit and inhale their breath! I know later on I shall be put in charge of those cows. Every one calls them already 'Mrs. Murry's cows'.

This letter must be posted, love. Do please forgive my two silly ones. I learn terribly slowly, my precious Veen, and I must not hurt you.

Ever your own
Wig.

I am making a cure of goat's milk — four times a day!

. . . .

£5 note enclosed.

(November 7, 1922)

My darling Bogey,

I had a letter from you today saying you had bought a pruning-knife. I hope you suceed with the old trees. Here it is part of the 'work' to do a great many things especially things which one does *not* like. I see the point of that. It's the same principle as facing people whom one shrinks from and so on. It is to develop a greater range in oneself. But what happens in practice is that no sooner do the people begin doing those things they don't like than the dislike changes. One feels it no longer. It's only that first step which is so terribly hard to take.

Are you having really divine weather? It's marvellous here — like late spring today — really *warm*. The leaves are still falling. The park belonging to this château is incredibly beautiful, and with our livestock roaming about, it begins to look like a little piece of virgin creation.

I am fearfully busy. What do I do? Well, I learn Russian — which is a terrific job — have charge of the indoor carnations — no joke — and spend the day paying visits to places where people are working. Then every evening about 50 people meet in the salon and there is music and they are working at present at a tremendous ancient Assyrian group dance. I have no words with which to describe it. To see it seems to change one's whole being for the time.

Until I came here I did not realize with what a little bit of my mind, even, I lived. I was a little European with a liking for Eastern carpets and music and for something that I vaguely called The East. But now I feel I am turned to that side far more than the other. The West seems so poor, so scattered. I cannot believe knowledge or wisdom are there. I expect this is a phase. I tell it you because I said I would tell you my reactions. . . . In three weeks here I feel I have spent years in India, Arabia, Afghanistan, Persia. That is very odd, isn't it? And oh, how one wanted to voyage like this — how bound one felt! Only now I know.

There is another thing here — Friendship. The real

thing that you and I have dreamed of. Here it exists between women and women and men and women, and one feels it is unalterable, and living in a way it never can be anywhere else. I can't say I have friends yet. I am simply not fit for them. I don't know myself enough to be really trusted, and I am weak where these people are strong. But even the relationships I have are dear beyond any friendships I have known.

But I am giving the impression that we all live together in brotherly love and blissful happiness. Not at all. One suffers terribly. If you have been ill for five years, you can't expect to be well in five weeks. If you have been ill for twenty years (and according to Mr. Gurdjieff we all of us have our 'illness') it takes very severe measures to put one right. But the point is there is hope. One can and does believe that one will escape from living in circles and will live a CONSCIOUS life. One can, through work, escape from falsity and be true to one's own self — not to what anyone else on earth thinks one is.

I wish you could meet some of the men here. You would like them very, very much, especially a Mr. Salzmann, who speaks very little. I must stop this letter. Is it a rigmarole?

I don't know what you mean, darling, by seeing me as an angel with a sword. I don't feel at all like one. There is another thing. You can't *really* be happy in my happiness. No-one ever is. The phrase is only a kind of buffer — don't you think? It's like people living through their children. Well, they may do it. But it's not life. Neither can I ever teach you how to live. How is it possible? You are you. I am I. We can only lead our own lives together. But perhaps I am treating too seriously what you said.

Goodbye for now, my darling heart,
Ever your
Wig.

I enclose a £5 note. Will you pay Heal's bill and keep the rest for any odd bills I may send you later. I know there are some. If you know anyone coming to Paris do give them two pairs of grey milanese stockings (for size five shoes) to post on to me. I need them awfully. *Merci en avance.*

. . . . .

(November 12, 1922)

Darling Bogey,

I am so sorry for you when you speak of your life as emerging from your study and disappearing into it again. Don't you *sicken* of shutting that door and sitting down to that table? One feels like a spider in an empty house. For whom this web? Why do I strain to spin and spin? Here, I confess, after only five weeks, there are things I *long* to write ! Oh, how I long to ! But I shall not for a long time. Nothing is ready. I must wait until *la maison est pleine.* I must say the dancing here has given me quite a different approach to writing. I mean some of the very ancient Oriental dances. There is one which takes about seven minutes and it contains the whole life of woman — but everything ! Nothing is left out. It taught me, it gave me more of woman's life than any book or poem. There was even room for Flaubert's *Coeur Simple* in it, and for Princess Marya. . . . Mysterious.

By the way I have had a great talk about Shakespeare here with a man called Salzmann, who is by 'profession' a painter. He knows and understands the plays better than anyone I have met except you. He happens, too (this is by the way) to be a great friend of Olga Knipper's.* His wife is the chief dancer here — a very beautiful woman with a marvellous intelligence.

Dear Bogey, I'm not 'hypnotized'. But it does seem to me there are certain people here who are far beyond any I have met —of a quite different order. Some — most — of the English here don't even catch a glimpse of it. But I am sure. I remember I used to think — if there was one thing I could not bear in a community, it would be the women. But now the women are nearer and far dearer than the men. Of course, I don't speak of Mr. Gurdjieff. I couldn't say he was *near* or *dear* to me ! He is the embodiment of the life here, but at a remote distance.

Since last I wrote to you I have changed my room. Now I am in another wing — another kind of existence altogether. Where all was so quiet outside the door, all is noise and bustle. My other room was very rich and sumptuous. This is small and plain and very simple. When Olga Ivanovna and I had arranged it and she had hung her yellow dancing stockings to dry before the fire we sat together on the bed and felt like two quite poor young girls . . . different beings altogether. I like being here very much. I hope Mr. Gurdjieff does not move us again too soon. But it is a favourite habit of his to set the whole house walking. Easy to see why when one saw the emotions it aroused.

About my stockings, darling. I heard from Ida today saying she goes to England tomorrow and would like to come to see you. She intends to return to France where she goes to work on some farm. Would you give the stockings to her ? I'll ask her to write to you. I

* Tchekov's wife.

never think of Ida except when I get letters from her. Poor Ida ! When I do, I am sorry for her.

I must finish this letter, darling. It is written on the arm of a chair, on a cushion, on my bed, as I try to escape from the heat of my fire. Oh, I have so much to do this afternoon ! It's terrible how the days pass. I had a bath this morning — first time since leaving England ! There's a nice confession. But it's wonderful what can be done with a basin and a rough towel.

Have you read Elizabeth's new novel ? What do you think of it ? Please tell me. How is your gardening getting on ? Have you learnt to drive the car ?

Goodbye, my dear darling.

Ever your
Wig.

. . . .

Sunday 6.30,
(November 19, 1922)

Darling Bogey,

I am thankful you have your little flat, darling. Rob mine to make yours snug. Take all you can or care to, away. But do you keep warm enough ? And what about food, I wonder ? I have asked Ida to buy me a number of things while she is in England and to bring them over to Paris with her. Bogey, I have not got a cheque book for the moment. Would you send her a cheque for £10.0.0 on my behalf ? I'll let you have it back in a week or two. But would you send it at once ? As Ida is going to stay such a short while in England. Thank you, dearest.

It is intensely cold here — quite as cold as Switzerland. But it does not matter in the same way. One has not the time to think about it. There is always something happening, and people are a support. I spent the winter afternoon yesterday scraping carrots — masses of carrots — and half way through I suddenly thought of my bed in the corner of that room at the Chalet des Sapins. . . . Oh how is it possible there is such a difference between that loneliness and isolation (just waiting for you to come in and you knowing that I was waiting) and *this*. People were running in and out of the kitchen. Portions of the first pig we have killed were on the table and greatly admired. Coffee was roasting in the oven. Barker clattered through with his milk-pail. I must tell you, darling, my love of cows persists. We now have three. They are real beauties — immense — with short curly hair ? fur ? wool ? between their horns. Geese, too, have been added to the establishment. They seem full of intelligence. I am becoming absorbed in animals, not to watch only, but to know how to care for them and to know *about* them. Why does one live so far away from all these things ? Bees we shall have later. I am determined to know about bees.

Your idea of buying some land and building a little house *does* seem to me a bit premature, darling. You know so little. You have never tried your hand at such things. It's not quite easy to change from an intellectual life like yours to a life of hard physical work. But your remark made me wish you did care for my ' ideas ' — I mean by my ' ideas ' my desire to *learn to work in the right way* and to live as a conscious human being. They are not much more than that. There is certainly no other spot on this whole earth where one can be taught as one is taught here. But life is not easy. We have great ' difficulties ' — painful moments — and

Mr. Gurdjieff is there to do to us what we wish to do to ourselves and are afraid to do. Well, theoretically, that is very wonderful, but practically it must mean suffering, because one cannot always understand.

Ouspensky came over last week. I had a short talk with him. He is a very fine man. I wish you would just see him — out of — let's call it curiosity.

I must get dressed for dinner. I badly need a good *washing*. Remarkable how clothes fall into their proper place here. We dress in the evening, but during the day . . . the men look like brigands. Nobody cares, nobody dreams of criticising.

Oh, Bogey, how I love this place ! It is like a dream — or a miracle. What do the ' silly ' people matter ? And there are silly people who come from London, see nothing and go away again. There *is* something marvellous here if one can only attain it.

Goodbye for now, my dearest.

Ever your own
Wig.

I will write Elizabeth.

. . . . .

(after Nov. 19, 1922)

My darling Bogey,

I hope you and Sullivan do find a place together in the country somewhere near Dunning. I am glad you feel Selsfield is too luxurious. It is very, very lovely, but it is not living. There is too much 'Dinner is served, sir ! ' about it. Do you ever feel inclined to get into touch with Lawrence again, I wonder ? I should like very much to know what he intends to do — how he intends to live now his *Wanderjahre* are over. He and E. M. Forster are two men who *could* understand this place if they would. But I think Lawrence's pride would keep him back. No one person here is more important than another. That may not sound much of a statement, but practically it is very much.

I shall be interested to hear of your meeting with Ida. That reminds me again of the stockings which arrived in perfect order. What an extraordinary brainwave to hide them in *The Times*! They are very lovely stockings, too, just the shade I like in the evening. One's legs are like legs by moonlight.

It is intensely cold here — colder and colder. I have just been brought some small fat pine logs to mix with my *boulets*. Boulets are unsatisfactory; they are too passive. I simply live in my fur coat. I gird it on like my heavenly armour and wear it ever night and day. After this winter the Arctic even will have no terrors for me. Happily, the sun *does* shine as well, and we are thoroughly well nourished. But I shall be glad when the year has turned.

Darling, I must sit down to a Russian lesson. I wish you knew Russian. I have also been learning mental arithmetic beginning $2 \times 2 = 1$, $3 \times 3 = 12$, $4 \times 4 = 13$, $5 \times 5 = 28$ and so on, at great speed to the accompaniment of music. It's not as easy as it looks, especially when you start from the wrong end backwards. In fact at 34 I am beginning my education.

I can't write to Elizabeth about her book. I thought it so dreadfully tiresome and silly. It didn't seem to me like a fairy tale; I saw no fairies. In fact, I saw nobody. And jokes about husbands, double beds, God and trousers don't amuse me, I'm afraid. In fact to me a sad tinkle from an old music box.

Goodbye for now, my dearest Bogey,

Ever your own

Wig.

(November, 1922)

My darling Bogey,

I understand affairs much better from your last letter. I am very glad you are going to be near Dunning. Of course, I do not feel that my way is 'the only way'. It is for me. But people have such hidden energy, such hidden strength that, once they discover it in themselves, why should they not do alone what they have to learn to do here? You were only joking, weren't you, when you said you might find Le Prieuré was your way? For one can only come here *via* Ouspensky and *it is a serious step*. However, one can always go again if one finds it intolerable. That is true, too. But the strangeness of all that happens here has a meaning; and by strangeness I don't mean obvious strangeness — there's little of it — I mean spiritual.

Are you having really perfect weather (except for the cold)? It is absolutely brilliantly sunny — a deep blue sky, dry air. Really, it's better than Switzerland. But I must get some wool-lined over-boots. My footgear is ridiculous when I am where I was yesterday — round about the pigsty. It is noteworthy that the pigs have of themselves divided their sty into two: one, the clean part, they keep clean and sleep in. This makes me look at pigs with a different eye. One must be impartial even about them, it seems. We have two more cows about to calve in three weeks' time. Very thrilling. Also our white goat is about to have a little kid. I want to see it very much. They are so charming.

You know I told you a Turkish Bath was being built. It is finished and working. It was made from a *cave* used for vegetables and of course all labour, including the plumbing, the lighting and so on was done by our people. Now one can have seven different kinds of baths in it, and there is a little rest room hung with carpets which looks more like Bokhara than Avon. If you have seen this evolved, it really is a miracle of ingenuity. Everything is designed by Mr. Gurdjieff. Now all hands are busy building the theatre which is to be ready in two weeks. I have to start making costumes next week. All the things I have avoided in life seem to find me out here. I shall have to sew for hours on end just as I have to puzzle over these problems in mathematics that we get sometimes in the evening.

But I wish I could tell you of the people I live with. There is not only my friend, Olga Ivanovna. There are the Hartmanns, husband and wife. He was — is — a musician. They live in one smallish room, awfully cramped, I suppose. But to go and sit there with them in the evening before dinner is one of my greatest pleasures. Dear precious people! She is very quick, beautiful, warm-hearted. No, it's no good. I can't describe her. He is small and quite bald, with a little pointed beard, and he generally wears a loose blouse spotted with whitewash, very full trousers, wooden boots. He is a ' common workman ' all day. But it is the life between them; the feeling one has in their nearness. But so many people come forward as I write. They are all very different; but they are the people I have wanted to find — *real* people, not people I make up or invent.

Tell me about your new plans when you can, my darling, will you? Was L.M. just the same? It is a horrible thing; I have almost forgotten her. And only two months ago it seemed I could not have lived without her care. Do Dunning's children have lessons? Why don't you offer to teach them something? It's good to be in touch with children; one learns very much.

Goodbye for now, my darling Bogey. I do feel we are nearer than we were. But there is so much — so very much one cannot write. One can only feel.

Ever your own
Wig.

. . . .

Friday: Piatnitse,
(December 1, 1922)

My darling Bogey,

I seem to have snapped at that £10 like a dog with a bone, and never even said *merci* in my last letter. I am most awfully grateful for it. I accept it with joy, though I *did* mean — yes, truly — to send it back to you. Did you see L.M. I wonder? Wayside Cottage reminded me of Rose Tree Cottage. The name only. They are of the same type. I hope you are snug in it. I suppose you couldn't (or wouldn't care to) snare L.M. as working housekeeper and gardener? I don't see Sullivan as a great help in such matters. But perhaps I wrong him.

About Christmas. I want to be quite frank. For many reasons I would rather we did not meet till the Spring. Hear my reasons before judging me for that, will you? For one thing the hotels at Fontainebleau are closed — the decent ones. You could not come to the Institute as a guest at present. It's not running smoothly enough. You would simply *hate* it. No, let me be very careful. I have not asked Mr. Gurdjieff if you could come. He might say 'Yes'. But I can't think what on earth an outsider could do here just now. It's winter. One can't be out of doors. One can't just stay in one's room.

Meals are at all hours. Sometimes lunch is at 4 p.m. and dinner at 10 p.m. And so on.

But the chief *reason that matters* is this. Physically there is very little outward change in my condition so far. I am still breathless. I still cough, still walk upstairs slowly, still have to stop and so on. The difference is that here I make ' efforts ' of a certain kind all day and live an entirely different life. But I have no life to *share* at present. You can't sit in the cowhouse with me at present or in the kitchen with seven or eight people. We are not ready for that yet. It would simply be a false position. Then, when I first came here, I had a most sumptuous luxurious room and so on. Now I rough it in a little, simple, but very warm room. But it's tiny. We couldn't sit in it.

Deeper still is the most sincere feeling I am capable of that I do not want to see you until I am better physically. I cannot see you until the old Wig has disappeared. Associations, recollections would be too much for me just now. I must get better alone. This will mean that we do not meet until the Spring. If this sounds selfish, it must sound selfish. I know it is not and I know it is necessary. If you do not understand, please tell me, darling.

I don't feel the cold as much as I have in other winters. It's often sunny, too, and I have just bought for 23 francs very good *boots,* lined with felt with felt uppers.

But I'll say no more just now. I hope you will understand and not be hurt by my letter, dearest heart.

Ever your
Wig.

                                    Wednesday,
                            (December 6, 1922)
My darling Bogey,
   Your Sunday letter arrived today. Until I have your answer to mine suggesting that we do not meet until the Spring, I will not refer to the subject again. . . . I think that's best.
   Your little house and way of life sounds so nice. I am very, very glad that you feel Dunning is your friend. Do you have something of your Lawrence feeling for him? I imagine it is a little bit the same. And Mrs. Dunning —you like her? And do you play with the little boys? There are nine children here. They live in the children's house and have a different mother every week to look after them. But I remember now I have told you all that before. I'll tell you instead about that couch Mr. Gurdjieff has had built in the cowhouse. It's simply too lovely. There is a small steep staircase to a little railed-off gallery above the cows. On the little gallery are divans covered with Persian carpets (only two divans). But the white-washed walls and ceiling have been decorated most exquisitely in what looks like a Persian pattern of yellow, red and blue by Mr. Salzmann. Flowers, little birds, butterflies and a spreading tree with animals on the branches, even a hippopotamus. But, Bogey, all done with the most *real art* — a little masterpiece. And all so gay, so simple, reminding one of summer grasses and the kind of flowers that smell like milk. There I go every day to lie and later I am going to sleep there. It's very warm. One has the most happy feelings listening to the beasts and looking. I know that one day I shall write a long, long story about it.
   At about 5.30 the door opens and Mr. Ivanov comes

in, lights the lantern and begins milking. I had quite forgotten the singing wiry silvery sound of milk falling into an empty pail and then heavier — plonk — plonk! 'Mr.' Ivanov is a very young man. He looks as though he had just finished his studies, rather shy, with a childlike beaming smile.

I don't know how you feel. But I still find it fearfully hard to cope with people I do not like or who are not sympathetic. With the others all goes well. But living here with all kinds I am simply appalled at my helplessness when I want to get rid of someone or to extricate myself from a conversation, even. But I *have* learnt how to do it, here. I have learnt that the only way is to court it, not to avoid it, to face it. Terribly difficult for me in practice. But until I really do master this I cannot get anywhere. There always comes the moment when I am uncovered, *so zu sagen*, and the other man gets in his knock-out blow.

Oh, darling — I am always meaning to ask you this. I came away this time without a single photograph of you. This is *intolerable*. I really must have one, Bogey. Not only because I want it fearfully for myself, but people keep on asking me. And I am proud of you. I want to show them what you look like. Do please send me one for Christmas. This is very important.

Goodbye for now, my own Bogey. I am
Ever your loving
Wig.

Don't forget the photograph.

. . . .

Saturday,
(December 9, 1922)

My darling Bogey,

I have never had a letter from you that I so 'understood' as your last about your house and how you are living and the wages you give to John and Nicholas. I can't say what a joy it is to know you are there. It seems to me very mysterious how so many of us nowadays refuse to be cave-dwellers any longer but in our several ways are trying to learn to escape. The old London life, whatever it was, but even the life we have led recently wherever we have been, is no longer even *possible* to me. It is so far from me that it seems to exist in another world. This, of course, is a wrong feeling. For, after all there are the seeds of what we long after in everybody and if one remembers that any surroundings are possible . . . at least.

What do you read ? Has Dunning any unfamiliar books ? You have rather a horror of anything at all . . . Eastern, haven't you ? I read Ouspensky's *Tertium Organum* the other day. For some reason it didn't carry me away. I think it is extremely interesting but—perhaps I was not in the mood for books. I am not at present, though I know that in the future I shall want to write them more than anything else in the world. But different books. There is Mr. Hartmann here with whom I have great talks nearly every evening about *how* and *why* and *when*. I confess present-day literature simply nauseates me, excepting always Hardy and the other few whose names I can't remember. . . . But the general trend of it seems to me quite without any value whatsoever.

Yesterday when I was in the stable Mr. Salzmann came up. He had just returned from his work — sawing logs in the far wood. And we began to talk about poverty. He was talking of the absolute need for us today to be *poor again,* but poor in the real sense. To be poor in ideas, in imagination, in impulses, in wishes —

to be simple, in fact. To get rid of the immense collection with which our minds are crammed and to get back to our real needs. But I shall not try to transcribe what he said. It sounds banal; it was not. I hope you will meet this man one day. He looks a very surly, angry and even fierce workman. He is haggard, drawn, old-looking, with grey hair cut in a fringe on his forehead. He dresses like a very shabby forester and carries a large knife in his belt. I like him almost as much as I like his wife. Together they seem to me as near an ideal couple as I could imagine.

Bogey, are you having fine weather? Today is perfectly glorious. There was a heavy frost last night, but it's marvellously clear and fine. No, I don't want any money just now, thank you, darling heart. What nonsense to say those W.S. certificates are mine! Why? They are yours! and don't go building a seven-roomed house. Seven rooms for two people! I will write again in a day or two. Goodbye for now, dearest darling Bogey,

Ever your own
Wig.

· · · ·

(December 17, 1922)

My darling Bogey,

I am so delighted to hear of your half motor-car. I think it is a most excellent idea. What fun you and Sullivan will have with it. It is so pleasant to think of you two together and I like to know that Sullivan will now understand you from a real standpoint — after sharing your life and working with you in the real sense. Do you teach him to cook and to sew and to knit? The fairies in the keyholes must have a quiet laugh or two of a gentle kind. As to those four little wood-gatherers, I love them.

I hope your tooth is better. Just the same thing has happened to me. My biggest and brightest stopping has come out. But I shall have to hang on until the Spring when I can get to Paris. So far all is well.

My fortunes have changed again. I have been moved back from my little bare servant's bedroom on the general corridor to my beautiful sumptuous first room overlooking the lovely park. It seems almost incredible grandeur. I suppose — I feel I have learnt the lesson that other room had to teach me. I have learnt that I can rough it in a way you and I have never done, that I can stand any amount of noise, that I can put up with untidiness, disorder, queer smells, even, without losing my head or *really* suffering more than superficially. But how did Mr. Gurdjieff know how much I needed that experience? And another mystery is that last week when it was intensely cold I felt that I had come to an end of all that room had to teach me. I was very depressed and longing beyond words for some real change and for beauty again. I almost decided to ask him to send me away until the weather got warmer. Then on Saturday afternoon when I was in the stable he came up to rest, too, and talked to me a little. First about cows and then about the monkey he has bought which is to be trained to clean the cows. Then he suddenly asked me how I was and said I looked better. 'Now', he said, 'you have two doctors you must obey. Doctor Stable and Doctor New Milk. Not to think, not to write. . . . Rest. Rest. Live in your body again.' I think he meant Get back into your body. He speaks very little English, but when one is with him one seems to understand all he suggests.

The next thing I heard was that I was to come into here for the rest of the winter. Sometimes I wonder if we 'make up' Mr Gurdjieff's wonderful understanding. But one is always getting a fresh example of it. And he always acts at precisely the moment one needs it. That is what is so strange. . . .

Dear Bogey darling, I shall not have any Christmas present for you. But you know that £5 I sent you. How much did you spend? Would you buy a book each for Chaddie and Jeanne for me and keep the rest for yourself? Jeanne would like Delamare's new poems, *Down-a-Down-Derry*, I am sure (it's 7/6 isn't it?) and Chaddie — h'm — that is difficult! Some book that looks pretty and tastes sweet — some love poems. Is that too vague? And may I ask you to execute these commissions for me? I hope there will be something left over for you, darling. Buy it with my love. I'll tell you what I want for a present. Your photograph. The proof of the drawing, of course, I should simply treasure, but why should you send me that? Keep it. Of course, if you could have it copied. . . .

There is a man here who is going to take a photograph of me one day. I have changed. I have no longer a fringe — very odd.

We had a fire here the other night. A real one. Two beautiful rooms burnt out, and a real fear the whole place would go. Cries of 'Vode! Vode!' (Water!), people rushing past all black and snatching at jugs and basins. Mr. Gurdjieff with a hammer, knocking down the wall. The real thing, in fact.

What is the weather like with you? It's so soft and spring-like here that actually primroses are out. So are the Christmas roses under the espalier pear-trees. I *love*

Adam et Eve, 1962 — by Georges Rohner

Le Radeau de la Méduse, 1963 — Salon de Mai — by Georges Rohner

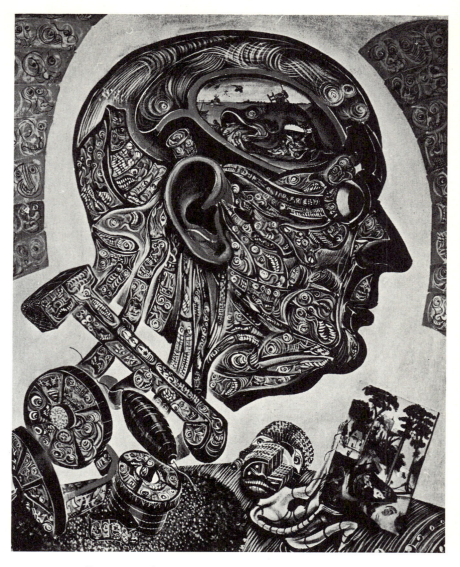

Portrait with Breughel and Bosch, 1952 — by Ferro

Ferro's wife, Bat-Yosef, poses for " Birth without pain "

Still from the Ferro film

Still from the Ferro film

Mecamakeup 1958
Ferro

Christmas; I shall always feel it is a holy time. I wonder if dear old Hardy will write a poem this year.
God bless you, my darling precious !
Ever your
Wig.

· · · ·

Saturday,
(December 23, 1922)

Darling Bogey,

Just a note to wish you a Happy Christmas. I am afraid it will not arrive in time for today is Saturday *not* Friday as I imagined. But there ! Put the blame on the poor Christmas postman. No, even to think of such a thing won't do at all. . . . A Happy Christmas, my dearest Bogey. I wonder very much how you who always says you hate Christmas so will spend it this year. Perhaps the Dunning children will make it seem real at last. Do tell me about them.

Here we are to have great doings. The Russian Christmas is not due for another fortnight. So Mr. Gurdjieff has decided the English shall have a real old-fashioned English Christmas on their own. There are so few of them, but that makes no difference to his ideas of hospitality. We are to invite all the Russians as our guests. And he has given us a sheep, a pig, two turkeys, a goose, two barrels of wine, whiskey, gin, cognac, etc., dessert of all kinds, an immense tree and carte blanche with which to decorate it. Tomorrow night we have our tree followed by the feast. We shall sit down to it about sixty. Whoever gets the coin in the pudding is to be presented with our new-born calf — a perfect angel. Would that it were mine !

I do love to hear about your Dunnings. What a queer

thing you should have found then just at this time. Not really queer, for it does seem to be a truth that when one is in real need one finds someone to help. Are you and 'Bill' friends? I mean more friends than you and Frieda were, for instance, for you had no separate relationship with her really, did you? I would like to know them both.

Darling precious Bogey, this is not a letter this time — only this note written on a table piled with paper chains, flowers, little bon-bon cases, gold wire, gilded fir cones — you know the kind of thing.

I attended the obsequies of the pig this morning. I thought I had better go through with it for once and see for myself. One felt horribly sad. . . . And yesterday I watched Madame Ouspensky pluck, singe and draw our birds. In fact, these have been gory days, balanced by the fairy-like tree. There is so much life here that one feels no more than one little cell in a beefsteak, say. It is a good feeling.

God bless you darling.

Ever your
Wig.

. . . .

Boxing Day: Tuesday
(December 26, 1922)

My darling Bogey,

I think the drawing of you is quite extraordinarily good — and in a very subtle way. I had no idea Rothenstein was that kind of artist. People will say it makes you look old. That is true. But you have that look. I am sure *c'est juste*. I am more than glad to have it and I shall keep it very carefully. Thank you, my dearest. The photograph I don't like so well for some reason. But photographs always pale before good drawings. It's not fair on them.

How is the old Adam revived in you, I wonder? What aspects has he? There is nothing to be done when he rages except to remember that it's bound to be — it's the swing of the pendulum — and the only hope is when the bout is exhausted to get back to what you think you really care for, aim for, wish to live by, as soon as possible. It's the intervals of exhaustion that seem to waste so much energy. You see, my love, the question is always: '*Who am I*?' and until that is answered I don't see how one can really direct anything in oneself. '*Is there a Me*?' one must be certain of that before one has a real unshakeable leg to stand on. And I don't believe for one moment these questions can be settled by the head alone.

It is this life of the *head*, this formative intellectual life at the expense of all the rest of us which has got us into this state. How can it get us out of it? I see no hope of escape except by learning to live in our emotional and instinctive being as well and to balance all three.

You see, Bogey, if I were allowed one single cry to God, that cry would be: *I want to be* REAL. Until I am that I don't see why I shouldn't be at the mercy of old Eve in her various manifestations for ever.

But this place has taught me so far how unreal I am. It has taken from me one thing after another (the things never were mine) until at this present moment all I know really, really is that I am not annihilated and that I hope — more than hope — believe. It is hard to explain and I am always a bit afraid of boring you in letters.

I heard from Brett yesterday. She gave a very horrid

picture of the present Sullivan and his views on life and women. I don't know how much of it is even vaguely true, but it corresponds to Sullivan the Exhibitionist. The pity of it is life is so short and we waste about nine-tenths of it — simply throw it away. I always feel Sullivan refuses to face the fact of his wastefulness. And sometimes one feels he never will. All will pass like a dream, with mock comforts, mock consolations.

Our cowshed has become enriched with two goats and two love-birds. The goats are very lovely as they lie in the straw or so delicately dance towards each other, butting gently with their heads. When I was there yesterday, Mr. Gurdjieff came in and showed Lola and Nina who were milking the cows the way to milk a goat. He sat down on a stool, seized the goat and swung its hind legs across his knees. So there the goat was on its two front legs, helpless. This is the way Arabs milk. He looked very like one. I had been talking before to a man here whose passion is astrology and he had just written the signs of the Zodiac on the white-washed stable door. Then we went up to the little gallery and drank koumiss.

Goodbye for now, my darling. I feel this letter is flat and dull. Forgive it.

I am ever your own loving
Wig.

. . . .

Sunday,
(December 31, 1922)

My darling Bogey,

My fountain pen is mislaid, so as I am in a hurry to write please forgive this pencil.

Would you care to come here on January 8 or 9 to stay until 14 - 15 ? Mr. Gurdjieff approves of my plan and says will you come as his guest ? On the 13th our new theatre is to be opened. It will be a wonderful experience. But I won't say too much about it. Only on the chance that you do come I'll tell you what clothes to bring.

One sports suit with heavy shoes and stockings and a mackintosh and a hat that doesn't matter. One 'neat' suit with your soft collar or whatever collar you wear and tie (you see you are my husband and I can't help wanting you to look — what shall I say ?) slippers and so on. That's all. If you have a cardigan of course bring it and a pair of flannel trousers in case you get soaking wet and want a change.

I am writing to ask Brett to go to Lewis' and get me a pair of shoes. Will you bring them ? I may ask her to get me a jacket too. But she will give you the parcel. Will you wire me your reply — just ' yes ' or ' no ' and the date, if ' yes ', of your arrival.

There is a London train that reaches Paris at four something. You could then come on to Fontainebleau the same day. Otherwise it's far better to stay the night in Paris as no cabs meet the late train.

You get out of the train at *Avon* and take a cab here which costs eight francs *with* tip. Ring the bell at the porter's lodge and I'll open the gate.

I hope you will decide to come, my dearest. Let me know as soon as you can, won't you ? I hope Tchekov's wife will be here. I have gone back to my big lovely room, too, so we should have plenty of space to ourselves. We can also sit and drink *kiftir* in the cowshed.

I can't write of other things in this letter. I hope to hear from you soon.

Your ever loving
Wig.

15

She Dies

This was Katherine Mansfield's last letter. She summoned her husband. A few weeks before, she was begging him not to come until the summer. He must wait. "I haven't yet enough life to share." She had not yet attained sufficient inner poise to be able to do full justice to her desire to change her love, nor to be so alive to the man she loved that their re-union should be experienced as fully conscious love. She had to reach the limit of loneliness before she could feel her " me " stable, strong, free and radiant, and only then would her love be so too. But, up till now the risk was too great of falling into the same lies and pettinesses inseparable from the weak love of ordinary lovers — slaves that they are to uncontrollable moods and chance circumstances — of slipping back into the old stale love of their former life. She wanted to complete her transformation first for, truly, love was too serious a thing to endanger before having acquired a centre of gravity, merely for the pleasure of an immediate re-union.

Then again, she wanted to wait until it should no longer be necessary to soften the truth. Up till then Katherine had glossed over the facts — to read her letters one would never have guessed that her condition was rapidly deteriorating, and that she knew it. But she had decided not to worry about her physical state as she would have done had she been under orthodox medical care. " If I save my soul I shall save my body too. It is quite natural that at first, while becoming aware of one's spiritual non-existence and of the tremendous work to be done to reach existence, that the body should tend towards death. One should not worry about it; it is only the first stage. A revolution will take place. First of all, the illusory personality that one mistook for oneself must be destroyed. Our very flesh admits it. What weakness and cowardice to try to go back to the old life at the very first trial ! " So she said nothing, but to spare Middleton Murry she pretended that she was not seriously ill so that he might continue to think calmly about their future together.

There were other things, too, that she glossed over. What love he had left for her was felt for the writer; very well then, to-morrow she would write. To-morrow she would produce work of much greater scope. But the fact was that, for the present, to write at all was quite out of the question. To have written as she used to would have meant to identify herself with people and things, and so increase her dependence on the outside world, it would have meant feeding on subjective lies that have nothing in common with the objective reality. No, it was no longer possible to write and all " literary " work was despicable. " Subjective art is trash," as

Gurdjieff used to say. Thus, the thing she loved best in life, her consolation and last resort, was taken from her. She accepted this, but lulled Middleton Murry with the story that she was staying at the Priory partly in order to broaden and strengthen the talent he so much admired.

Worse still, she said nothing about that key to the whole life at the Priory, that work of "death to oneself" which she was trying to carry on, as far as her remaining physical strength allowed. She said nothing because this work gave a tragic flavour to the days, and her husband could not bear tragedy. Another reason for her silence was that, had she told the truth, it would have meant denouncing their former life as false, illusory and pernicious, and would have implied an unfavourable criticism of Middleton Murry's general attitude. Nor did she say anything about the efforts she was making with herself, under Gurdjieff's orders. On the contrary, she took immense pains, in her letters, to pretend to be her old self, the Katherine who looked at the world of people and things with an amused and tender gaze. She described her life at the Priory as though she were in a rather unusual "pension de famille" with inmates whose inner lives were perhaps a little richer and more profound than is normally the case. This was, of course, to reassure her husband and make him think a little longer that nothing had changed. It was quite enough to have to ask herself hundreds of questions an hour about herself, without having to answer any that he, with his quick intelligence and liability to panic, might put to her, if she told him all about her life and her reasons for being there.

The time had not yet come for her to tell him the

naked truth, nor for him to bear to hear it; and though she knew how much work was entailed before she could " *change* " and was prepared for it, her illness robbed her of the strength of will needed and she was unable to make the first efforts required. So she remained on the threshold, profoundly humiliated by this bodily weakness that she could not control, and waiting to be able one day to join in the " work."

But suddenly she sent for her husband. There were fewer days ahead than she had expected, and it was not during their remaining days of life that she would be able to find her " me ", so mysteriously hidden away in the quicksands, but on the day of her death. All was over. It was Death's turn to play. Perhaps we all have to work during this life to acquire a soul, as Gurdjieff says, if we really want to profit by our sojourn on this earth, but we like to think that Death will give us a soul, we like to think that the great wrench of death is, *at the same time,* the tearing apart of the countless veils that separate us from our souls. And those of us who have had neither the strength nor the time to give our lives their full value, nor an awareness of eternity, put our final trust in Death.

She had felt this on Christmas night. She had suddenly left the gathering and taken refuge in her own room. Madame Kafian, one of the disciples who was very fond of her, had guessed and had forestalled her, she had put a log on the fire and lit three candles on a little Christmas-tree.

" Katherine came quietly into the room as usual," Madame Kafian told me, " and suddenly seeing the tree, raised her hand to her heart and cried: 'Adèle, why three candles ! ' " " Two for us," I muttered, confused, " and the third for — your husband." She smiled sadly and sat down by the fire. I wrapped her up in a big blue and white shawl (that I used myself when she was in bed), slipped a foot-stool under her feet and sat down myself on the floor, with my arms round her thin knees. We sat thus, silently, following our own thoughts and gazing at the Christmas-tree. One candle flickered and began to go out. " That's me," murmured Katherine.

Middleton Murry set out as soon as he received her last letter. No doubt, during these last months, he had forced himself to keep away from the torments of love for his sick wife, who expected so much from herself, and from him, and from love. He had retired, to live quietly in his country house, and to work at the literary criticism that Katherine rather despised, since living at Fontainebleau, where all ordinary ideas, knowledge and reason were treated with extreme suspicion. No doubt he was engrossed in his own affairs, and far from anxious to take part in Katherine's struggles. Nevertheless, he loved her, and understood all that was going on; he realized the tragedy and grandeur of this struggle, but it was for him an intellectual realisation that did not involve his whole being, and he remained shut up in himself, watching himself suffer.

They had done for each other, in their own ways, all they could, she with her passion and he with his subtle intelligence, and now they were to try to be truly united at last.

" I arrived at the Gurdjieff Institute early in the afternoon of January 9, 1923. Katherine was very pale, but radiant. We talked for a while in her room overlooking the garden. She told me that she had wanted me to come very much indeed, because the moment had come for which she had been waiting. She had had to disentangle herself from our love, because it had become an agony of concern for each other which threatened to strangle us. At the Institute, she had worked herself free of it, and from the fear of death, with which it was so deeply entwined. Now she could come to me as a free being, in a love that was purified of all fear.

The greatest obstacle she had to overcome in taking the plunge and making the final decision to enter the Institute had been her fear of losing me. But that fear had been the source of the falsity that had steadily grown upon her since her illness began. Only at rare and terrible moments had she dared — or been driven — to reveal to me the deadly fear that was taking possession of her soul, the blackness that engulfed her; and then I had been dismayed. When she had cried to me to help her out of the gulf, I could do nothing: I almost seemed to turn away as from something intolerable. And so our love had become a dream of happiness to be in some unattainable future. And she had had to pretend, and to go on pretending, to herself and to me that she was not the sick and frightened Katherine that she was, until her own identity was lost and she did not know which was her true self.

Suddenly, she had known that, if she was to escape this living death, she must make a clean sweep of all her fears. The Institute had offered her the opportunity. Even to enter it had been the cause of fear: she had been fascinated by, but afraid of its doctrines. She had been afraid of ignoring her illness. She had been afraid of finally alienating me. By acting in spite of her fears, she had overcome them. By risking losing me, she had found her love for me: it was entire and perfect.

And truly as I looked at her, while I listened, she

seemed a being transfigured by love, absolutely secure in love. She had no desire to defend the Institute; as indeed I had none to criticise it. She spoke quite quietly of her feeling that she had perhaps now gained all that it had to give her, and that she might be leaving very soon. When she did, she would like to live with me in extreme simplicity in a small cottage in England, and she would like me to cultivate the land.

It was a great happiness to me to be with her again. She led me out first to her gallery in the cowshed, then to where the company was putting the finishing touches to the dancing hall which had been erected in the garden. Though it was built with trusses, hangar fashion, it immediately impressed me by its likeness to a huge nomad tent, though I have never seen one. She introduced me to some of her friends — to Hartmann and Salzmann and Dr. Young, to Olga Ivanova and Adela, a young Lithuanian girl who was devoted to her. Under instruction I took a hand in painting coloured designs upon the windows of the hall. I met Orage again, for the first time for many years; and he seemed to me a changed man, much gentler and sweeter than I remembered him. Indeed there was a blend of simplicity and seriousness in most of the people I met there, and in the company as a whole, which impressed me deeply.

Many of them were very tired. They had been working against time, and often all night long, to finish the hall in time to open it on January 13. The work appears, in memory, to have gone on uninterruptedly all through that afternoon and evening. I cannot remember that there was any formal meal. But later in the evening Katherine and I went to sit in the salon. At about 10 o'clock she said she was tired, and began to go to her room. As she slowly climbed the big staircase to the first floor where her room was, she was seized by a fit of coughing. I took her arm and helped her into her room. No sooner were we inside, than the cough became a paroxysm. Suddenly a great gush of blood poured from her mouth. It seemed to be suffocating her. She gasped out, ' I believe . . . I'm going to die.' I put her on the couch and rushed out of the room calling for a doctor. Two came almost immediately. Wisely, I suppose, they thrust me out of the room though her eyes were imploring me. In a few minutes she was dead.

She died at the age of 34 and was buried in the communal cemetery of Avon, near Fontainebleau. On the stone was carved a sentence from Shakespeare which she particularly loved: ' But I tell you, my lord fool, out of this nettle, danger, we pluck this flower, safety.'

It is not for me to pass judgment on the Gurdjieff Institute. I cannot tell whether Katherine's life was shortened by her entry into it. But I am persuaded of this: that Katherine made of it an instrument for that process of self-annihilation which is necessary to the spiritual rebirth, whereby we enter the Kingdom of Love. I am certain that she achieved her purpose, and that the Institute lent itself to it. More I dare not, and less I must not, say."

M. Gurdjieff, at the head of the Russian group, attended the funeral unmoved. He held out to the people standing round the grave little screws of paper containing a mixture of corn and raisins called "Kootia," symbolizing germination and decay.

She had died without having changed anything in herself, or hardly anything. She had only succeeded in escaping from fear and in leading a less feverish and more ordered life; she had trained all her inner resources towards the hope that it was going to be possible to possess the truth in body and soul and to live and love on the level of this truth.

This was not much, but she had had neither time nor strength to gain more and at least this had given her last days a serenity that she had never known before. She was just becoming able to keep a certain distance from herself — from the self who was agonised at the prospect of losing life and love. She could also keep a little distance from her husband. The agonized Katherine had lived and suffered too close to John, too much involved in his every mood, word and gesture, identified with him, and John had lived and suffered in the same way, identified with Katherine. It was not Katherine's true " me," steady and free, that communed with John's real " me." It was their hundreds of little illusory " we's " that circled ceaselessly round each other, colliding, retreating, and colliding again, like motes in a sunbeam. It was the wretched love of ordinary human beings, not Love. As her husband said, she had long been searching for the way into the kingdom of love, but in order to enter it one had to change oneself, become a unified person, truly conscious and free. One had to kill what is called the personality — the endless flow of feelings, impressions, sensations, desires, associations, memories, and identifications with things and people. One had to reach the true, independent " me," gifted with objective consciousness. She finally knew this, and that there is a way to reach this state. All she had to do was to work with Gurdjieff, to obey him with courage and patience. She died before she had had time to effect a real change, but she died in hope.

In a letter to the "Daily News" that Middleton Murry wrote a few months after her death, he says: "What they are trying to achieve at the Priory cannot be explained in a letter like this, nor in many letters. But, as I see it, the Gurdjieff Institute did not solve the problems it set out to solve. It merely plunged its members for a time into a kind of unconsciousness. It was, in a way, a drug that was given them, a very effective and powerful drug, but who can say whether, in the end, they benefited, or whether there was any positive result?"

Thus, he had completely understood what it was that his wife and the other disciples were seeking from Gurdjieff, and had posed the great question: Does there come a time when their hope and work is justified, and they succeed in attaining a new state of consciousness in which they are as demi-gods?

But at least Katherine Mansfield found peace and hope at the Priory, the best thing that could be wished for her during her last weeks. This much Middleton Murry has made clear. It is possible she may have had to pay for it by shortening her life a little, but one has to pay for everything.

A few months after Katherine's death John became engaged to a girl of French extraction, Violette Le Maistre, and in the following May he married her. As for Gurdjieff, when anyone asked him about Katherine Mansfield he always replied, with apparent sincerity: " Me not know." For him, she had not attained to real *existence* in his meaning of the word, she had no true " me ", no soul. On the level of ordinary human beings, however noble their ambitions, and splendid their attempts, however great their sufferings, their intelligence and their sensibility, all is worthless, completely worthless. " Me not know " says Gurdjieff, the True Man. And on our own level, Middleton Murry says: "Alas ! I knew. But leave me alone to forget and console myself as best I can, as though I had not known."

She died, then, having apparently missed everything. John married again, at once, and Gurdjieff declared that she was nothing and had died without a soul. " You want to die like dogs ? " he used to ask his disciples, to spur them on. She had died like a dog — nothing had counted. She had lived, suffered, hoped and worked for nothing. It is true that during her last hours she had felt a certain exaltation, and this had touched John, but exaltation is itself worthless, and soon subsides. She had failed on both levels, John turned aside because he was a man, and Gurdjieff because he was, or took himself to be, a superman. All was lost on earth, as in Heaven. There was no salvation, and everything was completely wiped out.

Can this be true ? On the all-too-human side, the water was tainted, and on the super-human side it was polluted too. Is there yet a third source, from which the water would be pure ? This is the final question.

Part Three

MR. GURDJIEFF AND US

1
After 1934

After his serious motor accident Gurdjieff gave up the arduous work of running the Priory at Avon, sold the Chateau and, in 1934, took a flat in Paris, in the Rue du Colonel Renard, near the Etoile.

This was the beginning of the *exoteric* period. Recruitment of members was speeded up and the "Teaching" was given by instructors only distantly supervised by Gurdjieff, who himself gave up "working" with all but a very few disciples. When M. de Salzmann died, his wife became the effective leader and administrator of the "groups" which were springing up in Paris, Lyons, London and New York, as well as in South America and Austria.

It would seem that by allowing his doctrine to be taught in an elementary form by his assistants at the risk of many misunderstandings, Gurdjieff wished to attract the greatest possible number of people. He felt that time was short. Was he, perhaps, in casting his net so wide, hoping to find the *one* disciple to whom he could transmit his power and the essentials of his knowledge ?

It was at this moment that Ouspensky's book came out in London. Gurdjieff seems to have wished it success, in spite of his slight contempt for the " renegade ". The members of the " group " were responsible for its circulation in France. Madame de Salzmann's son-in-law, Philippe Lavastine, translated it. At the same time Gurdjieff's own writings, till then kept secret, were brought out of their hiding-places; part of *Beelzebub* was published in America and England, with the idea of a French version to follow. As Pierre Schaeffer says further on: " This modern miracle-worker, when he feels the game is up, that there is no-one and nothing more to be expected and that his hour is near, throws in his hand. In an instant, esotericism is over and all that used to be occult now sees the light of day. Yet how can one believe that the modern miracle-worker can circulate what should have been anti-ideas and anti-phrases by means of the printed word, which is necessarily imperfect ? This, however, is what he does, he who mistrusts everyone, above all his intimates."

It is not only his writings that are questionable, but the very form of the Teaching, the way it is circulated, and his obvious and growing contempt alike for his pupils and for all who showed any interest in his ideas. The Teaching exerted its greatest influence during the years 1934 to 1949, the year of Gurdjieff's death. (I mean " greatest " in the sense of being most widespread rather than most profound). But this influence was often sinister and several times there were hints of scandal. Some disciples were stricken by strange illnesses, in some cases fatal.

I cannot begin to describe, and still less to explain, Gurdjieff's changes of attitude. It seems to me that when he came to the West, in 1920, he chose to appear behind a mask, to give his undertakings an appearance of caricature in order to make them accessible to this century and to this civilization which he hated. The germs of radical destruction can only be introduced surreptitiously. Ouspensky broke away, frightened at this subterfuge and fearing that the falsity might not be only superficial.

It seems to me, too, that since 1934 and especially during these last years of world upheaval, of the complete collapse of old beliefs and ways of thought and action, of the disintegration of our intellectual, moral, religious, scientific and political tenets, Gurdjieff again changed his attitude. He scattered his secrets to the wind and went so far as to choose confusion; he allowed the good and the bad to run their course together, with an increasing contempt for the consequences and a deliberate bias towards the negative side of his work. Nietzche said: " I must put up a fence around my doctrine to keep out the swine." Innocent words ! Gurdjieff, with a laugh louder than Zarathustra's, pulled down the fence in order that, in his domain at least, the confusions and misunderstandings of his time should reach their climax. Let the swine in, and welcome to them, and to the lambs too, if there are any left ! Let the swine eat till they burst, and may the good that they consume turn to evil. And let the lambs find their own pasture if they can ! I believe he contemplated with dark satisfaction the spectacle of all these people stuffing themselves with his doctrines, and whether they prospered or died of it was to him a matter of complete indifference.

If we ever were in contact with what is known as an "esoteric school" it was only in the lurid light that seems to pervade all precious things in our time. It was an esoteric school under the sign of our own age. I will say no more. You will be reading the testimony of Pierre Schaeffer, to my mind a prodigy of insight into disorder which alas, is essential for an understanding of the Gurdjieff adventure, as for all other spiritual adventures in the Western world of to-day.

Hence the great interest and also the narrow limits of the confessions, analyses and judgments contained in this third part of the book. Here my own story begins, and it seems to me that we have all of us failed to extract the very real secret of the Gurdjieff affair as a whole. These confessions only express the contradictory aspects of our experience at a time when this experience was bound to be muddled and fragmentary. I feel that our accounts may prove disappointing, but this is an instructive disappointment. I believe, in fact, that in the present state of our civilization, inner experience can go no further than ours without as much confusion and as many dangers. I do not mean that inner experience has become impossible nowadays. On the contrary, I think the paths are being reopened, but, in this critical period, members of the expedition are not able to penetrate very far and have to pay a high price for every step, especially if they find themselves under the leadership of a master who seems purposely to add to the difficulties by reversing the signposts.

I repeat, then, that all I am concerned with here is to describe the reactions of living people with their particular types of mind, character, curiosity or hunger for knowledge. I am not pretending to unearth secrets, nor even to bring to light the super-human laws that undoubtedly appear to govern a man like Gurdjieff.

Thus, it will be understood that I am not trying to exonerate Gurdjieff from his responsibility for the evils which were, and still are, being endured by numbers of his pupils. Thousands of people in many different countries are still absorbed in this business, which goes on quite well without its master. Thousands more are ready to plunge in. This concerns the physical and mental health of an important minority of Western intellectuals. Yet for the life of me I still find it impossible to choose between the obvious advantages of good health and the secrets to be learnt through the serious disturbances that the Gurdjieff adventure can produce.

I must now say a few words about these disturbances. The people who are attracted by the Teaching all belong to a group with a bias towards mystical knowledge. Analysis of our modern modes of thought and reflection on their insufficiency are enough to turn us in this direction, and the actual events of our time force us to make this analysis. As M. Maurice Nadeau said of Ouspensky's book in the literary journal *Combat*:

"When we feel we have nothing more to lose and when our sciences, religions and ordinary ways of life can no longer disguise their inadequacy; when no one dares to assert without a laugh that knowledge and human evolution are advancing hand in hand, it is natural for the troubled and bewildered and for those who refuse to be duped any longer, to look for different kinds of nourishment." To that, for instance, offered by Gurdjieff, the most appetizing nourishment for critical minds.

Some people tend naturally towards a mystical

approach from a real vocation that is left unsatisfied by the official Western religions, which no longer appear to offer: "any concrete method or discipline for attaining the state of Fulfilment spoken of by their mystics and saints."

Others come to the Teaching through anguish — either physical or originating in psychoanalysis. I realize the mistake of referring to all kinds of anguish in medical terms, the mistake that caused Dr. Ménétrier, one of the greatest French biologists, to say of Simone Weil: "As I read her works I feel I am reading a description of a clinical case and I make out a prescription which, had it been followed, would have changed everything." Or the psychoanalyst who said: "Had he undergone my treatment, René Daumal would have been cured of tuberculosis and of Zen Buddhism at the same time." But I think it useful to say that the really anguished disciples approached the Teaching through their anguish, and that the troubles and disturbances suffered by some — of whom I was one — were primarily caused by their anguished way of approaching everything.

It was surely necessary to make these distinctions before introducing the witnesses for the prosecution.

The inner experience, once the preliminary stage of clearing the way to *being*, is passed, remains indescribable, at any rate through the medium of language in its present form. The experience of the "I" as they call it in the Teaching, of "Oneself" of the Vedantas, of the "inner man" of the Christian mystics, of the "transcendental *I*, completed and static" of Husserl, this experience, from which the Gurdjieff work *proceeds*, is impossible to put into words. We can only speak of that which precedes the experience, and if we had pursued it — given that it was possible to do so under Gurdjieff's guidance — we should now be in a state that would prohibit all *description*. We can only speak of the first stage to the extent to which we have failed to attain the second. This is the worst limitation of our testimonies.

Are there any disciples of Gurdjieff to-day who have succeeded in pushing their inner experience so far as the indescribable ? I do not know. All I do know is that those who have passed through the beginnings of the experience — however disappointing their descriptions may prove — consider it to have been the most important thing in their lives and feel that they will bear the marks forever in their hearts, bodies and souls.

WITNESS FOR THE PROSECUTION

2

Paul Sérant

I first knew Paul Sérant when I was chief editor of *Combat* and he was foreign correspondent. We used often to talk together at night, after the provincial edition had gone out and before the Parisian edition had gone to press. We met at the café where Jaurès was assassinated, at the corner of the Rue Montmartre and the Rue du Croissant. We could hear the roar of the printing-presses and the delivery-vans were drawn up along the pavements. We would stand at the bar with our colleagues, all of us drunk with nervous fatigue, and reel from our brandies to the slot-machines, amongst the nightly Paris tarts, tramps, drunks and madmen. The air smelt of printing-ink. No doubt we both savoured the absurdity of a fate that only allotted us this dizzy hour in which to discuss our " work " with Gurdjieff, and to compare our efforts towards finding a free and silent place within ourselves. We were at the heart of the turmoil, hearing the actual printing of all the lies and stupidities that a modern day carries with it. Meanwhile, with the tide of falsehoods rising around us, we talked of Tradition, of René Guénon, of gnosticism and the techniques of inner experience.

I shall always remember these strange talks and be able to recall the emotion that sprang from these muttered conversations, carried on through the souldestroying noise of the machines and of the men worn out by slaving at them all day.

Paul Sérant is, like me, in his thirties. He has published one novel, *Ritual Murder,* about his own and his wife's experiences with Gurdjieff. He has also just had published the first work of criticism to appear on René Guénon. Amongst our generation he is one of the greatest authorities on " traditional " thought. Here he is, in the witness-box.

Paul Sérant's Story

Why did I embark on the Teaching ? I can answer this readily in the words used by Fernand Divoire when asked the same question about occultism: " Because I was ripe for it. There are no other *reasons.*" But perhaps I can give some explanation.

The war was just over, and France had been liberated. I had finished with my studies and with family restrictions, and was free to come and go as I pleased and to choose my own vocation. In short, they were good times, and yet I was ill at ease and suffocating in the world that opened before me. I could see nothing but crime and absurdity wherever I looked — how could one believe in the future ? The future was either Soviet rule or the atom bomb, or one after the other. However, all around me people were completely " committed " and all kinds of movements flourished. But I felt paralysed; the horrible fate of sincere " collaborationists ", who were being massacred wholesale, while those who had made money out of the Occupation were allowed to enjoy their fortunes, robbed me of all wish to " serve ". On the other hand, cynicism does not come naturally to me, and success in the rackets of the day did not tempt me at all. Briefly, the outer world left me cold, so I turned inwards, to the soul and the eternal.

In that state of anxiety and anguish the religion in which I was brought up could no longer satisfy me. The Church seemed to me, as to so many others, to be too heavily compromised to be able to meet my needs. The truth is that there was too much sentimentality in the religious education of my youth not to provoke an equally sentimental reaction. No doubt I overcame this reaction later, when I discovered the tremendous edifices of the mystics and Thomists. But intellectual satisfactions are not enough.

In these circumstances, how should I not have welcomed with open arms anyone who assured me that there was a technique for giving Man true freedom, the inner freedom that alone can liberate him from the snare of external illusions ? I was all the more easily won over in that one of my chief " grudges " against religion was that it offered the layman no concrete method or discipline for attaining the states of fulfilment of which its saints and mystics speak. Without being in any way a specialist in these subjects, I was yet convinced that there must be physical and psychic exercises, not only in the East but also in the West, designed to encourage the flowering of the spiritual life; for instance, all that I had heard about

Hesychiasm had fascinated me. Then why not M. Gurdjieff ?

This need for a spiritual discipline seems absurd to many spiritual aspirants, probably because they have not yet reached that degree of anxiety that makes people feel their present lives to be quite unacceptable. When this anxiety becomes overwelming, and yet one still refuses death, one is ready to seek any possible way of escape.

And so I began regularly to attend the groups. You would no doubt like to know what we did. Well, some very surprising things certainly happened there, but I find it hard to describe them; not from embarrassment (and I would like it to be understood that I never saw anything shocking in the groups) but simply because it is not easy to describe the outer manifestations of an inner work.

This is what took place. We gathered together in small groups of five, ten or twenty people, under a " master," formerly Gurdjieff himself. We were taught to become conscious. The first stage of the work consisted in understanding that up to the present we had lived in complete unconsciousness, that in no circumstances or in any respect — physical, emotional, intellectual — had we ever been free, but always *identified* with our impulses, moods and associations. This side of the Teaching can be compared to psychoanalysis or Marxism. As psychoanalysis teaches us that such and such a noble sentiment is merely the sublimation of sexual inhibition, and Marxism, that religious belief is merely the result of economic constraints, so we were told that our normal behaviour, whether " spiritual " or " external ", was entirely due to mechanisms over which we had no control whatever. This control, the key to true freedom, was what we were going to be taught.

But if we are totally conditioned, how can we hope to escape? The Teaching said: Stop identifying yourself. Instead of being one with your automatic life, detach yourself from it. Learn to control it by watching yourself live. Say you are walking in the street: try, if only for five minutes, to keey yourself from being absorbed by what is going on around you, or by associations of ideas, and concentrate entirely on yourself. Say you are with other people: detach yourself for a moment from the game of conversation and watch them. Notice how completely they follow their own trains of thought, and how their ideas, far from being the fruits of a free choice, are only mechanical expressions springing from their own particular education, instincts or interests. These exercises in attention were referred to in the Teaching as " self-remembering ".

For a training in lucidity such as this, a concrete and practical grounding was needed, and this is where the exercises in relaxation came in. Control of organic life was considered the best means to achieve control of feelings and ideas. But the kind of relaxation we were taught was quite a different matter from what passes for relaxation in the training for certain sports. In our teaching, mental relaxation was intended to coincide finally, with physical relaxation, and for this, working together in groups was the greatest help. Alone, outside distractions soon upset concentration, and the very fact of meeting together regularly had the effect of reviving enthusiasm.

I repeat, enthusiasm. This must seem a strange word to outsiders, but you must understand that we were feeling the excitement of an undertaking that promised us *the possession of truth in body and soul*. The fact is that this adventure exalted us as probably nothing ever will again. For after a time, we really felt certain that everything had changed, not only our "view of the world" but our own inner lives, and that it now only depended on our own perseverance in order, one day, to attain to true freedom, the freedom of the man who, according to Chinese philosophy "is a law unto himself."

And yet I left the Teaching. Why?

Let me say first of all that perhaps a certain mental resistance prevented my receiving the Teaching as I should have done. I have been gifted by Nature with a lively mistrust, with a critical faculty that is often embarrassing, but which allows me to practise with no difficulty the "alternation" advocated by Montherlant. It was impossible for me to sit amongst the group — we sat on the floor with our legs crossed in the Eastern fashion, a position supposedly inducive to relaxation — without saying to myself every so often: "What the Hell am I doing here? Why am I not writing, or at the cinema, or by the Seine with a girl?" Of course these temptations were foreseen by our masters, who called them "negative feelings". But I could not manage to rid myself of them entirely. Besides, I couldn't believe that repudiating all one's critical faculties could lead to any real spiritual progress. I had no wish to lose my head (and I am now thankful never to have done so!) Even at the age of fifteen Pascal's famous injunction: "Make yourself stupid" puzzled me greatly. To say to an unbeliever: "Accept Holy Water, bow the knee, go to Mass and — you will see — faith will come", seemed to me to be going a bit far. That could only work, I thought for a special kind of unbeliever, one who was hardly an unbeliever any more.

My allusion to Pascal risks provoking cries of rage from some people who cannot take calmly the fact that one no longer agrees with them and who will complain that I have misunderstood, that the Teaching demands no kind of faith, but, on the contrary, requires that one should test and verify everything for oneself. Quite so. But all the same, one does not give oneself up to an experiment of this kind without having, from the beginning, a kind of hope that is very like faith. And it was precisely this kind of faith that I lacked when expected to admit that even the greatest intellectual and artistic achievements were merely the results of "associations" in irresponsible and unconscious minds. I could not help feeling this to be suspect.

But it was the realization of the strange state of mind of most of the people who had been in the group longer that I had, that really aroused my distrust. I perceived that the effort towards consciousness had created in them a suspicious mixture of pretentiousness, egoism and pride (or, more accurately, of self-satisfaction.) These faults are, of course, our common lot, but what seemed to me serious was the fact that they were being methodically cultivated in the name of non-identification, lucidity and consciousness of self. It is evident that if one holds the view that all men are machines, but that one is oneself beginning to be no longer a machine, a dangerous temptation arises: if others are machines, why not use them as such? Duplicity then becomes a quite legitimate means to an even keener consciousness of self.

It is then that a kind of spiritual inversion takes

place that is infinitely more dangerous than *immorality acknowledged as such*. When Machiavelli advocates for politicians the use of lies and subterfuge, he does so in the name of realism: he does not tell them that lies and subterfuge lead to a spiritual life but explains, on the contrary, that it is most regrettable that men should be what they are and that such methods of government should be necessary. In the same way, when Don Juan aims at possessing all the women in the world, he does not imagine that he is treading the path of saintliness, but knows, on the contrary, that he is giving up saintliness for voluptuousness. In neither case is the essence of morality endangered; the hierarchy of values is not questioned and the distinction between right and wrong remains intact. Wrong is still called Wrong, and Right, Right. Real spiritual danger only arises when Right is called Wrong and Wrong, Right. The perversion thus created is almost irremediable, and I think it is this perversion that was responsible for a number of tragedies, some of which are related in this book.

All these reasons for suspicion did not prevent my " working " for some time longer. Though at times revolted by it, my mind was able to accept in principle the methodical practice of " emptiness." How good it is, sometimes, to get rid of all the images that file through one's brain and jostle each other in one's memory! Those who succeed in this even for one second feel something that is impossible even to pretend to express, which in the Teaching they called the sensation of the *I* (or real *Self*, as opposed to the illusory *me*.) It is useless to try to describe the inexpressible.

When I had given proof of my ability to the group,

I was admitted to the "movements". These were physical exercises specially designed to develop the relaxation I have mentioned. I would like to be able to give an analysis of the "movements", but have to admit that my memory is unreliable. The movements themselves and also the strange music to which they were performed, were attributed to M. Gurdjieff, and all that I can now say about them is that they demanded as great a mental as physical effort; as in the relaxation exercises, it was above all a matter of noting "experimentally" the correspondences between the different levels of being. I can, however, remember the special difficulty of some of the movements, which consisted in relaxing to the maximum certain muscles, while at the same time contracting others as hard as possible. It seems to me that the concentration needed for success in these exercises is comparable to that required in Jujitsu (which, as few people realize, was itself conceived as a method for the harmonious development of man.) Finally, I can remember that there were movements that only the members who had been in the group longest were able to perform correctly: these, we were told, had been learnt by M. Gurdjieff from Dervishes and were performed at an extraordinary speed.

Then, one fine day, came what was for me a climax: I was invited to dinner with M. Gurdjieff. A strange dinner and a curious invitation! Gurdjieff's table was much too small to seat all his guests, only a few of his intimates could be accommodated at it. All the others, including me, had to eat standing up, as near the "master" as possible so as not to miss a word or a gesture. The impression that Gurdjieff was bound to make on someone like me who was seeing him for the first time was disconcerting, to say the least. Without his extraordinarily piercing gaze he would have looked more like a Taras Bulba run to fat, than to one's instinctive picture of a " spiritual master ". I once went to see Lanza del Vasto — there were no surprises there. Before a word was spoken I knew exactly what to expect. But this elderly Caucasian with a huge, bald head, proposing endless toasts to all the categories of idiots in the world, in a completely incomprehensible tongue, and bursting with such uproarious laughter that even the most hardened pupil dared not join in, this was really something amazing !

After dinner, at which a great deal of vodka and a large variety of Russian dishes were consumed, a chapter from Gurdjieff's interminable book, *Beelzebub's Tales to his Grandson,* was read aloud. We formed a circle round the reader, seated on the floor in the most uncomfortable position imaginable; while Gurdjieff, sunk in a huge arm-chair, smoked cigarette after cigarette (they were Celtiques, I remember. He refused the Gauloises offered him by a pupil, referring to them as shit.) Every now and then he burst into one of his gigantic laughs at certain passages in his work, which rolled on without any logical sequence and left his pupils completely stupified.

I went back two or three times to Gurdjieff's flat and always found the same atmosphere. I was particularly struck by the complete absence of any conversation between him and the pupils. People seemed really to be struck dumb in his presence. Once I requested a special interview which he gave me without difficulty. I was much impressed by the mixture of cunning, good-will and circumspection with which he answered my questions.

It was not because of the unusual side of Gurdjieff's character that I finally gave up the " work ". It was not the unpleasant attitude of some of the people in the group, nor was it my own intellectual rebelliousness. I stopped because of certain things I noticed about myself. I have already said that I came to the Teaching primarily in order to find some way of freeing myself from the anxiety that was strangling me. I am not, therefore, going to blame the Teaching for creating in me what was already there, like certain patients who complain, after a year's treatment: " If my liver is out of order it's that damned doctor's fault " when in fact they had consulted him precisely because he was a liver specialist. But, though I have no right to say that the Teaching produced my anxiety, the latter took on a new aspect more painful than the previous one. I was possibly less worried by the outside world, but on the other hand this exclusive preoccupation with myself finally produced an unbearable feeling of disgust. I had longed to be freed from the world; now I longed to be free from myself. Far from feeling that I was casting off my " mechanical " fetters, I had the impression of forging chains that were new but infinitely heavier, as they abolished the spontaneity of instinct and feeling — the spontaneity that can at times lighten so much the burden of being a mere machine ! Perhaps I was no longer a machine, but oh ! What nostalgia I felt for the mechanical state ! The self-consciousness which I had expected would produce the bursting of all barriers had in fact produced nothing but the worst of all tyrannies, the tyranny that no-one can be held responsible for but one's self.

It is plain that realities of this kind are not easily expressed in writing, and I did not, of course, experience these feelings with the same intensity at all times. But the question I began to ask myself: *Who is all this for ?*— drowned all other thoughts, and I could no longer answer myself: For my true self. I remembered other doctrines in which man did not sacrifice himself productively except to something greater than himself. This Teaching placed the "something greater than myself" within me and called it my *I*. But I felt most strongly that the object of my search should be outside myself. The more I plunged into my own depths the less I could discover the "something greater than myself." The " me " I could discern inspired me with a strong and growing nausea.

And yet I found it hard to stop the " work ". One only destroys what can be replaced, and in spite of knowing the Teaching to be responsible for the state I was in, for some time I found it painful not to be submitting myself to the discipline that had, up till then, entirely absorbed me; all the more so as my self-disgust persisted without the compensation that, in spite of everything, the regular practice of the " work " afforded me.

Ought I for all this, to condemn the Teaching as a whole ? That would be too easy a way of avoiding serious problems; and I should like to explain here about my novel *Ritual Murder,* that came out three years ago. This book, written shortly after my break with the Teaching, caused unbelievable anger among some members of the group. However, though no doubt the Teaching influenced the tone of the book (and I should like to know what novel is not influenced by its author's memories) it was neither autobiographical nor intended to portray real people. The plot was entirely imaginary—a young couple find that their love is being destroyed by a "spiritual master" who finally drives the girl to suicide and the man to cynicism. A certain similarity in speech between my "master" and Gurdjieff did not imply that I was describing the latter, or condemning his influence. Is a novelist who describes a wicked priest necessarily condemning the Church and Christianity? And was it not admitted in the Teaching that there were other schools which were pernicious and of which we should beware? None of these considerations were sufficient to prevent these people from feeling themselves immediately attacked. I had turned traitor and was trying to blacken the group. They certainly made me feel this! Poor young people, who were far less harmed by ridicule than by what they mistook for their consciences, went round the bookshops, begging them not to stock such a dastardly work! In short, it was sabotage. But their efforts to convince the uninformed that I had committed a crime against the Teaching and that my book should be boycotted, did not prevent it reaching its potential readers.

Their reactions led me to think: if these people took my words so hard, was it not that I had touched on a sore spot, and reproduced fairly accurately the atmosphere and dangers of the Teaching? But I should in fairness explain that the violent reactions came from the more stupid members of the group and it would be dishonest of me to attribute them to those who, since Gurdjieff's demise, had become the leaders. The people I refer to as "stupid" belonged to the bourgeois Parisian set that Max Jacob has so aptly described: "There are also families who think seriously about God; they are either slightly Buddhist, slightly Moslem, Christian Scientists or simply followers of Madame

Durand, the neo-vegetarian of the Rue Beaubourg. The essential thing is not to be Catholic." Max Jacob might have included in his list the disciples of Gurdjieff. And the inevitable weakness of these devotees lies in always thinking that it is they themselves who are being referred to. But, to finish what I have to say about my book, I am certain that if Gurdjieff had been alive when it was published, and had read it — a most unlikely hypothesis — far from being put out, he would, on the contrary, have enjoyed it very much.

So, I have no intention of condemning the Teaching as a whole. I am still convinced that there are aspects of it that no genuine seeker after spiritual truth can afford to ignore. I still believe that we live, if not all the time, then at least most of the time, in a state of unconsciousness, and that the first step towards awakening is the realization of our unconsciousness. I still think that we are too often apt to mistake our emotional or sentimental impulses for real spirituality, and that we too easily give ourselves credit for ideas that are only the product of educational and other influences. Further, I still think that the way from unconsciousness to consciousness must be helped by certain techniques. Finally I am grateful to the Teaching for having been, for me, a training in lucidity, scepticism and strictness towards myself, and at the same time a rejection of the modern mystifications based on sentimentalism. Briefly, I liked and I still like, the aristocratic, Nietzchian side of the Teaching.

On the other hand, I believe that the rejection of imagination, pushed to the point of contempt for all intellectual activity, can easily lead to the atrophy of reason and plain common sense. I have seen devotees who, in the name of non-identification, profess contempt for the lectures given by Philippe Lavastine, who has explained so much to his listeners and is himself a great admirer of Gurdjieff. While believing firmly that Spirit is infinitely higher than Reason, I do not hold that it contradicts it. In this respect I attach great importance to René Guénon's declaration that metaphysics is inaccessible without a very strict theoretical training. Perhaps it was because the Teaching denied the need for any such training that Guénon, I am told, when asked his opinion of Gurdjieff and the disciples, always replied: " Flee them like the Plague."

I come back now to the disturbing attitude of some of the group-members, to the kind of enlarging of the " me " revealed by this attitude. One could say that the disciples had misunderstood what they were being taught, but even admitting this to be so, the fact remains that any teaching capable of bearing such fruit is dangerous. One should consider whether the methodical practice of introversion is not bound to be fatally harmful to Europeans. I know, for instance, that there are certain Indians who strictly forbid the practice of Tantric exercises by Westerners on the grounds that they can only lead to insanity. So one may suppose that Gurdjieff's teaching would not cause the same disequilibrium in the East as it does in the West. One should never forget that Gurdjieff was a Caucasian. It implies no racial prejudice to suggest that the same methods cannot be applied to all peoples indescriminately. Remember, for instance, the description in Dostoevsky's *The Possessed*, of " a saintly person with a gift of prophecy and renowned, not only in our province but in the neighbouring towns and even as far as the two capitals." The " saintly man " receives his visitors in a manner that is at once generous, rough and off-hand, a manner curiously reminiscent of Gurdjieff's own. Such a man would surely not be honoured as a prophet in any European capital.

However, these differences between nations, though they may explain many things, cannot justify everything. At the end of Irène Reweliotty's posthumous journal, in which she often mentions the Teaching, is the following very touching passage: "How arrogant these people are! (the Gurdjieff group). It is not 'I am' that should be said, but 'He is.'

I give no *man* the right to take charge of my spiritual life.

My salvation is a matter that will be settled between God and me.

That is all.

And I have just come to realise that I loved God."

These lines were written on July 27th, 1945. Less than a week later (on August 2nd), Irène Reweliotty died at Salanches, where she had been taken after an attack of rheumatic fever. She was twenty-five. Reading her journal had very much upset me, as I had known her for rather more than a year before her death. I remembered her as an exceptionally live and sensitive girl, but I myself had not yet come across the Teaching and had no idea of her connection with it. When, later on, I read her journal, at the time when I in my turn was struggling with the difficulties she had known, I had the feeling that she was offering me a precious sign of friendship.

I say that the differences of race are not enough to explain everything, as Irène, who was Russian, has expressed with admirable simplicity the feeling that was no doubt the determining factor for many of the people who broke with the Teaching. For Irene, for me and for many others there can be no real spirituality without communion and without adoration. Asceticism, renouncement, detachment and emptiness only make sense when directed towards Love. This Love should not, I am convinced, be confused with the feeling in its most obvious aspects, and this is, of course, the opinion of the great mystics. But the point is, to avoid destroying in the soul the very possibility of adoration.

I know many people who have remained faithful to the Teaching and who claim to be finding in it, little by little, all they are seeking and I have certainly no wish to judge them. As far as I am concerned, Gurdjieff has probably paid a salutary part in provoking my reaction and I am grateful to him for having forced me to refuse what he offered me, thereby opening my eyes to certain realities.

Some of the faithful felt that anyone who left the group was committing treason, and it is, in fact, possible that the added clarity and strictness that we gained from the Teaching we used in the end against it. Yes, it is quite possible that we left it because of what it had taught us. If that is so, well, it is the way things are; it is for masters to provoke their disciples.

When the " moderns " maintained that the best way of remaining faithful to the traditionalists was to create boldly and freely as they had done in their day, I think they were speaking truth.

As for you, my former companions, who trample so happily on morals, culture, civilization and religion and who snigger if one so much as mentions a twinge of conscience, how can you be shocked when we react towards the Teaching in the way we were told to react towards everything else ? How can you fail to understand that one should be able to liberate oneself from this school of liberation ? It is true that you also despise logic. I only ask you to remember that you can no more judge our spiritual life than we can judge yours. "When it is a question of metaphysics," René Guénon says, "we must always keep a place for the inexpressible." Lao Tsu is even more categorical:— "Those who know don't speak and those who speak **don't know.**"

3

Aldous Huxley On Drugs

Pierre Minet was a friend of the poet Roger-Gilbert Lecomte and of René Daumal, who, together with Roger Vaillant and Roland de Renéville, founded the quasi-surrealist literary movement called *The Great Game*. The core of this movement was the assumption that poetic experience is the same as mystical experience.

Roger-Gilbert Lecomte died, before he was thirty, of drink and drugs. For his sake I should like to make a digression.

Amongst people with a leaning towards mystical knowledge, I knew, and still know, many drug addicts. The philosopher Aimé Patri and I were trying to clarify the relationships between drug-taking and mystical experience when, in April 1953, there appeared in the journal *Preuves* a very remarkable article by Aldous Huxley that dealt fully with this question. The article was called "Grace-Substitutes" and was an extract from his book *The Devils of Loudun*, Huxley says:

"From poppy to curare, from Andean coca to Indian hemp and Siberian agaric, every plant or bush or fungus capable, when ingested, of stupefying or exciting or evoking visions, has long since been discovered and systematically employed. The fact is strangely significant; for it seems to prove that, always and everywhere, human beings have felt the radical inadequacy of their personal existence, the misery of being their insulated selves and not something else, something wider, something in Wordsworthian phrase, 'far more deeply interfused.' Exploring the world around him, primitive man evidently 'tried all things and held fast to that which was good.' For the purpose of self-preservation the good is every edible fruit and leaf, every wholesome seed, root and nut. But in another context — the context of self-dissatisfaction and the urge to self-transcendence — the good is everything in nature, by means of which the quality of individual consciousness can be changed. Such drug-induced changes may be manifestly for the worse, may be at the price of present discomfort and future addiction, degeneration and premature death. All this is of no moment. What matters is the awareness, if only for an hour or two, if only for a few minutes, of being someone or, more often, something other than the insulated self.

" . . . In modern times beer and the other toxic short cuts to self-transcendence are no longer officially worshipped as gods. Theory has undergone a change, but not practice; for in practice millions upon millions of civilized men and women continue to pay their devotions, not to the liberating and transfiguring Spirit, but to alcohol, to hashish, to opium and its derivatives, to the barbiturates, and the other synthetic additions to the age-old catalogue of poisons capable of causing self-transcendence. In every case, of course, what seems a god is actually a devil, what seems a liberation is in fact an enslavement. The self-transcendence is invariably downwards into the less than human, the lower than personal.

" . . . This raises a very important and difficult question. To what extent, and in what circumstances, is it possible for a man to make use of the descending road as a way to spiritual self-transcendence ? At first sight it would seem obvious that the way down is not and can never be the way up. But in the realm of existence matters are not quite so simple as they are in our beautifully tidy world of words. In actual life a downward movement may sometimes be made the beginning of an ascent. When the shell of the ego has been cracked and there begins to be a consciousness of the subliminal and physiological othernesses underlying personality, it sometimes happens that we catch a glimpse, fleeting but apocalyptic, of that other Otherness, which is the Ground of all being. So long as we are confined within our insulated selfhood, we remain unaware of the various not-selves with which we are associated — the organic not-self, the sub-conscious not-self, the collective not-self of the psychic medium in which all our thinking and feeling have their existence, and the immanent and transcendent not-self of the Spirit. Any escape, even by a descending road, out of insulated selfhood makes possible at least a momentary awareness of the not-self on every level, including the highest. William James, in his *Varieties of Religious Experience,* gives instances of ' anaesthetic revelations,' following the inhalation of laughing gas. Similar theophanies are sometimes experienced by alcoholics, and there are probably moments in the course of intoxication by almost any drug, when awareness of a not-self superior to the disintegrating ego becomes briefly possible. But these occasional flashes of revelation are bought at an enormous price. For the drug-taker, the moment of spiritual awareness (if it comes at all) gives place very soon to sub-human stupor, frenzy or hallucination, followed by dismal hangovers and, in the long run, by a permanent and fatal impairment of bodily health and mental power. Very occasionally a single ' anaesthetic revelation ' may act, like any other theophany, to incite its recipient to an effort of self-transformation and upward self-transcendence. But the fact that such a thing sometimes happens can never justify the employment of chemical methods of self-transcendence."

Huxley, of course, makes the usual reservations and appears to condemn the use of drugs out of hand, while showing clearly that it is the same need that leads to drug-taking as leads to the search for mystical knowledge. He even goes so far as to imply that, in some cases, the revelations due to the effects of drugs can encourage the addict to seek in asceticism rather than in coma, the transcendental " me " which we were seeking for with Gurdjieff. Without insisting on this delicate point — the relationship between the highest and the lowest — (Plato says: " Inferior things exist in superior things, but more nobly than in themselves,") Huxley has pointed out very clearly the ties that unite the drug-addict to the ascetic. By ascetic I mean all who are in search of the divine.

But let us return to Pierre Minet. In an autobiographical work called: *"The Defeat"* he alludes to his brief membership of one of the groups. No doubt

Minet joined in order to remain with René Daumal, but he did not share his friend's urge towards Gurdjieff and was unable to pass the first trials.

In his testimony that follows, he makes some of the same criticisms as Paul Sérant, but the voice of revolt and despair can also be heard, feelings that were common to many of the pupils during their first weeks of the Teaching. It is instructive to hear their point of view.

4

Pierre Minet's Testimony

The desire to confess, to pour everything out, only came upon me after the death of my friend Roger-Gilbert Lecomite. Before that I was still inflated. The present stank, to be sure, but what of to-morrow? With a little care and will-power I could still make myself passable. I was sure of it. If I happened to think of the past and to be plunged in admiration for it, I suspected myself of shirking the future. That was the time when I was taking my soul in hand: concentration, discipline, don't allow the mind to wander, breathe with the mouth shut, take a deep breath and let it out slowly, fix the eye on a point and keep it there; try to be conscious, that's the thing, with no desire to ridicule the people who teach it. But it is not reassurance that I need. Wisdom does not tempt me, nor stability, nor truth. No, not even truth, and I mean to explain this — later. At the moment I want to insist on this effort of concentration and discipline. I am no more stupid than the rest; I succeeded sometimes in uncovering the authentic " me ". But then, I know only too well, I should have kept my mouth shut. Instead, I shouted and danced for joy; and the others, the rotten, stinking " me's," were soon back, and what looks they gave their new brother ! How greedily they swallowed him raw ! After which these cannibals returned to their usual hum-drum ways. What a result ! They got me at once, these people, by a revealing word, a whisper, compared to which my own most urgent exhortations were as nothing: — "Begin by absorbing the idea that you are nothing, no, not even a grain of sand, absolutely nothing — nil." This enchanted me, and was worth the whole of philosophy. It opened up infinite horizons. How much pleasanter it was, at first, to be nothing, than to be this mass of painful, talkative corpuscles, that had to be called something ! How restful it was, complete negation ! Not a thought nor a feeling that could stand up against it ! As soon as one or other appeared I cried : " Where do you come from ? What do you want ? " and, worthy or not, I pushed them mercilessly away. I wallowed in the void thus created.

This did not last long. " You are nothing. You can become everything. You can be. Only, look out ! Pay attention — more attention ! Always attention. Don't identify yourself with your feelings; you are like a baby learning to walk. Not so fast ! Follow Nurse ! " But I was the Nurse, too. How should I not go wrong ? However, I did my utmost to play the part properly. I forbade myself to criticise and was coming to live solely for the three hours a week of instruction in the way. We sat down. No cigarettes, please ! This is another little victory that you can gain over yourselves — little streams make mighty rivers ! So there we were, twelve souls sitting quietly listening to excellent metaphysical advice. All very sensible: undeniable that consciousness does not know itself, that man is mechanical, and even man No. 1, man No. 2, man No. 3 and man No. 4 — the man you will become when pigs have wings. But the further we got, the more theoretical it became, till we felt that instead of being flesh and blood we were turning into the graphs and figures and circles that were supposed to explain and solve everything and to lead straight to immortality. Cosmic laws, the influence of the planets on behaviour, the moon as guardian, no, it was too much and it bored me. I fretted, and felt I was being made to witness a conjuring-trick. So — whatever we might have been originally, we did not begin to exist till we had thrown overboard all our most characteristic attributes, our tastes, our most deep-seated sufferings and our dearest bonds. No, this was going too far ! And all to obtain peace and the blind faith of the novice ! If, while hesitating before this sacrifice, I dared to ask: " But what of my special favourites, Rimbaud, Lautréamont, Breton — yes, Breton, too, I can surely keep them ? " " Chuck them out at once ! They are false — sham ! " Finally I broke away. I refused to be stripped of any more. I preferred to stew in my own juice. True, it didn't smell nice but, smell for smell, I preferred my own to the new one. I was at least used to it !

5

Luc Dietrich and Irène Reweliotty

I cannot speak of Irène Reweliotty, who died at twenty-five, without emotion, any more than could Paul Sérant. I am not trying to stir up scandal in telling her story, but there are some things that should be said.

During the German occupation, Irène was stricken with tuberculosis. She went to the Haute-Savoie to be nursed. Thousands of consumptives go to the plateau of Assy, which is snow-covered for half the year. In the mornings and after their enforced siesta, one can see clusters of young men and women, with puffy pink faces and glittering eyes. For some weeks I was the guest of the local chemist, and from her balcony I used to watch these people, full of keenness for life, sensual, and charged with the secret meditations of their long confinement. They used to pass by, apparently well and happy, but one knew them to be fascinated by their temperature-charts, and familiar with all the frenzies, exaltations and questionings of their race against death. While we drank coffee and played the gramophone — we, the inhabitants of the living world sure of our own lives, would watch and listen to them, students of fear, at their recreations, while at the same time contemplating the vast, pure landscape.

The chemist, a disciple of Gurdjieff, had previously entertained Luc Dietrich and his friend Lanza del Vasto, as well as René Daumal. At this period I never wished to hear Gurdjieff mentioned again and, tactful hostess that she was, she spared me discussions about the Teaching and left me in peace to prepare the lectures on surrealism that I was to give in one of the large sanatoria of the district. But, as soon as Irène arrived, there were great reunions of the disciples and she naturally met Luc Dietrich, whose recently published book of memoirs, *Le Bonheur des Tristes*, written with the help and advice of Lanza del Vasto, had brought him sudden fame. Irène was twenty-one and wanted to be a writer. Luc Dietrich, who was a great charmer, soon exerted a strong influence over her, and what he knew of the Gurdjieff doctrine gave his conversation an added fascination, of which he made full use. He had to seduce. In spite of Lanza del Vasto's misgivings, he had gone back to Gurdjieff, who, in order to deliver him from his slavery to women, and to prevent him from identifying himself with his desire and confusing the desire of mechanical man with the real love that can only be experienced by a man with "objective consciousness", had condemned him to have one woman a day. Dietrich had accepted this as a "work" of liberation, and spent his whole time at it. Besides, he enjoyed greatly forcing his way into the hearts of others and making himself rapidly at home there. It was not a question of seducing Irenè there and then, but he could at least mark her out for the not-too-distant future, and, in the meantime, influence her profoundly by giving full play to his need for spiritual seduction.

Like many other young men and women of her age and distinction, Irène had as yet no real relationship with the outside world and other people, and still remained in adolescent solitude. This state of affairs was intensified by the war and other events in which the young felt they had had no part, and by the crumbling of their elders' values, beliefs, and ways of life. So Irène was inclined to live turned in upon herself. Her writings and paintings sprang from her unwanted solitude, and she knew herself that thoughts, images or words from this source were bound to be weak. Now, Luc Dietrich claimed, in the name of the Teaching, that it was possible to pass straight from weakness to absolute truth and beauty. He promised the solution of all solutions, wrapping it all in romantic mystery. Besides, he was a most attractive man with an intriguing past, an artist who was already well-known, considerate and playful, serious and mischievous, clever and affectionate, and surrounded by friends and admiring women.

It can easily be seen that Irène's adolescent troubles prolonged by the war, her natural tendency towards introversion, her literary ambition and the nobler ambition of wanting to " possess the truth in body and soul," her meditations on life and death occasioned by her illness, her desire to escape from the human condition of her generation and lastly, her amorous friendship for Luc Dietrich, together made a dangerous and explosive mixture.

Dietrich introduced her to several of the disciples, among them René Daumal, who dazzled her by his knowledge of Oriental philosophy. When she returned to Paris she plunged with her customary impetuosity into one of the " groups ".

However, she soon felt ill at ease. She experienced the revolt and despair described by Pierre Minet. A few days before his death, Luc Dietrich wrote to advise her to withdraw from the " work ". He felt her to be torn and distracted, and he suddenly took fright. But she continued with her group, in his memory. René Daumal died, too. She wavered and hesitated, and tried to break away. Then, at the very moment that she was beginning to doubt the sincerity of some of the members to whom she had become attached, and also the possibility of ever reaching the super-human state that had been promised her, one of the disciples offered to introduce her to Gurdjieff. She had not yet met him. Though she may have distrusted some of the followers, she had no doubts about Gurdjieff himself, whom Dietrich and Daumal had spoken of with such extravagant veneration. He would surely be *He who opened doors*, the " Master ". She was invited to dine in the Rue du Colonel Renard. Now her real adventure would begin, it was no doubt to be the first day of " another life ".

The dinner took place as usual. Suddenly, during the meal, the old man addressed her in Russian, a language that no-one else present could understand. He told her to pretend to go with the others after dinner, and then to come straight back again. She did not know what to make of it and was afraid. She left with the others and rang up Gurdjieff from a café in the Avenue Wagram. She told him her Mother was waiting and that she could not go back. Gurdjieff then insulted her in a way that left her in no doubt of his intentions. He was an incensed Rasputin. She felt something give way inside her, and was filled with the utmost horror and despair. The following day, she went to see the disciple who had introduced her to Gurdjieff and said she must leave the Teaching. She was treated in the way calculated to harm her most, slapped in the face and thrown out. Demented and completely shattered, she went off to Assy to try to regain some peace of mind. A few days after she arrived there, she had a heart-attack that no-one could have foreseen.

The last letter she wrote to her Mother, on August 2nd, started: "Dear Mother, I shall end by believing that Gurdjieff has cast a spell over me." She died on the 11th, and the doctors remained mystified.

While her brother (a well-known jazz-player) was watching beside her coffin he thought he saw an apparition that he *recognized* as Gurdjieff, though he had never seen him. One of his young friends went to see a well-know writer, a man who was well qualified to speak about Gurdjieff. He wanted to ask him about Irène's death. The writer answered: "If you value yourself, never meddle in that business."

The following chapter is an extract from her private journal.

Extracts from Irène-Carole Reweliotty's Private Journal

Six months later.

Saturday, March 27th.

To-day I went to see Luc Dietrich, overwhelmed with gratitude after reading his *Bonheur des Tristes*. He said: "Speak to me as to a friend. Lay aside all convention. Be the real Irène." I nearly succeeded. He talked about Art, which is true above everything, about goodness and beauty. He talked about himself and then about me. He encouraged me to resume this journal. I am happy about all this. It seems to me that I am now less fumbling in my thought.

I must be strict with myself. I must conquer myself and get the most out of me — not be content with the passable and easy. Oh ! I would like to achieve, to create. I am at the cross-roads in life. I am at last cured, and Life is before me. I must take the right road, now or never.

Work
(AND MAY IT LAST)

The study of myself will be the study of my falsehood. I will learn to know myself.

I will look into myself so as to make a choice. I will learn to choose. KNOW HOW TO CHOOSE.

Know how to choose without being a slave to likes and dislikes, know how to choose what I need, what I have to have. Learn what is good for me.

I want to nourish the multitude as an artist, and up till now, I haven't learnt to differentiate myself from the multitude.

In order to teach others to find themselves, to see themselves, I must find myself, see myself.

The proper business of childhood is to grow. To return to childhood means neither to delight in it, nor to return to puerility, second childhood or affectation — the whole scale of false sensibility. It is not a matter of falling back into childhood, but of rediscovering one's childhood, that is to say, of continuing to grow.

Going to the Circus

I am going to the Circus. The Circus is me. I am going to try to be the spectator at the Circus and the Circus itself, all at once.

I shall see all the different Irènes: the sincere one, the liar, the actress, the greedy one, the child, the false child, the generous one, the stingy one, the tender one, the hard one, the prosecutor, the vain one, the depressed one, the indifferent one, the enthusiastic one, etc.

NOT TO FORGET ONESELF. That is to say, to remember what one wants to be, to recall to memory the best of oneself. I am going to try to catch myself red-handed.

I am going to try to love and hate myself at the same

time, that is to say, to love in me what is true and real, but not what is small and feeble, and needs to be developed. Hate, hate like Hell, all the showily attractive parts, the gilt and tinsel, and all the showing-off and play-acting side.

Vichy. End of July 1942

I gain in intelligence, poise and lucidity.

I lose my heart.

When I re-read my memoirs of the time before I came here, I notice with amazement that I am quite changed.

Something seems to have broken in me.

Shall I find myself again as I was before, when I come out of this dream?

But I am not in the least the same. And I think of the " moulting " that Annette C. used to speak of. She was right. In two months I have abandoned my childhood.

June 11th 1945

If I cannot conquer my happy lethargy I am lost, paralysed by dreams that occupy my whole brain, and, I believe, all three of my centres at once.

How the devil am I to use the Teaching of the Gurdjieff group? All those people, and their questions, are so sordid.

I can only bear the beautiful. I am like Lanza del Vasto. I should like to know him better.

Wednesday, June 20th

An explanatory scene with Madame D. The abscess had to burst. This is all for my good. Luc hated compliance.

So, " they " are trying to track me down, and in the end they may succeed (the Gurdjieff group).

Even the exaltation of moonlight is not the truth.

But I am a word-machine; I write with all and nothing, and I hate myself and I'm sick of my vanity and laziness. The task is immense. Shall I ever succeed ?

This book. How do I dare attempt it, when I have nothing to say and everything to learn ?

Hallucination . . . I feel it is Luc dictating.

Practically. I want to make demands on myself, to force myself out of my self-satisfied retreat.

I am fine at holding-forth. Truly, I am wallowing in pride.

But this will change.

First of all, really set aside moments. That will be my first task.

Really, this evening I hate myself, and that's as it should be.

July 1st

I am detaching myself all the time and soon I shall love nobody and nothing any more, and I shall be ready for my book.

Alas ! won't it be rather like Dostoievsky's Idiot, my brother in weariness, whom I have only just discovered ? " Their " world of reasonings, exercises and ordered meditations, is not mine (the Gurdjieff group).

I can only feel. I cannot will.

July 11th

The Gurdjieff group. Oh ! the wretched creatures ! Demons of doubt are in me now. I call on God, but nothing, nothing, only fear. They have wanted to spoil Luc for me, and to spoil God. Am I really dirt — a prostitute ? Yes — I love myself. Can this be my religion, this comforting and monstrous contentment ? Yes. I have not been what I should. But neither has my religion.

At night? I writhe in the greatest anguish I have ever known because God, no, my belief in God, is in question. I am afraid. Nothing exists. Evil and slackness everywhere. Oh! to see CLEAR.

July 26th

It seems to me that my state No. 1, the physiological or essence-state, is an immense indifference, or perhaps a kind of unawakened inner monologue that only gives off a sudden spark at very long intervals. State No. 2, the acquired or personality-state, is the unhealthily distraught state of the hair-splitter.

To which state do my moments of illumination belong, the moments in which I see the end of the road so clearly, and even, sometimes, in a burst of splendid terror, the road itself? No doubt they are free gifts of state No. 1.

Am I a monster of egoism?

I no longer know. Are not my loves and enthusiasms, my joys and angers, and even my conception of God, are they not all an unseemly and stupid manifestation of egocentricity?

July 27th

I am a peasant. I belong to the earth. I come from it and shall return to it.

O God, in that dialogue with the wind you answered me.

No, my exaltation was not artificial. I prayed to you, spoke with you. I will return to the fight, as you wish it. But I belong first to you, because you alone know me and my true place, and you alone will be able to assign me to it when the moment comes.

How arrogant these people are (the Gurdjieff group).

It is not: " I am " that one should say, but: " He is ".
I allow no man the right to control my spiritual life.
My salvation is between God and me.
That is all.
And I have just realized that I loved God.
I sleep at the centre of the world.

7

René Dazeville

As I was collecting the final material for this book, I received a letter from an unknown young man, a barrister condemned to live for several years in a sanatorium. He was married and had a son a few months old. He wrote in the hope that I could get him a job as reader to a publisher or as literary critic on some paper. Incidentally he mentioned an article that I had published in May, 1952 in the weekly paper *Arts*. This article, on a posthumous work by René Daumal called *Le Mont Analogue,* describes Gurdjieff and the temptations and difficulties experienced by the writer while a member of the "groups". My correspondent explained that a friend of his had been a disciple of Gurdjieff and that, in his opinion, this friend had died through the Teaching. I looked upon this letter as yet one more of the many signs I had been given since I started this book, and I asked the barrister at once to let me know all he had seen and heard from his friend.

I was determined to publish whatever he might send me, so as not to lose the trail of any of these signs.

Six Months with a Gurdjieff Disciple

"Seven years in a sanatorium are not rewarding. This was where I was at the beginning of 1952. I had a strong desire to read a selection of Taoist translations that had appeared in 1951, but the library of the sanatorium contained almost nothing but detective stories and book-club choices, and I was too poor to buy the book. In the course of conversation I mentioned my disappointment to S.A., a charming fellow and a brave soldier of the 1940 war, but not one who was interested in Taoism or things of that kind. However, anything can happen. A few days later he burst into my room to announce joyfully that he had discovered someone who owned the book I wanted and was willing to lend it to me. The owner apologized for not bringing it himself but, like me, he hardly ever left his room. He hoped, however, to be able to visit me soon.

I hardly had time to speculate on what kind of inmate of such a sanatorium could posses a book like that, when one evening at the end of February or beginning of March my young friend introduced me to the follower of Lao Tsu, who turned out to be a man in his thirties. He was extremely thin, with an interesting face and the general appearance of a clean but unkempt Bohemian; his hair was rather too long, he had a drooping moustache and the bones of his head, above his long, thin neck, were very prominent, no doubt owing to his illness. His hands were long and large. Such was the man who was to be an almost daily visitor for several months to come.

We " clicked " at once, and curiously enough, it was

through our mutual friend the young soldier, who had himself knocked about a good deal before landing up in this place. At this our first meeting we all three stayed together till lights-out. Our talk passed from the Taoist book which had been the cause of our meeting to Far Eastern secret societies and thence to the strange sects that can still be found in the West. Suddenly, S.A. exclaimed: "What charlatans and swindlers they all are, the people in those circles! I have, for instance, a girl friend who belongs to the Gurdjieff groups. She doesn't tell me much but I rather fancy they make her swallow an awful lot of nonsense, and not for nothing, either."

This innocent remark caused a violent reaction in L.N., my new friend. Up till then he had spoken and listened quite calmly, but now he sprang to the defence of the Gurdjieff groups in a way that made it impossible to doubt that he was himself a member. He realized this at once and admitted his connection.

This was, for me, the second curious coincidence within a few days. I had just received Ouspensky's book *In Search of the Miraculous;* for personal reasons I had wanted to find out all I could about Gurdjieff and his Teaching from the "outside" — especially since I had read the various reviews of Ouspensky's book, which had already been out for more than a year. This time I was even more fortunate in having the opportunity of direct contact with a disciple.

It was a hard, snowy winter. I was rather weaker and even more breathless than my friends, so L.N. made a habit of visiting me two or three times a week, either alone or with S.A.

For various, easily understood reasons, I was determined not to ask L.N. any indiscreet questions about the Teaching, but to try to form an opinion on it from what he might tell me of his own accord. Also, I had Ouspensky's book which I began reading seriously, rather at the expense of Taoism. When L.N. found that I was interested in apparently the same kind of things that were all-important to him, and that I, too, took them seriously, he became more open in conversation, as long as we were alone. So much so, indeed, that in about a month we had covered a good deal of ground and exchanged views on esotericism, exotericism, and their connection, both in the past and present. We discovered that we agreed on many points, although there were some fundamental questions that I was careful never to ask and that L.N. never brought up. I did not think much of this at the time, knowing that discretion and reserve were habitual to men of his type, and rightly so in matters relating to the practical details of an esoteric spiritual training.

Then two things happened to change our habits: first, the departure of S.A., whom I shall always remember warmly as an excellent companion to have in such a place; and then more seriously, the deterioration in L.N.'s health. If I remember rightly, this was at the end of April or beginning of May. It now became impossible for him to visit me; he was unable to leave his room and was hardly allowed any visitors. However, as we had become good friends, whenever he felt slightly better he begged me to go and see him for a few minutes, usually in the evenings. This I was glad to do, for apart from my desire to form an opinion on the Teaching, I felt keenly that behind his impassive exterior he was very lonely in this sanatorium, and was thankful to be able to talk quietly and calmly for a little while about the things that most interested him.

Perhaps his physical condition at this period was responsible for his revealing certain things about the so-called "Unknown Teaching" which, since the publication of Ouspensky's book, was for a time common gossip.

This is what he told me. He came from a large and humble family and had contracted tuberculosis while still a young man. He had been treated for two years before he was finally considered cured — *that is to say twelve years before his return to the sanatorium.* He lived with his family in the outer suburbs, and when he was strong enough to work, he set himself to various trades, all of which he considered of secondary importance. His real ambition was to paint, and he taught himself the rudiments of painting in his spare time. I am sure he was gifted, from what I have seen of his work; he gave me some of his pictures, which are much admired by those qualified to judge. He managed to live a normal and active life, which shows that he had quite overcome his disease. It was through his student and artist friends that he first came in contact with the Teaching. I never knew the exact date, but it must have been in Paris after the war, and he was immediately "bitten," as they say. He did not tell me much about the "doctrine" that cannot be gathered from Ouspensky's book, but he let out some practical details of his experience that made me deeply aware of the dangers of the Gurdjieff method. He was obviously a particularly keen "subject" and gave himself up completely to complicated breathing exercises. During some of the collective "seances" he took part for hours on end in extremely strenuous symbolic dances that he would never have been able to keep up if he had not been in a kind of trance. "I came out literally dripping with sweat from head to foot," he told me on several occasions. And all this on top of his work, his painting, and the many practical difficulties of his life ! At this period, if I remember correctly, he gave up completely his home in the relatively fresh air of the suburbs, to live wretchedly in Paris, entirely absorbed by his new friends.

Then, sure enough, the inevitable happened. Because of his exceptionally strong nervous energy he held out longer than seemed possible, but soon after having had the honour of being present at the " Master's " demise, and following eleven years of health, he suffered a bad relapse and had to be rushed off to the hospital with bronchial pneumonia, which all but finished him. He came out of hospital with his health permanently impaired and in very poor general condition. I think it was his new-found " friends " who had him transferred to the sanatorium in the mountains where I met him. But he did not know what I learnt later — from a medical point of view he was considered " lost," without the faintest chance, either from treatment or drugs. However, though he realized, up to a point, the seriousness of his condition, never once during our conversations did he so much as hint at a possible connection between the methods of the Teaching and his relapse. What did he think about it, in his heart ? I cannot say, but I believe that, being so certain of his instructors' infallibility on all points, he simply refused to recognize the connection. Leaving aside for the moment the physical dangers of the Teaching, one can count amongst its favourable effects, as exemplified by L.N., a remarkable self-control, a highly-developed willpower, great physical and moral courage, and strong powers of concentration. On the psychic level it seems that he had obtained results, but in my opinion this is no proof of the intrinsic value of the Teaching.

In spite of my liking for the man, I always felt a certain indefinable uneasiness in his presence, caused by the impression he made of a "hardening" that was incompatible with true spiritual development. Let there be no mistaking me, *all real "esoteric asceticism" necessitates a progressive detachment and a slow acquisition of outward impassivity, the visible sign of an inner stability.* If this asceticism does not follow the path of exoteric mysticism and does not attach the same importance to acceptance and morality that purely religious methods do, neither can it fall into "immorality," not even unconscious immorality. *Who does the greater can do the lesser, and, if I may put it so, the Sage's morality is extra.* Now it seems to me that, in many "para-esoteric" questions, my unfortunate friend used arguments and upheld a view of life that was quasi "Luciferian," to borrow a Christian expression; which proves, in my opinion, that though the Teaching may well have led to the acquisition of certain "psychic powers," it in no way facilitated the attainment of a true spiritual state. Despite several discreet suggestions by L.N., I never allowed myself to be tempted to join one of the so-called "Master's" groups.

In June or July, L.N.'s general condition again worsened. He was as thin as a skeleton and could no longer eat, but he nevertheless retained enough energy and lucidity to keep up a correspondence with his "friends," who came to see him sometimes, and to read and meditate and talk to me for a few minutes every day.

His friends and I had been trying for some time to

obtain a new remedy as a last resort, encouraged by the fact that, apart from his miserable general condition, his disease seemed no worse than two months before. But the end came swiftly, so swiftly that it surprised everyone, though of course one became used to every kind of surprise in the sanatorium. A day or two before August 15th, I left him as usual at about nine-fifteen, apparently perfectly calm and in a condition that gave no fore-warning of what was to come. At half-past ten the night-nurse heard a faint ring of his bell. When she reached him he was already dead. He had died of an internal haemorrhage.

I was informed of his death the next morning, although it is not usual in sanatoria to notify the patients of events of this kind. But one is, of course, bound to find out. As I was his only real friend, I was visited later by his "friends" of the group, who, though much distressed, were chiefly concerned to get back certain papers. Unfortunately, I was unable to help them, as the authorities had sent all his belongings to his family. A few days later, a young woman came to see me, and gave me more details of his life before and after he joined the Gurdjieff group. They only confirmed the fundamentally amoral nature of my poor friend's bewitchment.

I might well end this narrative here were it not that I feel that the testimony expected of me requires a more definite conclusion.

I wish to emphasize that I have not written these lines for the pleasure of appearing in print. Until Louis Pauwel's book comes out I have no idea what conclusions he will draw from his collected material. Some may object that my testimony comes only from the "outside" but perhaps I had my own private reasons when I agreed to make available such confidential material.

Let me now say, then, that on the one hand it seems to me incontrovertible that L.N. was, *at the very least, the physical victim of the teaching, owing to the practical methods he was forced to pursue without regard to his past illness.* On the other hand, any so-called esoteric teaching that advises its future disciples against putting their faith in one of the existing exotericisms, whether religious or not, that appears systematically to scorn all metaphysics and theology, and to rely exclusively on " psychic powers," seems to me the teaching of a false " spiritual master," and a very subtle act of subversion, *all the more dangerous in that its theories on some levels are both interesting and valid.* The fascination of this teaching is enhanced by the fact that it condemns the obsolete forms of occultism and theosophy, which have long since been discredited.

I will end by paying tribute once more to a man I shall never forget. No doubt in our age men will continue to die around us in terrifying numbers, but there will be fewer and fewer able to consecrate, still less to sacrifice their lives, it may be mistakenly, in the single-minded pursuit of Truth. My friend was one of these. May he even yet find his way.

René Dazeville.

WITNESS FOR THE DEFENCE

8

*By Dorothy Caruso. Extracts from
" A Personal History"*

Two nights later on the ship, twenty-four hours out of New York, I sat unconscious of time and sea, conscious only of a conversation.

In darkness, on a deserted deck, I looked up into the black, unmoving sky and listened to words that lighted the universe.

They were words that contained thoughts of such power and abstraction, such virtue and vastness, that I sat speechless, overwhelmed by the magnitude of ideas of a kind I had never heard.

All my own thoughts, all my uneasy, unsuccessful efforts to create within my troubled mind a mental chart that I could follow toward what I hoped would be a wonderful experience, became puerile, pitiful, in the face of an immense unknown world that was opening before me. It reached far beyond the mind and yet was a part of it, or the mind a part of its immensity.

In my flash of understanding, the words I was hearing were consumed, forgotten forever, and I saw instead a way of life, a road as clear, as straight, as the road I saw in that instant when I looked at Enrico Caruso from the top of a flight of stairs.

· · · ·

At two o'clock I went to my cabin. The children were waiting for me. " Something has happened to me," I said. " I have heard things tonight that may change the course of our lives."

But I could not repeat the words I had heard — even today I cannot remember a single phrase of that conversation. It had to do with a system of knowledge concerning man's relation to God and the universe, as taught by a man called Gurdjieff. He lived in Paris and for many years had been teaching there. From a name and an outline of an " unknown doctrine," there arose for me a total vision of a new world. What was important, now, was how soon I and my children could enter this world.

And suddenly I realized, as if through revelation, that on this night, on a ship sailing toward New York, I had come at last within sight of a land I had sought since childhood.

The magnitude of the revelation, the quality of the disclosure and the immensity of its effect upon me, erased from my mind all dread of the future. Nothing could ever take from me this night's apperception of a new world; and my only wish was to meet the man called Gurdjieff who had explored to its limits this unknown world, who had travelled all the way along its roads and welcomed all those in need who came to him to learn.

· · · ·

The person who made this conversation was Margaret

Anderson. Later she told me of her life — how she had founded the first of the little magazines, the *Little Review,* and how, after publishing it for ten years, had left America and gone to live in France, to be near Gurdjieff.

I decided to look for a place in New England—white farm-house with a red barn, or a salt-box on a village green — and live among people of this kind while waiting to return to France to see Gurdjieff.

I found it in Sudbury, Massachusetts, eight miles from Concord . . .

I had gone to Sudbury not as toward a dream, but with a conviction. I was certain that in a community of thoughtful, natural, understanding people I could express my own reality, and that among realistic New Englanders I would be allowed to be my authentic self.

In New York I had often listened to Gurdjieff pupils talking about their " inner life." I was unconscious of an inner life. " Either I have none," I thought, " or else it is buried too deep in me to be felt " . . . buried under reflections of everyone I had ever known, a thousand reflections superimposed upon my own reflection. It was as if I wore ten hats at once. What would I look like, I wondered, without any hat at all ?

And so from the beginning I was natural in Sudbury. I answered the usual questions about Enrico and told all my stories; but I also talked from myself, from my own ideas, not only in relation to him and the children; I talked as a separate entity.

But soon I discovered that my way of being natural was not the Sudbury way, and that my kind of conversation belonged to a different category from Sudbury conversation. On the day I heard a woman say, " We don't care about all those ideas and things — tell some more stories about your life with Caruso," I realized how much the Gurdjieff teaching had sharpened my appetite for real communication — talk that led toward something — and how dissatisfied I felt telling stories or listening to the dry-leaf rustlings of flat events.

Unexpectedly I had come upon my inner life . . . *Paris, June 1948.* In spite of all I had been told, I had made my own conception of Gurdjieff. He would have the tongue of St. John, the inspiration of St. Paul, the sanctity and remoteness of the Reverend Mother. I would be filled with awe and exaltation, and when I left it would be with a high sense of humility for the privilege of having met him.

It was in this fervent and expectant state that I entered his Paris flat in the Rue Colonel Renard on the last day of June.

But when I saw Gurdjieff all my preconceived ideas vanished. For I saw an old man, grey with weariness and illness, yet whose strength of spirit emanated with such force from his weakened body that, save for a sense of fierce protection, I felt no deep emotion at all.

I could not understand his English. His low voice and muffled Asiatic accent formed syllables that had no meaning to me, and at the same time I realized that at this moment ordinary speech was unimportant. It was as if we had already spoken and were continuing to speak, but in a language without sound.

After lunch he invited me to have coffee with him in his store-room. There, in the midst of fruits and sweets and wines, with slender sausages of camel's meat, bunches of scarlet peppers and sprays of rosemary and mint suspended like a canopy above, as I watched him pouring coffee out of the battered old thermos bottle,

I suddenly felt as young and trustful as I had felt when Mother Thompson watched over me in the Convent. Years of worldly experience fell away and I was a child again.

Gurdjieff offered me a piece of sugar. " You want to ask me something ? " he said. I didn't want to ask him anything — I wanted to tell him something. But I was unprepared for this direct and simple opening. I could not quickly think of any abstract or esoteric question, so instead I blurted out what had troubled me ever since I had been going to his house.

" Everyone here seems to have a soul except me. Haven't I any soul ? "

He didn't answer immediately, or look at me. He took a piece of sugar, put it into his mouth and sipped some coffee through it. Then he said, " You know what means consciousness ? "

" Yes," I said, " it means to know something."

" No. Not to know something — to know yourself. Your ' I '. You not know your ' I ' for one second in your whole life. Now I tell and you try. But very difficult. You try remember say ' I am ' once every hour. You not succeed, but no matter — try. You understand ? "

At this first interview I said none of the things I had planned to say. Instead I told him about my childhood in my father's house, of the goodness of Enrico and my despair when he died, and about my children and how deeply I loved them. And then I said, " I don't know anything about the things all the others know. I don't even know what to ask you. What can I do when I have nothing to start from ? What shall I *do* ? "

" You must help your father," Gurdjieff said. I

thought he had not understood, that I had spoken too quickly; so I told him again that my father was dead.

"I know. You tell already. But because of your father you are here. Have gratitude for this. You are your father and you owe to him. He is dead. Too late to repair for himself. You must repair for him. Help him."

"But how can I help him when he's dead? Where is he?"

"All around you. You must work on yourself. Remember what I tell — your 'I'. And what you do for yourself you do also for me."

He said no more, but I felt as if he had spoken great things, and not in ordinary words; and when I left it was with something rich and strange and full of meaning . . .

. . . Message came from Paris late at night. Gurdjieff had been injured in a motor accident. His condition was critical; he was lying unconscious in a hospital.

When we arrived in Paris he was already at home. He had fractured ribs, lacerations on his face and hands, and many bruises. There was a danger of internal injuries.

"Is he conscious now?"

"Oh yes," they said, "and he wants the readings and meals to continue as usual. He came in for a little while after lunch. He'll be at dinner — thirty are coming."

But the next day he was worse and the doctors held out slight hope that he would live.

We stayed that night in a small hotel near his flat, waiting for the telephone to ring. It never rang. On the third day he was seated again at his dinner table. His head was still a shining dome, smooth and high, but his face was a dark shadow. There were purple bruises on his lips and he wore a piece of gauze around his throat to hide a wound.

"I cannot eat," he said, "my mouth all cut inside." Painfully, with his lacerated fingers, he divided a trout, handed me a piece across the table.

"You like?" he said. "Then take."

For the rest of the meal he sat in silence. In his eyes was the same blind look he had when he played the prayer music. As we rose to leave he got up too. He lifted his hands against his ribs. "It hurts," he said, "great suffering I have." I could only stand there looking at him. Before I could wish him well, he said, "I thank you. I wish for you all that you wish for me."

. . . .

He cured himself, no one knows how. He had refused X-rays and the medicines prescribed by doctors; yet his recovery was so complete that he looked younger after the accident than before, as if the shock had strengthened his whole organism instead of weakening it.

In the late afternoon he sat, immaculately dressed, outside a café near his flat, with a panama hat shading his eyes and his cane lying across the table in front of him, talking with pupils, drinking coffee, watching people pass. At other times he sat alone, speaking with no one, noticing no one until at last he rose and, in the long dusk, through quiet shuttered streets, walked slowly home.

There, after resting for a while, he changed into a loose grey cashmere suit, open white shirt and soft kid slippers, gave instructions in the kitchen, then came to sit with us and listen to the reading of his book, looking from one face to another, recognizing yet withholding recognition. At dinner he welcomed us as he had always done, talked of the same subjects in the same words; and, as usual, halfway through the meal, placed on his head his tasselled magenta fez. It was good to know that he was recovering, and it was good to see and hear intimate small ceremonies repeated — the ritual of the toasts, the offering of bread, or fish, across the table in his hand. And as I sat observing, absorbing, rejoicing, I grew aware of a swelling sense of harmony that related everything within the room to everything else — gestures, faces, voices, food, my thoughts vibrated in unison like a chord in music. I began to understand something that I longed to go on understanding. I wanted to achieve the " I " he had told me about.

Long before his accident Gurdjieff had said, " I cannot develop you; I can create the conditions in which you can develop yourself." For weeks I had fought against the conditions he created — I had been angry, impatient, judicial. But I had concealed these emotions; raging inside, I had appeared outwardly calm . . . the habit of a lifetime — good manners, instead of an effort to act honestly. It would have been better to burst forth in defence of what I thought unjust, to ask him point-blank why I should sit through endless meals, eating food I neither liked nor wanted. That I had felt compassion or anxiety or even deep affection for him was beside the point. It was good to be concerned about him; it would have been better to have been concerned about myself: to have begun to change, to develop myself. Once he had spoken to me about my great aim. " I haven't any aim," I said; " what should my aim be ? " He said, " Do you want to perish like a dog?" I answered, "Of course not." He didn't explain, he simply repeated what he had said before: "Remember your 'I'." ...

I never saw Gurdjieff again. He died in Paris, two days after we landed in New York. And so, scarcely before it had begun, a great experience ended.

Whatever I may have learned about his work, during the two years I knew him, might, as time passed, grow hazy in my mind; but what I felt when I was in his presence, whether he spoke or sat in silence, I would remember clearly always. Those feelings live forever that are born in the soul's heart.

Gurdjieff was gentle with my soul. It was a soul that had not grown up, as I grew up. It had been timid, but trusting. Often it had been betrayed, but it had not been murdered. Nanna had found it first, and she too had been gentle with it. Enrico had loved, moulded, sustained and protected it. Brother had fought for it.

Gurdjieff gave it courage. From his mysterious and conscious world he guided it with the kind of understanding he called "objective love" — the "love of everything that breathes"; and "it" responded with unlimited trust — the highest type of love there is, I think, in this immediate and unconscious world.

Nothing is so great or so true as the trusting love of a child. It doesn't matter whether he has understood your words or not — it is the way they are spoken that matters. And the way they are spoken creates in the child the love and trust he returns to you. This is the emotion that Gurdjieff, and the "conditions he created," created in me.

I can repeat our conversations, interpret his silences, describe his appearance, define his doctrine, yet I can only give the slightest indication of the change that took place in me after knowing him.

I was aware, before he died, of this process of active and increasing change. His death, instead of ending the process, accelerated it. And then, one day, I understood what had been happening. I had transformed something in myself: the change was Me.

A mystery is something that cannot be expressed, something beyond human comprehension.

Man is a mystery.

The cosmos is a mystery.

Man in relation to the cosmos is a mystery.

Everything is a mystery, and everything is a paradox. To understand this takes more than human comprehension, and more than human comprehension means: to know.

Gurdjieff knew.

He knew from his " being," as he called it. And he knew all the time.

I know only for an instant at a time. That instant is a spark of understanding — it belongs to the person of my essence. During those instants I am aware of a division of identity — a separation between my essence-person and what I have always called " myself."

When those moments are past they do not become simply memories like other memories. Something else raises and widens and deepens the perceptions.

The substance of that " something " I do not know— all I know is that it is a substance; it is not merely an idea.

*By Georgette Leblanc. An Extract from
" La Machine à Courage "*

Circumstances allowed me to see Gurdjieff continuously until war was declared. I can only convey the steady relationship with him and with the work — the " development " that no other happiness can ever equal for me — by giving extracts from the journal I used to write from time to time, during long, sleepless nights.

I am a little afraid of the absurd interpretations that could be given of the struggles recounted in this journal — faults to be conquered, crimes to be expiated, childish mortifications, false mysticism — when all I was really attempting was to awaken and enlarge what was already within me, as it is within everyone. I shall not speak of the principles of this science. I have no right to. I shall simply try to describe what happened, which was, for me, the culmination of life.

FRAGMENTS OF A JOURNAL
(1936 - 1940)

June 1936—Constant suffering. A painful period. Have at last found a flat in the Rue Casimir-Périer, between the church and the trees.

A wonderful end to the month because of my recent meeting with Gurdjieff. He has been living in Paris for some time and I decided to say to him: " Time is passing and I am making no progress. I haven't much longer to live. Will you let me read the new parts of your manuscript ? " He looked at me for a long time and at last he said: " You still have time to live. Yes, come to lunch to-morrow and you shall read."

He murmured something that I couldn't understand. At length I grasped it: " Liver out of order. All organs clogged." Again he looked at me for a long time, and he then said: " Yes, I will do it for you."

I wanted to cry out my thanks, but I knew that I should keep calm, that he would understand me. With difficulty I got out: " Thank you."

I lunched with him and his family and a few pupils. After lunch he fetched his manuscript and showed me a cupboard in a small room next to the dining-room. He would leave it there for me, and I could come and read whenever I liked.

So I go there nearly every day. I read with concentration, as though my life depends on the difficult thought to be gleaned from those pages.

June 28th and 29th—A bad liver attack. (This was to be the last).

Thursday, July 16th—I tell him I have changed. I haven't had any pain for the last fortnight. This has never happened before in the last twenty years. He was glad and not surprised. He said that he had wished this, that he had an object. He repeated for the second time: "You are young." I understood later that he thought it a question of glands. He explained that there was hope for me, but that the work would take five years. One achieves nothing if body and soul are not keeping pace. It is faith that purges the flesh. In Tibet, priests are doctors, and vice versa.

He tells his pupils that my case interests him. " She was a candidate for death. Now she is a candidate for life." At lunch he looked at me mischievously : " I only said, read the book, madame, read the book."

July 22nd—Physical and moral delight when every night I can stretch out on my bed. Amazement of the body, when the expected suffering doesn't come. I often feel a strong, internal heat, as though I were pleasantly near a fire. I sleep peacefully. I believe a deep and beneficial upheaval has taken place. My mind is overflowing with astonished gratitude. I understand what is happening, but living through it is amazing.

July 27—Yesterday I dragged myself to his flat, exhausted. I read the book for two hours, and when I left I felt light and strong. I walked for miles without tiring. Physically, I am experiencing spring, in this cold month of July. I feel charged, like a dynamo.

July 30th—Gurdjieff came in while I was reading. I was finishing a chapter on the religions. I told him of my exaltation, with as few words and gestures as possible. He doesn't like too much enthusiasm. He was obviously pleased. He thinks my health is improving all the time. He added: " This is nothing as yet. Soon something else will begin."

August 1936—No more pain. I can't feel my organs. My body knows it is living through a miracle. Morally, I am not yet accustomed to marvel. I am assisting at something immense that is taking place inside me. The brain is not our sole control; some of our organs register what is happening in us more accurately than the brain. At the moment, I have the impression of a perpetually turning wheel within me, embracing my whole body from head to foot, inside and outside. The wheel is moved by the relief from suffering of my organs, and by my conscious will to receive what I am being "sent." It is also the wonder of experiencing something that is not hereditary. I could not have conceived it, but having always been searching unconsciously for it, I was ready. Otherwise there could have been no result.

August 1936—If I succeed a little in grasping this Master as a whole, it is because I have been seeking and studying him for thirteen years. The humility of Jesus was in tune with his bare feet, the desert and the epoch. Gurdjieff's humility looks like a grimace, or a joke. Really, he seems to me almost a messiah — a messiah with no followers, no setting. He "is," but the blindness of the civilized world turns him into a negative prophet. He has, however, a few disciples, enough to ensure that he will be "understood" in one hundred or two hundred years. Humanity is powerless without pregnancy, and becomes aware of its condition through growth. It takes centuries for it to give birth to a messiah.

September 27th, 1936—For several months it has been clear that man's unconscious is producing what he calls destiny, that is, war, while at the same time he declares, in all sincerity, that what he wants is peace.

September 30th, 1936—I go every day to read his manuscript. I consider it the decisive event of my life.

The time of destruction — war — is near. However,

we go on arranging our flat, which is getting prettier all the time because of the arches I have made everywhere. We shall lose it. There will be war, external or internal, or both.

I am anguished by the strength that has been " restored " to me. For three years I had accustomed myself to the idea of death. Now I'm full of desires, enthusiasm, plans.

October 28th, 1936—"He" still does me good, but, being now no longer torn by constant pain, a release of tension is taking place in me. And then winter is coming. My body is adjusted to the changes of the earth, beneath the pale colours of the cold. The trees stretch their branches towards the sky with mechanical gestures. One's body has bad habits; having suffered too long, it wants to suffer still. It is more on edge, more sensitive. And I feel I'm slipping. I have moments of discouragement. I try not to admit it, but it's true.

October 31st, 1936—I explained to him my condition, my distress. He knew . . . the usual reaction. From the beginning he had said to me: — "I can stop the pains and so prepare the way for something else."

I know that there is some special work to ensure that my psychic life shall keep pace with my physical cure, but shall I have the strength to undertake it ?

He went back to his studio, and I began my reading. A minute later I felt enveloped in vibrations. I remained there, reading and resting, from two o'clock until six. The next day I felt renewed.

Monday, November 2nd, 1936—A great day. When I arrived at his flat he opened the door himself. I said at once: " I am in a new body." The light from the sitting-room fell full upon him. Instead of withdrawing, he leant back against the wall. Then, for the first time, he allowed me to see what he really is—as though he had suddenly dropped the mask that he is obliged to wear. His face was stamped with a goodness that embraced the whole world. Transfixed before him, I took him in with all my strength, and experienced so deep and painful a sense of gratitude that he felt the need to soothe me. With an unforgettable look he said : — "God helps me."

November 15th, 1936—The efforts required are infinite and almost hopeless; but to believe at last that a truth exists, is there, and that one can go towards it, is enough. I understand, now, that happiness was nothing, that the delights of love and art were nothing but pleasurable soul-deceivers evoked by a desire for self-manifestation. I am aware that my sub-conscious has lived in spite of me, like a deeply buried treasure. It was necessary to have lived first for a long, long time, according to the usual laws.

November 20th, 1936—One of Gurdjieff's greatest virtues is having been able to make accessible to human understanding, truths almost impossible for the human brain to grasp.

End of November, 1936—After dinner he played. A unique sight — Gurdjieff playing on his little organ. One can see the music "pass" through him. He plays it, but is not the player. He is the direct means of expression of an "impersonal thought" — the perfect vehicle of an idea. One is watching a man—a circle—live. One hears a language that borrows its very essence from art, in order to adjust itself exactly to the form to be communicated. And what an extraordinary look !— the richness of his smile—the richness of kindness, the richness of truth.

December 25th, 1936—Extraordinary gathering at

Gurdjieff's. In another age, a patriarch distributing bounty. The little flat was full—of relations, friends, the Concierge and his family, and old retainers. The Christmas-tree was so tall that it was squashed against the ceiling and its stars fell off.

The distribution began with real ceremony. About fifty numbered cardboard boxes stood in a corner of the room. He stood at a table, with his glasses on and a list in his hand, calling out names that corresponded to a number. The person called came up, and into each box that was put in front of him, Gurdjieff added one or more hundred—or thousand—franc notes. Then he handed over the box with a small gesture that meant " No thanks," and muttering: — "Off with you" he passed on to the next one. The ceremony went on from 9.0 o'clock until ten. A Russian publisher received a dressing-gown, a doctor received woollen underwear and a thousand-franc note. As Gurdjieff dropped the note into the box S. said: — "He's lucky —that one." Gurdjieff replied in a flash: — "Not you?"

At ten o'clock we dined. On each plate there was a huge chunk of mutton, with pickled gherkins and pimentoes, and a Russian roll—all things I can't bear; but there were splendid desserts spread out. Cake, fruit and sweets of all kinds. At half-past eleven we left, and others took our places. The Russian maid told me: — "After one o'clock until daylight the poor will come . . . and the place will stink."

We know that after this feast there will be, for him, a more or less lengthy fast. Thus he will compensate for his material bounty and fulfil his duty.

December 28th, 1936—A resurrection is beginning in me — the all-powerfulness of the spirit. A passionately interesting and fundamental question for me—the successive deaths and perpetual re-births. Illness devours life: resurrection—the sum of what was, is and is to come—goes beyond.

My intelligence—no, I don't believe in it, but I have an element of lucidity that, through all the disasters of life, has never failed me. Before my present experience, I saw the time approaching when this element would be all that remained to me, like a flag on an empty house.

My notes from January to December, 1937 describe only the long months of effort, of discouragement and exaltation, of fall and ascents well-known to all who follow the difficult path of consciousness.

But what does that mean? —"the path of consciousness"? One has heard this phrase all one's life without attaching any precise meaning to it.

It is the same with everything that touches on the secret history of humanity, of which Gurdjieff and a few others believe themselves to be the trustees. But on what basis, precisely, does this science of the soul rest? Philosophers are satisfied in saying that: "this interpretation of the Universe, this anthropocosmogeny is the highest, the greatest, the most admirable, the most invulnerable that has ever been conceived; it overflows man's thought and imagination in all directions." (Maeterlinck.) "But," they add, "what influence will a revelation such as this have on our life? What will it transmit to us, what will it add to our morals, to our happiness? No doubt very little. It will pass over our heads. It will not descend to our level. It will not touch us, we shall lose ourselves in its immensity and, in the end, knowing everything we shall be neither happier nor wiser than when we knew nothing." At the same time they admit that our moral evolution lags several centuries behind our scientific evolution—and that it is solely on the former that man's happiness and future depend. They maintain that all one seeks can be found between four walls, in books. What could one gain from such an arm-chair search ? Anyone can read Hermes, Pythagoras or Buddha and remain blind to these secret codes, without undergoing any change in himself. These are special teachings that do not reveal their content. Man has something more to do than to read, admire and speculate. The study of "Know Thyself" demands special work and a dedicated life. To those who think that by work they will obtain results beyond their comprehension, one is tempted to say:— "First begin to work."

All work imposes the same laws. The road that looks vertical flattens out as one mounts it. This hesitation to dedicate one's life is due mainly, I think, to fear. Every initiation involves a time of panic. The first gulf is between "knowing and incorporating."

I will include from my journal some extracts from this painful period of incorporating. Resurrection and Fall followed each other for a long time. Then there was a long, slow period of stabilizing without which there could have been no construction. It was like flood-water finding its level, and bringing its fruitful desolation. Neither despair, nor hope. I lived in a tunnel.

Journal, October 10th, 1937—I know that I am approaching serious moments, morally and psychically. I know about the equilibrium that has to be maintained during these trials. I understand about the balance that is required between the three centres, and that a whole life-time is too short to attain it. A few lines from Goethe constantly haunt me: — "There is no path. Nothing but the untraced in that which nothing can tread . . . You will see nothing firm to catch hold of in the eternally empty distance."

I know and I detest my anguish. Great as it is, I count it little.

But I am afraid. Afraid of what ? I have a hundred fears that haven't all a name. It is my parents, my ancestors, who are afraid in me. Then why do I listen to them ? I had less fear of death. Was that, then, more natural ? Yes, surely.

Others before me have done what I want to do; but that doesn't help, because, for the first time, everyone is himself, each experience is new, as it adjusts itself to an immutable truth. I envy the impatient ones who plunge in with no hesitation. I am not, however, afraid of being mistaken. My confidence has been strong enough to enable me to withdraw from the outer world. I have already refused the easy way of life many times, but now, faced by what is still to do, I see that that was little enough — perhaps, even, it was laziness, the boredom of beginning over again. Has anything changed ? It is impossible to know.

No sacrifice is demanded, but time cannot be stretched. One has to choose. A small life for a great truth. It is little enough. One must pay. The price rises with the quality of the experience. I am ashamed of my hesitation. It seems that I am haggling with myself. However, I must discuss with myself while this self is still mine. You will go on, into the darkness, without knowing anything. You will see no progress. That which seems is abolished for the sake of that which is. The hardest moment is yet to come. You will only know it by living through it, by feeling yourself lost beyond help. The Master will look on at your painful stumbling and say nothing. He has said: — "I cannot develop you. I can only create the conditions in which you can develop yourself."

October 12th, 1937—The important moment has come. I cannot ignore it. I even think it would be idiotic not to notice it. But my decision is still the same: I would rather risk "all" than watch myself slipping, slowing-down, diminishing psychically, understanding less, taking in less . . . No, not at any price. Let it be enough to suffer, to struggle, to look death in the face from nearer all the time. *No*, I will go on risking.

They could say: — "You are losing your reason." What reason would they mean?

October 13th, 1937—I had a dream. I had been walking for years in search of a planet. At last I arrived on it, through space. I thought at first that the towns, the people and the things on it were the same as our own. I soon found that there was little in common. The people loved one another and didn't speak. The animals spoke.

I had a long conversation with a white horse as big as a Cathedral. He explained to me his two-dimensional view, and his dreads. He realized that I was burning hot, so he let his mane fall like rain round my body, to relieve me. It was he who told me about the celebration of a feast that is unknown to us. Three of the seasons had beaten the fourth. I was seeing the triumphal return of the troops—the regiments of all the summers of the world were advancing, their banner streaming, flanked by high spring-times and barely turned autumns. They had killed the winters. They bore neither good nor ill with them. Their songs were bells, their laugh was the laughter of the sea in sunlight. To amuse themselves on the way, they had chastened plagues and banished pain and calumny —those scurges of humanity. My companion said:— "With winter they have killed the inevitable. Death will be only a result, the consequence of not having understood."

Suddenly, one of the men fell from a great height on to the ground at my feet. He split in two. He was empty.

October 18th, 1937—Tomorrow we will ask him, Margaret and I, if the time has not come to attempt the personal experiences.

When I "really" begin the trials nothing will have altered outwardly. I shall have my same name that I don't like, I shall wear the same clothes. No sign will be made, nor promise. I shall go, to-morrow, and simply say:— "I will do." It will not be "I want to" or "I shall". It will just be those three words. But for me, for me alone, for myself, it will be the biggest event of my life. When I say that, I shall see before me, in spirit, a succession of mysteries without end, that I shall pass through, come what may.

For those who haven't been wishing and seeking all their lives it is almost easy. But for me it is the perilous end of what I have always been seeking, and seeking without hope. I thought, like everyone else, that my end would be my death. But this end is in order to gain life.

I cannot write the words:— "I will do" without trembling.

October 19th, 1937—Five o'clock in the morning, in my room in the Rue Casimir-Périer. The sky is a deep blue behind the still spring-like trees. It is cheerful and calm. My God ! Why have I known that one can live on another plane than the easy, human plane, which seems to me more and more like a bed of roses. I loved that life. I had at last reached a life turned entirely towards the spirit, and softened by a perfect tenderness, with never a shadow of misunderstanding. How far will it be modified by a new sacrifice ? I don't know. At eleven o'clock Margaret and I will ask the Master to "begin".

October 19th, Evening—He consented, and gave us an appointment for one o'clock to-morrow at his flat.

October 20th, 1937—As soon as we arrived, he explained again all that we already knew : the need to be certain; to realise that the work would become more and more difficult; that it was not too late to say NO. He didn't mention the rewards. The first one for me is this, that he wants us to help each other.

October 21st, 1937—A heavenly day in the Luxembourg Gardens, with dead leaves swirling about. I have begun the new work, explained by Gurdjieff in such a clear and complete way that I understood without exactly knowing the words. For me it is a long-awaited revelation, this fact, this real, tangible happening, that has infinite repercussions in my being.

Long ago, perhaps forty years ago, I wrote to Maeterlinck : " I don't know if you are aware of it, but I am like a soap-bubble that floats in the air and is not attached to anything real; even in my depths I feel that I am nothing. Only one worry exists, perhaps, in this void, that is, my dissatisfaction at being the way I am It is as though, in order to change, I had to accomplish something I ignore. This comes from far away in me, like a lost thought, a commandment I can give no form, and I search and search . . . "

To-day, a life-time later, when I know what I have to do, I see these words again: "As though, in order to change, I had to accomplish something I ignore."

Eleven o'clock at night—To sum up, this 21st of October I have lived real moments.

End of December, 1937—I live too hard. I am tired. If I saw death coming now, I should not accept it as easily as I accepted it in the hospital beds where I have spent so many years. That is because now my time is heavy with a real substance, that I had no conception of before.

I said to Gurdjieff: " I am almost afraid, life is rising in me like the sea." He repeated: " This is only a very small beginning."

10

By René Barjavel

I met Gurdjieff only once. That is not long in which to form a judgment when, clear as one is about oneself after a lifetime's acquaintance, one knows that one is nothing but a little heap of dirt that possibly reflects a ray of light here and there. The dirt must be re-absorbed before the light can be set free. But, having devoured himself with relish during the long years, man nearly always dies simply of indigestion, without having made the smallest progress.

All this is far from Gurdjieff's teaching. It is only to say that I shall be careful, not only not to judge him, but not even to attempt the smallest appreciation. I met him in Paris during the occupation, at one of the dinners he used to give for his pupils. There were ten of us at table. He looked at us and laughed. He had good cause. As it pleased him to embarrass a newcomer he offered me a raw onion. He did not realize that I was from Provence, and that to me an onion was a dainty titbit. But it turned out to be slightly rotten, so that it proved, after all, a bit of an ordeal.

I never went back to dinner there, and never saw Gurdjieff again. Why ? Lack of time, of money, of food tickets, two young children and material worries that excluded spiritual preoccupations. Very bad reasons — excuses. To-day, after many years, I think it was because I was afraid of him. I had been working for a long time with one of his disciples, through whom I received his teaching shorn of his personality. And this teaching, this doctrine, was as lucid as mathematics. But when I found myself in Gurdjieff's company, his volcanic temperament hit me in the face. I turned away from the volcano and returned to the clear stream that flowed from it. Later, I even left the banks of the stream. That was long ago. But I know that I drank truth there, from that fount of truth from which flows all the wisdom of the world, the fount where religions are formed, those rivers that are constantly flowing further from their source. If I ever become anything better than dirt it will be the result of a long, slow struggle that I would probably never have engaged in if I hadn't come across the Gurdjieff " group." This is all I can say now, but it is the truth.

THE OLD MAN AND THE CHILDREN OF THE AGE

11

A Non-Conformist Catholic

An esoteric school under the sign of the children of the age, with the defects, absurdities, confusions, contradictions and ambitions of the age. A fitting master for the false light in which we live, capricious, scornful and kind, cruel and good, indifferent and supersensitive, full of a dark humour, despotic as Stalin and apparently as lenient as a workman-priest, noisy as a publicity man or a politician, and secretive as a poet in revolt. A string of disciples in whom are found all the elements of our decaying society and every aspect of our troubled contemporary thought, sensibility and morals. And yet a teaching, a master, disciples, a school, such as one might conceivably have found in the great ages of mysticism.

A complete description of what we learnt, suffered and hoped with Gurdjieff in those years after the War is given, I think with great skill and accuracy, by Pierre Schaeffer in the testimony that follows. This account deserves, I believe, close attention and several readings. It contains the analysis and provisional synthesis of every aspect of the Gurdjieff adventure during its last years. The drama of the old man is properly depicted for the first time, and the general significance of the movement, at least in so far as it narrowly concerns our own time, is well given by Pierre Schaeffer, who is, I repeat, without doubt the possessor, above all others, of that insight into disorder unfortunately so necessary for the elucidation of the problems of our time.

To the cursory reader his testimony may appear contradictory. More exactly, his testimony is that of contradiction itself. Permeated as he is by the vital need of antagonistic realities, he follows his Master with enthusiasm and reticence, love and cynicism; tries, in fact, to be faithful to him in *essence*.

This is perhaps why Pierre Schaeffer was bound to give us an unconventional picture of Gurdjieff, without (as yet) the glow of devotion, or the sneer of sarcasm. This versatility is reflected in his life and is, curiously enough, the mark of his career. Trained, against his will, in engineering, the writer in him was at loggerheads with the mathematician: a musician with classical tastes, it seemed almost in spite of himself and against his natural bent that he invented "concrete music". But it is above all through an understanding of his spiritual life that one will be able to appreciate the fundamental continuity of this testimony. An unconventional Catholic, becoming more unorthodox with the years, he only withdrew from his pre-war companions to the extent that they lost interest in him, refusing to understand his book *The Choristers*, in which boy scouts' games suddenly take on an unexpected importance, and even forbidding the reading of it. Probably his testimony on Gurdjieff will receive the same treatment, among the "groups."

His professional attitude is just as significant. A well-known figure and experimenter on the Paris Radio, he never gave up the search for some way of arriving at a deep, spiritual contact with people through this medium, at present given up entirely to the deadening and dehumanization of the masses. Needless to say, this attitude, both organic and anarchistic, made it hard to fit him into any Government post, or the Church, or later into the Gurdjieff "groups," where he was always the *enfant terrible*, a true child of his time.

12

By Pierre Schaeffer

Everytime I Lose Sight of Myself

I go on long journeys. I am away for months at a time. In Scandinavian hotels, and in Pacific towns, on floating airfields, in the middle of African marketplaces or Aztec churches, I sit as I have been told to sit. I try to discover peace in myself, and, knowing only too well that it is useless to look for it in my head, I try humbly to find it in the tranquility of the body, through the relaxation of my muscles. I sometimes succeed, especially if I do the exercise daily.

But if I neglect it, even for a few days, on the grounds that my general condition doesn't require it, or that my journeys, professional duties, social responsibilities or legitimate pleasures excuse it, then I go adrift at once. Meanwhile, they continue their meetings in Paris, that distant metropolis. They go on obstinately with the same thing when you would think they would be far better employed in some proved branch of instruction, or in going to Church. They had made me promise to force myself to "self-remember" for a quarter of an hour every day. I don't often manage it.

Back in Paris again, and the months of forgetfulness over, I know where to go to re-discover the self that, vainly, I have been trailing over the surface of the globe, only to lose it more completely. I go then, or, rather, I went, for in a sense all this is already over. Though I went, it was unwillingly; one doesn't go with alacrity to have one's blood tested or one's teeth examined. I felt that my soul, or whatever one likes to call it, is an organ, too, and deserves to be properly looked after. And so I went to see Gurdjieff.

I had passed the stage of questions aside, absurd requests and interminable waits. I knew beforehand that he would be kindly but ironical, looking at me with his weighty brown look, so concentrated that it was not Gurdjieff I saw at all, but a mirror reflecting life. But whereas a mirror demands nothing and sends back merely a harmless image, the intensity of this look I knew would demand nothing less than myself, which was more than I would be able to give. He would wait for me to speak and I would have nothing to say. It was not to Gurdjieff that I would describe my journeys: he had done them all himself; nor my adventures: as an adventurer he beat all records. My successes then, my merits, my faults? Neither merits nor faults concerned him, but only a state, a weight. Like the weighing-machines in airports, Gurdjieff, the precision instrument, would unmercifully calculate the rate of my energy, the tension of my potential. But the instrument was sensitive in all meanings of the word. How disappoint him again?

Not having enriched myself by a single extra spiritual atom, I would refrain from meeting him face to face; I should see him, but buried in the usual Wednesday evening crowd. I would hardly be noticed. The others, who had persevered and remained at home, had no need of India or Tibet; I should soon be able to tell, by imperceptible signs, whether they had made any progress and if I had lost much ground.

A Modern Miracle-Worker

It is not impossible that a miracle-worker should appear in this Age, in spite of its sterility. But that's wrong — it is far from being sterile. It is fertile and cannibalistic, attributes that go together. Are these the most likely conditions for the appearance of a miracle-worker?

A miracle-worker, by definition, is recognised by his miracles, or at least by the prodigies he performs. But as for miracles, how spoilt we are in this Age! Everything touched by its clay fingers turns to sun, uranium, heavy atoms. What good for a miracle-worker to walk on the waters, invent serums or multiply loaves? Let him, at a pinch, be a biologist, for this Epoch, in search of Life, could use his powers. But the modern miracle-worker is too wise to perform an unconditional miracle in biology. No, with hearts beating peacefully in bottles and tissue living happily by itself; with the states of our souls soon to be reckoned in PH, and our passions in endocrine equations, the modern miracle-worker, whom one must presume to be fully aware, will not be found meddling in biology.

It is in man's dominion over man that the modern miracle-worker stands a chance. Nothing in the hands or up the sleeves. The rule of the game is to seem ordinary. A few hypnotic powers as a stand-by — one abstains from using them. There is our man. The modern miracle-worker seems like anybody else.

If he's a fount of knowledge, there are others more knowledgeable than he; should he be a saint, then we know all about him, he has followers who belong either to East or West, and the modern miracle-worker doesn't appear for the Chosen but for the Gentiles. Above all he does not present himself as a hero. As for heroes, there are train-loads of them, entire camps full of them; huge crematoria have to be built especially to get rid of them. And as for the witnesses one has to believe in because they get themselves slaughtered, one should point out to Pascal that not everyone lives in a happy age when a little blood is sufficient to carry conviction. No, more likely one would find the modern miracle-worker a disgusting cynic, a ferocious cad. Anti-hero and anti-saint, he would appear, rather, in the guise of a scarecrow to keep off both vice and virtue. For it is not the interweaving of these that gives the age its curious flavour ? At the height of civic virtue we have atomic explosions and guided missiles. At the height of social responsibility and the welfare-state, the inevitable destruction of one half of mankind by the other. It is too easy for one side to accuse the other of being the depository of all immoralities and absurdities, this is not so. The heroes and the saints, and especially the believers, are exactly evenly divided. No, the modern miracle-worker owes it to himself to be neither hero nor saint, but the offending counterpart of their failure, of their gigantic folly.

In this aspect he is not reassuring. It is regrettable, to begin with, that he should dabble in science with no qualifications. That he should teach (on what authority ?) is also disturbing. But that he should supply no references or good conduct medals, and keep silent about his youth and antecedents, which we are bound to imagine rather shady, is more than we can swallow. However, in the matter of modern miracle-workers, we have some experience. Hitler and Stalin are examples of what persevering and unscrupulous characters can achieve in the dominion of man over man. It is surely from want of magic that their destinies misfired and are mere history. But who can fail to feel their secret desire to have appeared as a kind of magician in the eyes of their people ? Who can fail to feel, in the people themselves, a passionate longing for a magician ? Who can fail to remember when, after the false war in disappointed France, the magic photograph of the Marshal appeared, quickly followed by that of the General ?

There is something one is bound to respect in this anxious awaiting for a Master. The professional thinkers will not admit it. Convincing others of their importance by their conceit, they pay no heed to magicians. As soon as the masses become mystical, the élite cry out: " The Salvation of the universe depends on experts." Once again, the Pharisees form a syndicate. It is a fact that this clay-handed epoch, so wasteful of uranium and blood, is disorientated between too much and too little knowledge, too much and too little feeling, too much and too little conscience. For the modern miracle-worker in such chaotic circumstances, there is an abyss to be filled: his destiny is not necessarily fixed because he is destined to upset history. He is " irregularity according to law." The fate that awaits him is neither the Cross nor insulin; amongst so many charlatans he will necessarily be valued according to custom. He will be judged *in camera*.

Awaiting M. Gurdjieff

One had squeezed oneself in as best one could between a shin-bone, a knee and two thighs — that is to say, three neighbours; but more were arriving. One was thankful not to be in their place. Not only did they have to face the unnatural silence and concentration, but there was now not a square inch of space. They stood hesitating as though overcome with giddiness. Was it because from their height they could look down on so many crouching bodies, folded legs and fixed looks, or because those already firmly settled and therefore safe, formed such a hostile barrier as almost to force them back down the stairs, on to the pavement and into the jaws of the Metro — and urgent business?

These poor herons, balanced precariously on one leg, searched in vain for a resting-place. The room had its accustomed look: a clutter of knick-knacks, paintings and prints; falsely-exotic window-panes; the annual Russian Christmas-tree that for weeks on end took up an undue amount of room; and precious *objets d'arts*, not a corner of which hadn't at one time or another grazed a back or bruised a knee. These things could not be compressed, but the audience, after the application of what must be magical force, is miraculously able to assimilate everyone really determined to find a place. The peace is disturbed by scuffling and scraping as bodies are squeezed tighter and tighter. But the fixed looks remain. Perhaps some of this constraint springs from queasiness here and there. To be so uncomfortable after a hard day's work, and all for the sake of an evening such as I am about to describe, is not conducive to concentration. How can sardines so closely packed be expected to improve their souls? Some of the novices showed faint signs of indignation — it was too much. The more experienced turned everything to their advantage. They knew that with a little ingenuity a twisted knee can become a spur to flagging strength. The small physical pain has to be carefully tended; without it they would already be asleep. The overstretched muscle forms a small centre of consciousness; they spread out the irritation among the surrounding muscles, as they have been taught. From the knee-joint, the little kernel of pain, as it becomes diffused, loses its sharpness and awakens the calf and the thigh; then it reaches the stiffened buttock, and so to the trunk. Then there is a set-back — it goes no further. The other day it reached as far as the chest, the nape of the neck, and even the head. For a brief instant, the whole body from the knee had become sensitized, awakened. But tonight, there was less, but still it was something.

The latecomer, full of fresh air from the outside world, and inner confusion, knows all about it. He also knows that, so long as he arrives before the appointed time, he is not causing undue disturbance, on the contrary, the place made for him with so much difficulty is his by right. The moment of shame soon passes. It can't be helped, he must go through this upheaval amongst the rapt audience before he can settle down and make himself at home. He will get his revenge. Forty people had squeezed up for him, in a final effort. A minute later another arrives, then two more, then three together, then six, then another, and another, then finally seven, who remain in the passage, no-one knows why, perhaps by special permission or for important duties distributed with discernment and precision amongst the old-timers (washing-up or laying the table). Now the important ones arrive, whom " Monsieur Gurdjieff " has no doubt received privately, and whom he will probably follow in a minute; the making way becomes respectful, more room is somehow found, more and more room. Thus, one of the laws of energy is verified: the more is spent the more there is.

One has a gift for certain things. I had a gift for being there; I know it, and am not particularly proud of it. But I had the greatest contempt for those who were too fussy to squeeze themselves in. Some people came and went away again, outraged. Others one couldn't even imagine coming. Some were frightened by the surroundings or put off by the neighbourhood; they would have preferred vaults and a pulpit, or chairs and a platform, or urbanity and diplomas. I must admit that I liked the place because of its wonderful absurdity; I was touched by the frantic patience of the audience, by the universal law that corresponds with mathematical strictness to that of the Tube-train — many second-class and few first. The XVIe *arrondissement*, with its exclusive but powerful scents (Dior and Lanvin) perfumes the slightly exotic proletariat. There is a gypsy who wears an ear-ring (only one). There are a banker, two duchesses and several typists. There are the bearded and the clean-shaven, garrulous painters and silent Government inspectors. There are wigs and blondes, the nerve-wracked and placid, distinguished and common, Northerners and Slavs, extroverts and introverts. Anything can happen. Péguy's wise words again come to mind: "And you realize by that how man flatters himself when he says he descends and when he says he ascends. That he has not measured how flat is his life between the point of honour and the level of shame."

I have never hated crowds and have often found in

them a better kind of solitude. One's experience in this place is that of mankind in general. Men believe themselves greatly different from one another, but they are much more alike than they think. They surely differ more from a dog or an angel. However great our personal gifts, the idea that collectively we have access to a certain level of understanding, neither higher nor lower, is a salutary one. A gathering of dogs or of sardines can only have a dog's or a sardine's conception of the Cosmos. It matters little, therefore, that such a gathering should trouble about either quantity or quality. It is good for us intellectuals to be jostled. And so, let come who may: the Grand Turk and two Mormons, Lord Mountbatten and Louis Pauwels, the Contesse de Noailles and her maid, it doesn't matter. We have enough to keep us busy in ourselves.

The Modern Miracle-Worker Must be Shocking

I can never repeat often enough that the modern miracle-worker must be shocking. Even believers can admit scandal. Christ caused a scandal, there is the "Scandal of the Church." But, like the military experts just able to prepare for the next war, they must have a well-tried scandal. Humility and poverty and renunciation, all hated by the Romans and the Pharisees, is what one expects. But, supposing the modern miracle worker had the bad taste to love this life as much as the next?

It would be an even greater scandal should the unconventional miracle-worker lay no claim to the exclusive representation of any known God. Far from presenting himself as invested with power from Above, this topsy-turvy miracle-worker would identify himself completely with the man in the street, and so would not even attempt to be exemplary. Furthermore, going astray himself and holding the ends of threads that no doubt soon become tangled, he would collect groups around him like sporting teams, mountain climbers or explorers. The strict discipline of such teams is well-known. Individual success matters little provided the end is attained, but it doesn't matter either who is spared. Thus, the modern miracle-worker would not necessarily be beneficent; aggressive and costly, he would be as dangerous as Everest or the Orinoco, as expensive as aureomycin, as exacting as a lover. It would not be the good miracle-worker that we expect, nor the anti-Christ. This dangerous adventurer would demand not only our time and money, but also our life-force, our psychic energy, for ends that we ignore and for which he, against all prudence, takes the risk.

Some, however, can understand the interest of meeting the modern miracle-worker. After all, it is not so much his life as our own that matters. We don't ask that he should be exemplary but prodigal. If he takes our money, it is because he needs it; if he wants our energy, the essential is for him to help us cultivate more, and it's up to him to give us back a fair percentage. In other words, it's spiritual trading; supply and demand, a very different thing from beggarly devotion. It is more like the bracing atmosphere of the Old Testament, battles with fierce angels and an unscrupulous Jehovah.

Generalization of the Notion of a Modern Miracle-Worker

If on meeting, someone imposes himself on us whose being awakens ours with sufficient force, this person could, for the time being, play the role of the modern miracle worker. Supposing we impose this someone or other on ourselves ? When the Grand Lama dies he is immediately replaced. A few precautions only are required, then all that remains is to accept him cheerfully. The difficulty would be transporting this prodigy to the Rue des Colonels-Renard.

Continuation of my Inner Monologue in M. Gurdjieff's Drawing-Room

In a few minutes he will be here. I don't yet know if I am going to hide. If I had had the guts I would have gone to see him. Having been back a month, I first of all postponed the test, then put it off and finally rejoined the herd. Will he catch sight of me, behind so many backs ? I recognize the familiar smell of the picture-coated walls, and the absent expressions of those present. But enough of impressions and reporting, enough historical surveys. This is a matter of my own salvation.

I have a look round. In six months they have aged. Have I a new wrinkle, too, and the first white hairs ? I find the poeple depressing. (Myself . . . . .) Do I despise or envy them ? I am attracted by their enthusiasm but irritated by their docility. Some of them run to Gurdjieff with nothing more than a cold. They are flies caught in his web, and perfectly contented. At last a guide, an expert, a magus. M. Gurdjieff knows, has known, will know. Pills for some, tasks for others. Very special invitations to dine. For those less favoured, a cup of coffee in the little room from the ceiling and walls of which dangle all the fruits of the Orient and food-stuffs from all the Russias—eels, sturgeon, caviar from the most distant seas. By what grocer's miracle, with what cash and for what esoteric-culinary fantasy are they gathered here ? Questions that many a journalist would ask if he had access to this holy of holies, but journalists are kicked, flabbergasted, down the stairs. The devotees and fanatics dare not ask. M. Gurdjieff knows what he is doing. I don't ask myself, what is the use ? Gurdjieff doesn't hand me a slice of special water-melon or Turkish Delight. He plays the game one wants—if one doesn't defend oneself (I defend myself like the Devil) in the end he plays his own game.

I like to imagine George Ivanovich younger, full of fire, ambition and passions; a kind of Caucasian Lawrence, or a secret agent of the Intelligence Service and of the Heavenly Government at the same time. Either one has dominion over people, or one hasn't; there is no pretending. One moulds and reshapes them, squeezes out the juice and picks out the strong and tough, those with whom an exchange is possible. Alas, Alas ! What loneliness for a man like Gurdjieff ! Who can he ever find to stand up to him, or even to keep him company ? Too strong for everyone, he will search in vain. To the "Groups" who press round him he has only promised the exchange of a contract: give me your energy and I will do something with it, so that you get something back. This mysterious exchange of vital substance frightens even the bravest—the strong escape and the cunning hide. Only the wets are left among this lot. The big names in the movement have all gone, either cursing or scared. The frauds, the prattlers and the humbugs have all gone too—the Devil take them.

Others are dead. A curious hetacomb — Salzmann, Daumal, Dietrich. One couldn't do better in a mystical-detective story in which a wicked God, pursued by Inspector Gurdjieff, strikes down all who come too near. Wars have come and gone, reconstituted continents, invented by the prodigious Gurdjievian imagination, are again swallowed up by the Ocean. How many men and women, roubles and rupees, have passed through his hands? In vain—he is alone. He is the bearer of a radical and overwhelming message, ambitious, urgent and unrealizable? It crushes him even more than the weight of his years. What is he waiting for, in his bourgeois flat, that anachronistic den whose shutters are never opened? Some last-minute disciple whom he will at once recognize, and who, after an authentic struggle, will be able to seize by force the trust which, according to the rules, must only be relinquished to someone stronger than he? Well, it certainly won't be any of these docile pupils, these pretty, saintly women (there are lots of women) these amateurs (of whom I am one) who will be either capable or wishful of it. And the others, fled, hidden or dead, is Gurdjieff aware of them, are they concealed, like a terrible regret, behind his sombre gaze? Bring me people, more people, he commands his intimates. Not that the number makes much difference, but it is a great net that Gurdjieff is trying to throw over his elusive successor. And, indeed, the attendance grows and the space diminishes. Who will be prepared, in a minute, to respond to the old man? Who will be able to bring something forth? "Have you anything to offer me?" he will repeat, and everyone will be silent. I, too!

So instead of thinking of my own concern, of my destiny and my salvation, I find myself thinking about Gurdjieff.

A Dealer in Hearts

The modern miracle-worker examines his world as a horse-dealer his animals—their teeth, their hoofs, their rumps. He uses his own system of reference. One can refuse to accept his findings but one cannot defend oneself from being weighed and sized-up—one just is.

It wasn't even necessary for me to meet this man to be rescued from spiritual bankruptcy, five or six years ago. Other, less eminent people had been able to form relay stations. Should he disappear, these relay stations will still operate in the same way for others, teaching them such simple things as, for instance, that they are, above all, their own victims; that they are machines that automatically wind themselves up again, that they consistently take chalk for cheese; that they waste their energy; that their generosity and greatest virtues are, more often than not, mere booby-traps benefiting no-one, neither themselves nor others.

But the modern miracle-worker warns his world—leave me, leave me quickly, or beware ! We all know how much good we derive in the beginning, from the "purification by emptiness". It is easy to cleanse oneself to the bone. Those who lend themselves to this purification have, as a rule, nothing more to lose. But the modern miracle-worker follows the Scriptures:— "To those that have shall be given". The man who thinks he can pursue this teaching without giving himself completely, without re-making himself out of a purer substance, without being willing to expend this substance in its turn, that man is threatened with exhaustion and a slow death. At this point many quit, it is too much for them. They complain that they cannot breathe, that the whole thing is lacking in love. The gaze of the modern miracle-worker is certainly not pleasant, the dealer in hearts is not accommodating. Love, in these conditions, is impossible. No convent could be worse, no rule more unliveable. Change nothing in your lives, says the modern miracle-worker, live as before, but change everything from the inside.

In a few months and with no other help, the modern miracle-worker saved me from despair. There is one of his sayings that the enlightened often repeat to themselves: " I am only here for the despairing." My cure turns against me. How shall I be able to persevere, without the energy of despair ?

" Work " Begins

The resistance was futile that I was putting up against the work, only an hour ago. *Unum necessarium.* All religions say the same thing. Three minutes of immobility were enough. Mounting this staircase and re-entering this lumber-room were enough to free me from time, that we cannot stop in this life, and from the unrolling of events that are complicated by false necessities, by many undertakings and duties that we like to think imperative. Where the springs meet the heavens, the spirit can make a false bound. If the kingdom of God is anywhere, and it is certainly well hidden, it is here and now, at this moment and in oneself. The monstrous phenomenon that makes one despair of man, is his inconceivable capacity for forgetting this, for forgetting his all-powerfulness, which can abound at the slightest stimulus. What is one to make of this inhibition against the act of recollection, of the panic fear and obstinate unwillingness to unleash this power ? Man's tragedy is his inability to live within himself. He who is at peace with himself and with the Universe, should be able to find in himself his happiness and fulfilment. God, if He exists, would come and call . . . God is everywhere and nowhere. The spirit bloweth when it listeth. Let us enter the great All. But there is Nature that invites and loves us. I have spilt a drop of my blood for you. Here are the Sunday crowds and the Eternal idlers. If it were really a matter of life and death, they would be more serious. Peter is mortal; we live dearly. Time passes wearily, then we go. First Communion was long ago, circumcision was long ago, initiation through red ants or grandfather's brain, was long ago. Sounds and scents float in the evening air . . . melancholy tunes and languorous memories.

But keep calm — restrain yourself. If you are a coalman, have faith, that's all you need. If you are an intellectual, stick to your party. The Sorcerer can. The Party knows. The Church exists. The Lama is in flight. So be quiet. You have your leaders, your dogmas, a tradition, so what the hell! There is historical determinism. At the worst there is the Void.

So — for a second's attention, five minutes of dreaming. Associations, mechanically unrolling without beginning or end. It is not done to be frightened or moved in the Catholic Church, either.

Pray, just pray. Time belongs to God. Don't let the hands remain idle, nor the head either. A good monk hasn't a minute to himself. Here, too, dreaming is considered despicable, but one can't stop thought any more than one can stop a haemorrhage. Some other activity must be engaged in, energy must be diverted to some useful work. So I start again at the knee. The knee must be felt through and through as well as on the surface. Then the leg. Then, for the sake of symmetry, the other leg. Try to equalize the two sensations, try to give them weight, to feel the two legs as one whole. Then, given that one's extremities are more accessible (mine are), the hands. The right one first, then the left. I do get something but, it seems, by an excessive expenditure of will-power. If one exists, why doesn't one's body, like an obedient animal, lie down at the foot of one's consciousness? My forehead is puckered. How can I smooth it? I have four members, good, and for the moment they are keeping me pretty well occupied, but I am no more aware of the rest of my body than usual. I am a tiny creature with four thin little legs, an insect's abdomen and a separate head. A sigh. It's true — I have a heart. A wave of feeling. The feeling is a kind of autonomous emanation, almost independent of any object and disengaging itself like hydrogen, liberating forces that are there, however lacking one may be. Now I've forgotten my hands and my thighs, immersed as I was in that sigh, in that rather feeble effort that, nevertheless, demands immediate attention and nourishment. I'm no longer a piece of chewed string, nor a machine for wrong thinking. For an instant, in becoming aware of myself I felt that I belonged to the whole world, that I had a part to play in it and was no longer completely useless. The old fears receded before this sense of deep and justified calm. To recapture this feeling in memory, I would have to go back to certain communings of my schooldays. Had I succeeded in stopping thought then, too? Perhaps what the child took for awareness of God was really awareness of self?

I called a truce then, and allowed myself a rest, as one does at the end of any prolonged physical effort. One soon tires. Men of all times have muttered: "I have worked well."

But the evidence refutes them. All religions start with work.

"You — Absolute Dirt"

The modern miracle-worker disconcerts everyone. Does he preach a religion? Has he doctrines or practices? Hardly. They vary so much with the clients, countries and seasons of the year that he may be a philosopher, a gymnast, a healer, a dramatist or a business-man. Why not, as life, the whole of it, is merely an exercise? The basic exercise, "self-remembering," that beginners think so easy and that causes so much misunderstanding amongst practitioners of Yoga, is, for the modern miracle-worker, only a preliminary. That self-remembering does in fact bring back and provide the clue to all the strongest emotions and most sacred moments of our past life is yet another source of misunderstanding. Here questions merge, questions that the modern miracle-worker doesn't even trouble to answer. What is the use if, from the Western believer to the Indian polytheist, from the Benedictine monk to the Dervish, a whole universe of phenomena, concealed by dogmas and superficial customs, corresponds to laws that are fundamentally common to all? What are these laws, and to what creed do they belong? Have you a doctrine? Is it right to believe in God, in Christ and the Church; should one believe in Buddha and detach oneself from appearances?

But the modern miracle-worker confounds his world. He is like an alchemist administering potions. He separates a phenomenon from its context, isolates it in his prosaic, concrete, irrefutable experience. A doctrine ? Not as much — there is no language. These people communicate well enough in broken French, English and Russian. They might otherwise be tempted to enter into explanations, but the most subtle of disciplines awaits them, that of language. Should one of them get excited and wish to find out more, all he gets is: " You're dirt." The old hands know — the newcomers suffocate. With a pleasant smile: " You understand, you dirt ? " Yes, is the answer, full of goodwill. One certainly requires goodwill ! Sudden fury, violent indignation, and the modern miracle-worker's moustache bristles. " You not understand. You complete idiot. You filth." Silence. The poor man, caught between humility and humiliation, tries to save his face. Why ? For his own sake or that of others ? The others, who have all had it said to them before, chew over the words in silence. Perhaps, after three years and when applied to someone else, the meaning has suddenly burst on them ? There is no malice in the attack, but the truth is so blinding when it concerns another ! There is a pause, which is a good thing for everyone. Then, as though nothing had as yet been said or heard, the modern miracle-worker, who talks no language properly but mangles many, invents a phrase. Others do likewise, for less good reasons. He finishes up with: " You all absolute dirt."

The foul-mouthed prophet looks round. The first man is no longer attracting attention, but there is general discomfort. Everyone is shaken; the Christian, who is re-discovering his lost or fading humility; the unbeliever, who has never been called such a thing before; the hardened man whom nothing affects, who this time is forced to take notice. Self-pity is out of the question. The masochist can't wallow in dirt for there really isn't any in what has just been said. The word re-echoes in the depths of their being. Who feels inclined to laugh? Human weakness is not even disgusting; the nullity of the human creature is not even humiliating; the misery of man without God is suddenly blinding.

The modern miracle-worker surely has no need to make speeches, he has the gift of tongues.

The Modern Miracle-Worker Between Tradition and the Science of Tomorrow

I have not come to deny but to fulfil. The modern miracle-worker continues the pious work. It would not be correct to say that he takes the good where he finds it. It is not a matter of expurgating the Upanishads, the Koran or the Evangelists, of mixing up Buddha, Mahomed and Jesus, in order to produce easily digested nourishment for his Anglo-Saxon clients. The modern miracle-worker is a lawful follower of these masters, but at the same time an underminer of their Churches. He makes no choice.

First and foremost he teaches understanding. "All is yours" as understanding grows. It is the eye that must be made clearer.

The modern miracle-worker adds his iota to the annals of Revelation. From Buddha to Christ, God always provided a humble setting for His incarnation. After untold years the Creator draws nearer to His creature. From Vishnu with his hundred arms and thousand heavenly faces, veiled by the firmament of waters, from the enigma of the beasts and the mystery of re-incarnations up to the modern Christ, human in form though divine in nature, there is an incontestable economy of means. Thus from amongst all His dubious inventions, the Creator of the Quarternary and Tertiary periods opted for man. Thus, starting off with an Asiatic taste for dragons and levitating hermits, the Creator became Greek and Roman in culture and Jewish through grace, ended up in a quieter, and what we like to think a more rational, vein.

Sometimes one has to re-trace one's steps; the mystery of the Incarnation is not in one direction only. It requires an effort at divinization on the part of man. What is divinization if not, on the part of the creature, a super-human, super-natural effort to associate itself with the process of creation? One has to draw the greater from the less, to suffer the pangs of this unnatural birth. You are all Gods, said the bad Angel who knew much, and who surely spoke truth, surely too soon.

So the modern miracle-worker will attempt the most audacious synthesis. Immersed in tradition, he will be outrageously modern. The order of things is itself the miracle. He doesn't unloose the strap of any sandal. He preaches a massive respect. All future science and all past tradition are in accord, which pre-supposes, for the present, the most caustic criticism and outbursts of laughter right up to the altar rails. The fact is that at every stage, respect for the essence prevails over mockery at appearances, faith in the Father resolves the doubts of His sons, the Word triumphs where the word fails.

The modern miracle-worker holds the two ends of a chain; one end plunges back through lost oceans and is anchored to broken traditions; the other is joined to the sciences of to-day and to those of to-morrow, which are hinted by reality to mankind, already at the full stretch of invention.

The modern miracle-worker is like Mendelief, and boldly classifies the energies of creation from God to the Moon. He is like Descartes and enumerates, not wishing to leave out anything from a creation which surely must make a single whole, and in which everything is related. What matter if he is mistaken; if, through lack of time and of knowledge past and forgotten or future and still inconceivable, he invents, invents both what might have been in the beginning, say ten thousand years ago, and what will be in the near future, in a few hundred years? Are these constructions of his ingenuous or inspired? To dare to imagine what could be, is to say that it will be! Descartes, too, thought he could deduce the laws of optics from his arm-chair. He discovered four laws, two of which were false. The fact is that it is possible to have invented a system and yet be incapable of applying it. But systems give birth to epochs; they name them, as stone and iron have done.

The modern miracle-worker is, perhaps, only a minor prophet. He guesses, he indicates how things will happen.

M. Gurdjieff Comes In — And Goes Out Again

At last he comes in. The waiting arm-chair receives his corpulent form. No-one stirs. There is an atmosphere of courtesy, deference and a pleasant work relationship on both sides. " Carry on," says Gurdjieff.

It is good to sleep, even in these uncomfortable conditions, as long as the weather is set fair, and a good breeze blows one away from the shores of one's wretched self. I was drifting peacefully towards the future when the schoolmaster, the quartermaster, the grandfather instructor, called me back: "Your exercises, your mental sums." "I have counted as you told me," says someone, "and I find it helps me. One, one hundred, two, ninety-nine, three, ninety-eight, etc.: it helps me." " What in ? " " In retaining the sensation of my arm." A grunt. The pupil continues: " I have even complicated the counting. The more difficult it is, the more my brain is occupied and I manage, sometimes, to have a very strong sensation of my whole body." Now everybody is prepared for anything. Congratulations (rare), insults (frequent), sarcasms (the most frequent of all). " How long you do that ? " " A fortnight." " Enough, enough, then. You do no more counting. Already mechanical. Already you sleep counting new way. Understand ? " It was obvious. Who could fail to understand when he said it ? As soon as it becomes easy it is useless. The engine must never tick over. " Next, next ? " says Gurdjieff. A heavy silence. Who has something to say ? A small, oversensitive woman in a green hat cannot stand the silence any longer. She says just what comes into her head, but quite sincerely of course. She says that while " working " she has felt a lump in her throat rise and fall and fix itself, finally, in her solar plexus. Relief amongst those at the back. They are allowed to giggle occasionally for a few minutes. It never fails: " You idiotic, you hysterical . . . how you say in French ? " Gurdjieff turns with a broad smile. " You crazy— dotty." Dotty ! The lady in the green hat grovels. Everything the Beloved One does and says is right. She blushes and stutters. " You in mad-house soon, eh ? " " Yes, M. Gurdjieff," she answers humbly, feeling certainly the better for a glow in her heart that will probably send her home to work even harder than before, in the wrong way.

But who are we to judge ? A little less silly, a little less nice ? Why doesn't Gurdjieff send her away ? He never sends anyone away, because everyone needs everyone else. The confessions of the silly are needed in the whole symphony. Who dares to lift his head and say: "Thou fool ! You absolute dirt." The silence is only heavy with our complete nullity, but there is a tension in it that, like all human energy, can be of use. Even the lump in the throat of the lady with the green hat is a useful lump, if not for her at least for the others.

"Squeal, squeal ! " mocks Gurdjieff. But no-one utters. The silence becomes colder. Those who have only been there for six months or two years glance at the old-timers. Have the seventh-year veterans nothing to say ? The silence is painful, rarified like the air at high altitudes. What could have been said, at a pinch, a little while ago, would now sound impossible. Everyone was more or less prepared for this. It is now too late. Gurdjieff is no longer mocking but disappointed.

Nearly everyone sits with head bowed, but to-day I keep mine up and don't even try to avoid his glance. I notice his clothing, slippers, a gaping waist-coat, a stained jacket, a chechia: it's my grandfather. I haven't been able to do my sums. I don't know my verbs. I haven't worked hard enough. I haven't worked at all.

My grandfather is dead, and so is my childhood. After the reproachful look, I used to go off without a word and draw back the curtain from the kitchen window down which the rain would be streaming in rivulets. The country, so limited and given up to its long, slow labour, stretched away beneath the downpour of the long winter months of Lorraine, which would give way at last to a late spring and langorous summer. Then there would be winter again, more winters and more years without end or aim. I would grow up, but would I ever become my own master? Beyond the limited horizon, and the sums and the verbs, would I ever find the meaning of anything? I would cast a furtive look at my grandfather. He was perhaps mending the pump at the sink, winding it with a big rusty spanner. The rabbit stew was simmering gently on the stove. Soon we would eat. But what right has a child who has done no work to eat? Why should the rabbit that they had killed and so painfully skinned, the day before, why should it be allowed to suffer and get cooked? For an idle child, who does nothing but gape through a wet window-pane, under the reproachful gaze of a Master, who only wishes him well?

Another exchange of glances. He doesn't seem surprised at meeting my eye, amongst all these bowed heads. It is not childishness that is overcoming me now, but manliness. I want to be a man, to have done, at last, with this absurd situation, to smash the window-pane, to interrogate the earth, to justify my food. I have been alone for forty years in this human family where everyone chatters, everyone pretends, everyone hugs his anguish to himself. Miraculously, I find my grandfather again, after so many years. I murmer, as I used to:—" You are not alone—God loves you." The hot

THE OLD MAN AND THE CHILDREN OF THE AGE 425

brown eyes rest on me for a moment. A fatherhood exists in the world. A mind responds to the question posed by the agony of the rabbit, and the sodden fields. I am the son of Some-one.

I dare to look round. Time stands still, but the silence seems to have lightened. The atmosphere is easier. Gurdjieff now expects nothing of us, nor we of him, nor anyone of anyone, nor of himself. There is a truce. Dense and less cold, the silence falls on us like snow, the snow of an interminable winter.

I don't at all like these people. Some of them profit, others are victims. One of them, a bad angel who has understood more than the others, pulls a grimace. He said to me, one day:— " Gurdjieff has brought us a doctrine of haste." " Of haste ?" " Hurry, if you want him to help you understand the rule of three." I do hurry, but I shan't succeed. He passes a hand over his forehead. They are freckled, like my grandfather's. I am touched by his unbuttoned waistcoat, and creased trousers, but resist the *chechia,* it comes from another country and proves that we have grandfathers in all corners of the world, that God's gaze rests on us from the Caucasus to Lorraine. Do I really hurry ? No, not really. I play truant, I sleep on my feet. Gurdjieff breathes heavily and gets up. Perhaps, like my grandfather in his last days, he cannot contain himself for so long.

This man, I know, is going to die—to die before I have time to ask him *my* question.

The Modern Miracle-Worker and the Jansenist Quarrel

The modern miracle-worker declares:— " You go on like this, you die like dogs." A surprising statement equally strange to all creeds, lumping together as it does those who believe in Heaven and those who don't. Here is a fresh difficulty: to possess a soul or not would be too simple. Souls have to be made and it's every man for himself. Hence the haste.

And, after all, why should one possess a soul any more than the rabbit one eats or the dog one runs over? Here, both the rather facile affirmations of eternity and the rather narrow denials of anything to come, are both surpassed. Hell, for materialists, would be annihilation, the return to chemical substances. For anyone who wishes to make the attempt time is short in which to try his luck. It is a question of a subtle synthesis, of *restricted* efforts and uncertain methods. It is tempting but bitter.

One can imagine the longings of this ship-wrecked crew, the horror of this Medusa's raft. If it really is a question of sucking energy from one another, what will these *machine-creatures* do, with their blessed egoism?

The longing is absurd, the egoism deadly, the concentration useless. There are no tricks for gaining salvation. In the new terminology it is called "hydrogen grade N," but it is still divine grace which falls on us when it wills and not when we will. The modern miracle-worker cannot bring it down for us by saying "filth". This is the Jansenist quarrel again in an unexpected and rather abrupt form—my grace suffices you. It's back to the Classics. All religions are the same.

The " Reading " Sessions

One Wednesday evening when the silence had become more oppressive even than usual and I dared not meet Gurdjieff's eye, he growled significantly "Well, if this is how it is . . ." From that day on there were no more questions or answers, but only "readings". As it might be a schoolmaster sick of his lazy pupils who, instead of inflicting the expected punishment reads to them *Round the World in Eighty Days*.

Already, during the preceding months, when things became sticky and we no longer got anything from one another, Gurdjieff would make a sign and a reader would try deciphering the bundles of papers brought out with infinite care from amongst the treasures of the back shop. There were several type-script copies of these chapters, which were tremendously sought-after. A rich American had paid a thousand dollars for twenty pages; another had given a hundred for the privilege of looking through them, shut up in a room in the Waldorf-Astoria. The French, less inclined to spend, especially on their souls, patiently awaited their turn which, by their impotence at the meetings, they brought considerably closer. So now, instead of questions and sarcasms, there were readings. Against a background of vague uneasiness, the squatters of the Rue du Colonel Renard lapped up the still uncorrected chapters of *Beelzebub,* or, to their great surprise, of Ouspensky. By a sudden change of heart Ouspensky, banned up till then, was now again in favour. This very Russian process made me laugh and cry at the same time as I was in no way taken in by it. It was Gurdjieff himself who suffered most by his apparently vindictive revenge. By what insight had he timed so well Ouspensky's re-instatement? He had allowed just the two or three indispensable years in which to weigh up the terms and verify the "information" which hence-rth was to appear in print, explicitly in Ouspensky's work and deeply hidden in *Beelzebub*.

I watched this reversal in consternation. The esoteric teaching about which I had understood at least that it was neither exotic nor even occult, but could only be communicated directly from man to man, without the need of fine language, this teaching, then, that I had not had time to absorb but only to catch a glimpse of, was now going to be closed to me and I, with many others, was to be plunged back into all the misunderstandings of the written word. It was useless for Gurdjieff to multiply the difficulties. Being unable to alter Ouspensky's air of respectability, he insisted that nothing should be cut out of *Beelzebub*, none of the untranslatable puns, absurd truisms or bawdy jokes, that so evidently had nothing to do with the subject-matter. It was all right for us, we knew. But the general public would be reading from bound volumes that they could obtain without humiliation, robbery, or the expenditure of a thousand or a hundred dollars. We had it read aloud to us while crouching in uncomfortable positions, a very different matter, and we understood that it was all part of the "work", this curious alchemy between intellect and muscles, this secret interchange between cramped legs, restricted breathing and the racing of the imagination.

Further, Gurdjieff was listening with us, punctuating the reading with discreet sounds. There was no commentary or explanation, and only occasional laughter. Gurdjieff was already dead, hearing from his coffin how his future readers would devour and digest him.

By an absurd but quite understandable turn

of events the text that was so soon to become common property and available to the most idly curious, to outraged experts and to the higher "scientists", the text that was soon to be torn to shreds by the critics and treacherously turned to ridicule by absurd subtitles, was kept under lock and key where the faithful were concerned, and only brought out as a special favour. As in all parties where, rightly, intellectuals are mistrusted, so in this group the intellectuals were treated with special suspicion. The devoted typists redoubled their precautions. The book was about to be launched and would have a right to its publicity and puffs. The manuscript, preserved like a relic, the mystical double of the one that would appear in the bookshops, retained its quality. The readings from it were a magic rite. Try experimenting thus with Proust or Rabelais (I name these two advisedly) and note the results.

According to Gurdjieff the book was to be published by subscription. The expenses would otherwise have taken a very large part of his income. The plan was to bleed the rich in order that the rest should have everything for nothing. A *de luxe* edition, carefully enhanced by snobbery and enveloped in piety, was to rake in the dollars, of which Gurdjieff, seemingly, controlled the miraculous source. Then many thousand pocket-size copies on India paper were to be distributed free at street corners, in pubs and in the ports. Tons of seed. Wastage is one of the attributes of Divinity. We French didn't care, we were pleased to think of this free distribution, mostly among ourselves, not only because we are the stingiest of people, but also the most incredulous. God needs the incredulous.

The Modern Miracle-Worker and the Blessed Gibberish

The modern miracle-worker throws in his hand when he feels that the game is up, that there is no-one and nothing more to be expected, and that his hour is near. In an instant esotericism is finished and all that used to be occult now sees the light of day. Yet how can the modern miracle-worker circulate what should be anti-ideas and anti-phrases by means of the printed word, which is necessarily imperfect? This, however, is what he does, he who mistrusts everyone, above all his intimates. He casts his bottle into the sea, he baits his most treacherous hook, to draw the big fish from the depths.

"Your modern contemporaries . . ." This is how Beelzebub contemptuously refers to mankind when he tries to explain to his grandson, Haroum, with what a strange collection of dreamers, of pretentious ghosts, of *machine-creatures* he will have to spend his time on earth. But even if these modern contemporaries are put out by the coarse Gurdjievian humour and vexed by the Caucasian jokes; even if, amongst so many bestsellers and book club choices, they can't be bothered to crack this rather vulgar shell to discover the hidden kernel, they will have to admit that, at the very least, they are faced with a literary phenomenon the like of which has rarely been seen before.

Ouspensky's work presented little difficulty to a public used to hearing and devouring all kinds of things. Though the table of hydrogens was rather a stumbling block, the anecdotal parts were easily absorbed. But the translation of *All and Everything*, which would be appearing forever in instalments, was a very different matter. Indigestible, obscure and involved, it constitutes a remarkable feat: communication by language in despite of language, by words beyond words, by an anti-literature. Such an attempt is not new, we have had *Pantagruel* as well as *La Recherche du Temps Perdu*, *Une Saison en Enfer*, as well as *Maldoror*. But one expects the result to still conform, to a certain extent, and not to dispense altogether with rules. Gurdjieff's writing shows a complete lack of respect for literature and this is hard for writers to forgive.

As for other people, they will long dream about Beelzebub's stories to his grandson; they will descend into those depths by whatever glimmer of light they can provide for themselves. They will reach the central chapter where, in an unknown Tibet in an unspecified epoch, the last scene of Gurdjieff's cosmology is enacted, the scene in which the possible salvation of our planet is pushed into a distant future. There, man was at last about to succeed, in that country that until then had remained almost inviolate. He had prepared himself, with complete devotion, for the final attempt. The philter of immortality, so naïvely conceived by the magicians of the Middle Ages, was at last within reach, but in a different way. Triumph over death was not to be achieved by any magic spell, nor yet by a blind faith, but by the ultimate understanding of the mysteries of life, and by gigantic efforts on the part of men especially trained and equipped for this merciless struggle. For the mastery of living matter, a perfect knowledge of and respect for the uses of inanimate matter were needed. But life can be violated in other ways, by pure destructiveness and idiocy. Such are the **ways of our modern conquerors and Empire-builders,** as savage as the Visigoths or Neanderthal Man. How can one explain to an Englishman that the fate of the world is being played out in Tibet and that the Tibetans must be left in peace for another few years (perhaps even a few weeks) to enable them to achieve success ? To put it briefly, it was the English campaign in Tibet that caused the downfall of the Men of the hour on whom the fate of the world depended. A pull on the trigger by a *machine-creature,* who is himself functioning automatically for the greater glory of Albion, and the world has to wait another hundred thousand years.

Such is Beelzebub's story to his grandson. One can smile and shrug one's shoulders, but the story that Gurdjieff tells is as probable as the Last Supper and perhaps not so very remote from it. It is evident that the modern miracle-worker has unpublished material to add to the Atridae, to Abraham's sacrifice and to the various happenings under Pontius Pilate.

Your modern contemporaries, O Haroum, talk their heads off. They imagine that they choose their own leader and do not realise that it is the Master (and they are lucky if they find one) who chooses them. Generations may pass without their finding one, even though they may have deserved him. Then there may be others who, not having deserved it, yet meet with two or three. Some are prepared to go to the ends of the earth in search of the Successor. But the story of the World is not written on this level. The very most we can expect in our lifetime is one short and abridged chapter of the Universal story. That is why we can begin and stop anywhere. We are told more than is necessary for understanding and, usually, more than we can grasp. This blessed gibberish, these dynamic sugar-sticks, will henceforth be on sale in the bookshops. Between the two covers of the enormous book are set traps into which will fall elephants, and not small elephants either. A rare kind of intelligence will be needed. Some will read it as a detective-story; others will settle down to esotericism as they settle down to a meal. Incense will burn in new sacristies, a new Church will be born, with Ouspensky as writer of the Epistles and Beelzebub as Evangelist. It will at once be expurgated and a careful choice made for anthologies, of passages not too obscure nor too licentious.

The wave closes over the Pirate. Perhaps a big fish is on the look-out and will follow him down into the depths.

A Session of "Movements"

For those who get no more answers because they ask no more questions there are still the "movements." These "movements" brought together the groups of different standards into a larger and in some ways more open group, and the necessary qualifications of the members also seemed rather different. The large number of new arrivals necessitated the continual division of the classes and the formation of more and more courses for beginners. Here again there were two opposite streams, like those I tried to describe with regard to the "work." The fact was that the "movements" satisfied so well these cravers after inner stability (some of them at first did not even suspect the existtence of Gurdjieff and had no idea that the "movements" formed part of a wider teaching) that they would come flocking to take part, and were strangely punctual and strangely persevering for a time. They reminded me by their assiduity of two apparently quite dissimilar kinds of people, on the one hand of novices in a convent, and on the other, of members of a rugger team. But can this have been Gurdjieff's aim ? Did he really take all this trouble for the sake of the performers, arranging, manipulating, and, with his sharp eye, sorting out the best ? The best for what ?

Any description, however clever, would fail to convey these " movements." All I can say is that thanks to them, work of an extraordinary precision took place in our moving centres, a skilful disconnection became apparent in the functioning of our muscles and we acquired an intimate insight into the workings of our bodies. The stricter the execution of a movement, the greater the possible control and supremacy over every aspect of co-ordination. Once the machine was wound up and running by itself the exercise was made complicated to a degree never dreamed of by the beginners, given up as they were entirely to the joys of an apparent harmony. With intense difficulty the intellectual centre was first of all brought into play, then the emotional centre, or possibly both together. How can I explain this to someone who has not experienced it ? To the outsider, what significance can there be in the efforts of these people to make asymmetrical movements with arms and legs, at the same time doing more and more complicated mental arithmetic and, to crown all, being told to perform in a religious spirit ? What a wonderfully conventional phrase ! What religion ? It didn't matter in the least. It was not enough to emerge from the Metro, one also had to emerge from one's own private tunnel. To those who were striving for the most intimate physical co-ordination while at the same time keeping to the rhythm and the steps and making mental calculations, the extra command to do it all "in a religious spirit" involved no misunderstanding. The difficulty lay not in grasping the meaning but in acting on it.

"You now say God have mercy" Gurdjieff would say. The docile ones at once cried out in a loud voice "God have mercy." ("You not shout loud enough.") Then there were the believers for whom the words did, after all, hold a meaning; they were astonished at the gymnastic prayers. It seemed that they were asked to perform a spiritual exercise the wrong way round, first to make a physical effort, then a mental one and lastly to bring in the emotions. Here were no comfortable hassocks, no glamour, no stained glass or soft music. To the strains of middle-Eastern music on a piano tuned to augmented seconds, (not everybody's taste) muscles stiffened as arms took up the required position, relaxed again for a skilful movement of the legs, while all the time the mental calculations were proceeding. Each one took his turn in a kind of gymnastic canon without loosing his proper place in the row; no-one was able to imitate the one in front but the slightest mistake threw out the row, if not the block, or even the whole forty-two performers. On top of all this, at the word of command, all inhibitions and fear of ridicule had to be cast aside and the words "God have mercy" shouted out loud.

There were no down-cast eyes or false ecstasy. Sometimes, if the "movements" went well, if exercise no. 27 (there were no names, only numbers) reached the required standard, it became possible to catch a glimpse of the goal, that is, collective liberation from mechanicalness, and the running of a machine now under full control. The spirit, now served by the body, attained a higher sphere, but this was nothing like the feeling of being moved or exalted. Rather, it resembled one's feeling on gaining a hard-won height that had to be quickly abandoned because of giddiness. This experience was like the super-effort of the man who, to save his skin, runs faster than ever he thought he could. It would come in a flash, especially if Gurdjieff wasn't there. When he was there he was always complicating the exercises and inventing new ones, and never, never gave us time to draw breath or to take stock.

He would walk amongst the dancers, straightening a row here, bending a torso there, correcting the position of an arm or leg and then moving on to the following line, making it do the next figure so that when all were once more in motion the exercise moved on from line to line, like a wave. Never mind about your bodies, it's your state that counts. You are nothing but the hieroglyphs of an inexhaustible language that I shall continue to speak through you and whose secret I shall guard with my life. Though you may be clumsy, slow and lifeless, go on, write, write in your muscles, in your heads and, if possible, in your hearts. These are texts to be deciphered inwardly; only those who transmit them can understand them. You are living ciphers.

Some of the instructors were outstanding; they were usually girls who were the most gifted. They would note the hieroglyphs on little diagrams, receipts for the exercises, a collective score. Occasionally there were public performances. Gurdjieff, in one of his irrepressible freaks, would dress everyone up in Turkish costume. This just had to be borne. Misunderstanding would reach its height. The idle curious, to whom the aesthetic side mattered most, would go away, outraged; the other, less snobbish spectators, might guess that something important was going on, in spite of the fancy dress, something incomplete but possibly prodigious. As for the corps de ballet, these Parisians in Turkish slippers, Gurdjieff would simply throw them handfuls of boiled sweets.

The Modern Miracle-Worker, Matter and Spirit

Every new approach to reality confounds by its simplicity, but all true simplicity is inexpressible. If the knowledge acquired by a man who has been touched by grace is not at once apparent to others, he tends to be shocked, forgetting that before the touch of grace he had been as blind himself.

What is true of a man is equally true of a civilization of an epoch. Twenty centuries of Greeks worshipped Zeus, the Thunderer. If anyone had dared put forward the notion that it was not a God but electricity that caused thunder, he would at once have been put to death for blasphemy. Many now-a-days are put to death for much less; but for as much, no-one is punished, people merely smile.

The modern miracle-worker raises a smile. People are baffled by his complicated exercises. If, at least, they were all of a piece—medical, "folky," monastic or artistic—"all of a piece" meaning that they belonged to some known category and could be easily pigeon-holed for the peace of mind of all concerned. But he who interrogates the clouds, who applies to Zeus the theory of ions, is impure, confused and questionable. However, every monadology comes in its right time.

The modern miracle-worker suggests that the Kingdom is of this world, that matter, sufficiently accelerated, becomes spirit. Matter is generalised spirituality, as soon as it breaks through the wall of the body. The suggestion is that we should, so to say, release God as, for example, we release atoms or rockets, even at the risk of one's skin. Meditation becomes an exact science, prayer a dangerous sport. God is no more to be found through dreaming, nor is He surrounded by anthropomorphic concepts disguised by clever definitions. God is apprehended through an experience that is unmistakably material since the body participates in it. All this can, of course, be easily misinterpreted and give rise to the most grotesque misunderstandings.

But the modern miracle-worker is alone in trying an experiment of this kind. One may smile at his arranging his flock in the Salle Pleyel in figures of five and making them perform exercises which are too difficult for them and the product of a thousand years of monastic discipline, but one is nevertheless nervous of experiments on human beings and afraid of accidents. There are no safeguards and no checks.

However, the orthodox God's teaching to his intellectual followers is comforting: your body is the temple of God. These athletes of the mind are not unaware that the ancient Egyptians believed in the connexion between body and spirit, but having such puny bodies themselves they prefer to stick to metaphor, it is less tiring. The modern miracle-worker works in the flesh, having exploded the metaphors and wrecked the analogies. If our separate bodies are temples, and our combined presences a living harmony forming another temple, (where two or three are gathered together in My name there am I in the midst of them,) and if this by any chance should be one of the highest aspects of accessible Reality, then let us beware. Play with fire if you like but not, if you can help it, with high-tension wires.

Dinner with Gurdjieff

Once the intolerable silences and interminable readings were over and the cramped limbs completely petrified, the Wednesday-night company was allowed to relax. In spite of aches and pains, it invaded the dining-room. There were places for twenty people seated and forty standing up, including those in the corridor. But, as we have already seen, space creates itself and if there is room for thirty there is room for sixty. A chain of plates linked the kitchen to the dining-room and M. Gurdjieff himself served out the food. Special helpings were destined for special people—for the Platinum Blonde, for the Director, for Misunderstanding, for Sewer, for Alfred. Then, as soon as M. Gurdjieff came back from the kitchen, glasses were filled with peppered vodka and a master of ceremonies proposed a toast to a certain category of idiot (the first, or ordinary category) to which I had the honour to belong. I never troubled to find out exactly how one was promoted from the different categories (round, square, polyhedral, psychopathic or hopeless); like Napoleon snatching his crown from the Pope, I had shamelessly appropriated the category I liked best, the lowest, that of *ordinary idiot,* and this for two reasons. The first, that as the hierarchy appeared to be upside down the ordinary idiots seemed less foolish than the others (I thought, and still think, that I was right.) The second was, that as most people had a tendency to raise themselves in the hierarchy of foolishness. I thought it more classy and also more in keeping with my exceptional humility, to include myself with the lowest grade. So the first toast, drunk to the idiots of my category, put me in the lime-light. However, I had fallen into the trap: having been informed, everyone chose well and truly the category that pleased him. I had examined myself, and received the right answer.

To M. Gurdjieff, these toasts to idiots were a never-failing source of amusement, (and how I agreed with him !) He used to turn to the category of fool in question, and raising his glass in their direction, give them a broad smile. This smile showed his affection both for their wretched selves and for their indescribable idiocy. As far as I was concerned, I must admit that I always thought I caught an appropriately ironic glint in the eye of my host. Where does that fool come from, with his pretentions to being an ordinary idiot ? The sudden spark moved on to damp some other fire. From this simple setting sprang the most improbable incidents. What is more, those who were scared of alcohol were forced to drink large quantities of vodka; those who relished sweet things were made to eat the hottest paprika, and vice versa. Sickened either by onions or halva, we were all both spectators and victims, and could only properly appreciate the situation as illustrated by our neighbours. A tenth glass of vodka was irrevocably poured out for the non-drinkers, causing a rosy glow to spread over normally abstemious faces, while the gay dogs, unfortunately all too rare, who would willingly have indulged themselves, were, of course, strictly brought to heel. The unworthiness of their habits was pointed out to them, and the vast expense in which their excessive appetites were involving their host ! " How much you think this cost ?" M. Gurdjieff would ask, holding out the smallest radish. " Special radish specially sent for me from Caucasus." It actually came straight from the Neuilly market.

It has been said that the comic is essentially a phenomenon of liberation in which two paradoxical elements are at work: terror and ease, privation and abundance, the solemn and the grotesque. The meals with Gurdjieff were a good example. For while these outlandish skirmishes were taking place in an atmosphere of the greatest solemnity, the web of silence that had accumulated during the last two hours was not so easily broken; it could still be felt through the smiles and the jokes. If anyone should put a foot wrong, and behave in a manner either too formal or too ribald, he would immediately be crushed under a weight of ridicule and contempt. An atmosphere at once pious and Rabelaisian, exotic and monastic, bantering and contemplative, was created by the obligation we were under to eat and drink more than was reasonable, to be on the look out for so many traps, to take part in complicated rites and at the same time to pursue the " inner work " which, though nothing had been said, was quite evidently expected. (It was popularly held, and even verified, that a meal with Gurdjieff could always be digested.) I was in my element at these dinners, which were dreaded by many, I came away light-hearted, rejuvenated, restored in the real sense of the word, and greatly helped in my struggles against sleep and pessimism, "idées fixes" and stomach-troubles.

Not least among the comic elements of the situation was the extraordinary submissiveness of the guests and their fanatical determination to find instruction and significance in Gurdjieff's slightest word. As for me, I said nothing and blasphemed inwardly. Though I was touched by the old man's truculent lavishness, by the enormous burden he saddled himself with, by the immense trouble he took with us all, by a kind of prosaic goodness that turned the offer of a piece of halva, a small gherkin, or a spoonful of sauce, into a gesture full of significance and of special meaning for such or such a one, I could not but be aware of his great fatigue and of the tragedy that was playing itself out in these obscure surroundings.

Why did he accumulate so many contradictions? What over-subtle rules were hidden by these rules altogether too crude? Sometimes, owing to fatigue and the lateness of the hour and also, no doubt, to the vodka, he would stumble over his words and I, for one, was far from expecting a dead shot every time, as some of the other guests did. On the contrary, what I admired were the sudden changes of atmosphere, the quickness of his repartee and the liberation of the emotions when, after three quarters of an hour in which nothing much had happened (without, however, my being able to relax my attention, which was constantly held by many different things) he would suddenly, and with no warning, violently attack one of the guests, either in a most personal or purely impersonal manner. No one ever left without feeling, in one way or another, stirred, moved, fascinated.

Whereas, when "working" in solitude there was nothing to control the degree of objectivity and seriousness that we put into the "work", on the other hand, during these love-feasts a chain reaction took place in which nothing any longer made ordinary sense. Eating and speaking became momentous acts and remarks exchanged across the table seemed like the stabs of a knife. Everyone, picked out by a search-light, was caught in the very act of desertion and had to be brought back between bayonets. Failing trial by red-hot iron or poison, the glass of alcohol became a kind of judgment from heaven. What spiritual progress can be claimed by one who hasn't even the grace to allow himself to be made drunk ?

This great feast—can I say it without shocking ?—reminded me of another. It was impossible not to think of the Last Supper. Bludgeoned into life, we were taking part in tragic agapes. We dipped our hands in the dish with a Master. The figure of Judas or of the favourite disciple was enough to give one a fit. Our indomitable friend, the Banker, whose face was aglow with the vodka that he detested ("you drink another toast, Director, you not drink anything !") was Peter. There were swooning Mary Magdalens, incorrigible Marthas and Nicodemuses painfully full of goodwill. Was Gurdjieff himself aware of these resemblances ? The very act of eating, if surrounded by rites, however incongruous, could not fail to make us think of Holy Communion.

I need hardly say that everyone of us kept this experience to himself. Just as communicants never exchange confidences about their participation in the Sacrament, so, as far as I know, none of the guests ever spoke about the meals, and although I am doing it now, it goes against the grain. But how could I conceal such an important aspect of my testimony ? So long as the secular controversy goes on about Holy Communion, I feel obliged to state that anything (gherkin or pimento) can, with the necessary concentration and human tension, become the way to communion, without recourse to magic or collective hypnosis. When I say communion I mean to emphasize that it is the pattern of a sacrament, not outward and by analogy but inward, by the equivalency of spiritual and sensual experience.

Any other man would have exploited this result, but Gurdjieff let it speak for itself. Everything is food, but all depends on how much of the food that one eats one is capable of assimilating. This universal mastication is either destructive or creative according as to whether it conforms to the World's laws or to God's Will.

Money, about which Gurdjieff so often spoke, (I need not repeat what has been said a hundred times about the rather dubious analogy between the role that money plays in Gurdjieff's eyes and in those of psychoanalysts), the money spent on all this food and the fact that it was distributed indifferently amongst the worthy and the unworthy, signified, on the part of the Father a kind of wound inflicted continually on his Treasure. The lavishness of the Host, the frenzied wastefulness of which he was capable (as a young man, he burnt his roubles every evening so as to plunge himself and his group into difficulties which had somehow to be overcome) placed side by side the value and the contempt that he attached to money. The false notes of meanness and haggling grated against his inexhaustible generosity.

Thus, communion is achieved in spite of everything, through our senses, thanks to the law of supply and demand and to the relationships between host and guests.

Gurdjieff's meals, though cooked in an oriental way and garnished with aromatic herbs, had no especial virtue, as some people said. The cucumbers, certainly, were Russian, the sweets Greek and the water-melon Spanish. It was significant that the whole world should have been ransacked to provide food for the feast, heavily supplemented from the back room. The fact that Gurdjieff took the place of my grandfather and, at the same time, of Christ, did not offend me at all. On the contrary, the idea that one needs Christ in order to reach the Father had often been drummed into me, but though I felt I knew a little about Christ, I had never really understood the need for the Father, nor His strangely passionate nature. Christ had been tortured, but only once, however often it may be repeated in the Mass. But the Father suffers eternally and at every moment. He sustains His world and offers it the fruits of its soil. He does it like an old moustachioed Caucasian, like an old-fashioned school-master of the days when a school-master was as good as a priest. The real, moustachioed, if not bearded, God then became comprehensible to me. Communion in the world could take place in all kinds, provided the communicant was worthy, that is attentive. The rabbit had suffered before it was cooked, and child though I I was, I was right to be horror-stricken by its agony. Gurdjieff did not teach us to do without meat but, on the contrary, he bared his big teeth and accepted the human situation and his proper, not very elevated, position on the ladder of creation. But if the rabbit suffered, and if the Father suffers, and all his treasures are put on sale or return through the lack of understanding and stupidity of his guests, it is because it is a matter of the accomplishment of the greatest mystery in the world, of universal manducation. We were a long way from the carefully whitened and purified unleavened bread. For us there were sauces, such of which it is written: he who dips his hand in the dish with me will betray me.

I never think of the Last Supper without being reminded of these times with Gurdjieff. Leonardo's picture is much damaged and the paint is peeling off, leaving horribly deformed silhouettes, but the mystery of the picture remains. A few traces of paint, even mouldy paint, and the presence of Christ and His companions shines forth as the painter first conceived them. Anyone who wishes can take part in the Last Supper if he will but open his eyes. Last Suppers, alas, are always among the last moments of the Masters, they will be their Memorials.

Though I mocked at the feasts with Gurdjieff, knowing all the time that those moments vouchsafed me were an inestimable blessing, now I never go to Mass without thinking of him. Had he not invited me to the last hours in the Upper Room ? Had he not taught me not to despise any of the earth's sacrifices ?

Farewell to the Old Man

The modern miracle-worker dies in his bed. Perhaps, for the period, that was rather inadequate. No hemlock, no hyssop, no gas. Possibly cirrhosis of the liver—in any case a natural death. A burial a bit more Russian than others. The Rue Daru is a small islet of Slav Atlantis in the middle of Paris, and much impaired by its separation. There followed flowers and wreaths at Fontainebleau-Avon. O Institute for the Harmonious Development of Man ! O Katherine, who wrote in vain those little letters to her man of letters ! Gurdjieff himself keeps her company now.

There was much weeping. I was interested to note how my own tears would taste. I know this crocodile, and tears seen through a microscope are not pretty. I contemplated the dead face that I had tried so hard to fix in my mind, that I knew so little, and had interrogated so poorly. I wept, and they were real tears.

To die like a dog. And you, George Ivanovich, have you saved your soul ? Have you extracted it from gross matter, from mortal functions and the hindrance of the senses ? Have you, by dint of attention, have you quickened the beat of energy ? Has God inhaled you?

If there were those who awaited a strange event and hoped, on the fortieth day, for some Tibetan prodigy, then they were disappointed. Only a new Christ is resurrected. The modern miracle-worker is merely a man.

All the same, he didn't die like a dog. In death he made a difficult, indefinable movement with his extraordinarily contorted muscles. There was a force behind the mask, apparently so calm, a gaze behind those lids that would never open again. This gaze imprinted itself on our pupils. Every eye caught a gleam and we assimilated this food, too.

Once more the thread is broken, the track comes up against the future. " There you are, in a fine mess ! " he had murmered, before departing. Already at his bedside I could see incurving the spiral that he used to draw for us to show us where the straight lines of our evolutions would begin to turn.

They will turn you into a scare-crow, an old fossil, a pope, an ordinary idiot, or perhaps even a philosopher.

I shall never again know a more brazen seeker after God, nor a heathen more ambitious for his soul. You were Pascal and Proust, Descartes and Rabelais, Lucretius and Gulliver, Tobias and the Angel, and I salute you! If Christ leads to the Father, it was you who led me back to Christ. Others drew signs and taught by words: you gave us yourself. You sketched out the symphony of creative Awareness, of unimaginable Attention.

Who has dared to live your life, and who will fulfil it ? In the end you have drawn real tears from me, M. Gurdjieff. I must have loved you.

Postscript

That my insight and understanding, and even my good faith, should be in question is only fair. The testimony is worth no more than the witness. But being what I am this is what I saw, felt and understood, and my only obligation is to testify according to my own truth, the only living truth, which, like everything that lives, bears within it its own destruction and reparation, its own ferment and poison.

Am I for or against Gurdjieff ? Both, of course, as one is for and against God, for and against oneself, for and against one's life. Hagiography is a different thing. It matters not who is shocked. If everything was clear there would have been only one explanation, one moral code, one faith, for the last hundred thousand years. Or, more exactly, there would be no faith. Read

Ouspensky and say whether you are for or against him. To my mind, those who swallow the Gurdjievian cosmogony whole, and those who reject it out of hand, are equally wrong and, above all, equally superficial. Those who study Gurdjieff, alive or dead, without either fear or respect, are equally naïve. From such a man one takes and rejects, one is both wary and receptive. One struggles with him. To struggle with Gurdjieff (and not against him) is to understand him, to know him, and, in the end, to love him.

As for putting him on a pedestal, especially after his death, that is the most sinister trick that well-meaning Gurdjievians could possibly play on him. That is to show true disrespect.

However, if, in this particularly confused age, in which no attitude seems to make sense any longer, one has to care about what people will think and, bearing in mind the words of the Evangelist, take notice, not of the scribes but of the lesser ones, then I must add the following: —

Those who want to get the most out of Gurdjieff's life and work must, first of all, rid their hearts and minds of the habits of a limited logic and of a morality based on fear. Questing souls fall into line too readily with their predecessors. Great examples from the past are always, for them, fatal mirages. With intellectual growth they inevitably become conformist philosophers; commitment in action leads them straight to heroism; and supremacy of the feelings, to religion. There is no mixing of kinds.

This is Gurdjieff. No blood or tears. A struggle with bare hands. No intellectual prestige, no commitment, no emotion or reverence. You come because of your craving and your terror, and you will not be comforted, reassured or illuminated. You will only find a man who will make you understand what it means to be a man, a man alone.

You are not asked if you are good or intelligent, or if you have faith. You might, perhaps, be asked if you are courageous. But you will be asked if you *are*, just that. You should be warned that this is the question that will give you vertigo and that unless this undertaking is absolutely indispensible to you, you had much better leave it alone. One can very well live as one is, and it is far better to be only half alive than not to exist at all because one's curiosity has led one to the terrifying point where one loses all sense of one's existence.

One can, of course, turn back and say, as one might of a mountain peak, that it was too high and without a good guide . . . and even with a good guide? Or, again, one can persevere, knowing how much is at risk.

But to describe the experience of Gurdjieff without pointing out the dangers or giving any words of warning would be stupid and dishonest, and would also be treating Gurdjieff as though he were of no importance.

As for the comic parts and the occasional dirty word that my regard for truth has compelled me to quote, those who are offended by them lack, to my mind, the minimum of humour needed for getting on with Gurdjieff, and they will do well not to risk an encounter, even a posthumous one.

Lastly, if the thread of my gratitude and respect, discreet as it is permanent, that runs through this testimony cannot be detected, it is because I am nothing but a clumsy fool, which is quite possible.

One final remark. To my way of thinking this testimony would only make sense if completed and backed up by testimonies from others who had really worked with Gurdjieff (and if possible not writers or journalists). By definition these people would not write willingly or well, but they might, at least, have tried. Others, who were both writers and disciples, have died. In particular, Luc Dietrich and René Daumal. I knew Luc well enough to be certain that he would have become a writer, but I did not know Daumal and can say nothing about him. Now, Louis Pauwels loyally meant to include all testimonies in this book, and my own account of my clumsy and ridiculous experiences was not intended to be the only one from a " disciple." What I left out, or distorted, or was unable to convey, should have been supplied by others. But they have abstained.

For the living, it is their own affair. For the dead it is more serious. The dead, as always, are gagged by those who think themselves their heirs. Which means that neither Daumal nor Dietrich are represented here by indispensible extracts from their notes. The most contemptuous refusal was made in their name.

I gladly take this contempt upon myself, with a lively feeling of apostolic satisfaction. Gurdjieff re-taught me about Christ so effectively that I cannot but feel more at home with the publican, even if a journalist, or with the multitude, albeit uninitiated.

I do not want to heap coals of fire on anyone's head, but I would like to advise those who keep the living thought of the dead hidden away in cardboard boxes, to pass on as quickly as possible such explosive material, whose only legitimate heir is the whole world, that is to say, my neighbour.

And as for my neighbour, I beg him not to rest content with a testimony as unsatisfactory as mine. The dead will surely speak in the end and amongst them Gurdjieff himself, whose difficult book (already published in English) will at first disappoint but later, cruelly and grandly, give a new vision to any man willing to take part in the " work."

POSTSCRIPT

A Few Words at Parting
or
The Fable of the Monkey and the Calabash

All that remains now is for me to thank the readers who have reached the end of this big book. They are, I believe, members of the family that I belong to, and that I think I know quite well. In the bosom of this family, civility is not convention but invention; not sedative, but stimulating. So I cannot thank them better than by indicating the best way, in my view, of taking leave of " Monsieur Gurdjieff."

When I was a child there was a fashion for toy projectors. One of my friends had one of these marvels and we used to shut ourselves up in his room to watch pathetically short documentary films tremble on a bit of sheet we pinned to the wall. Although this was twenty years ago, it still moves me to think of it. One of these films showed the capture of monkeys. One saw negroes tie a calabash to a coconut-tree, throw in some pea-nuts and go away. The monkey came, slipped a hand through the narrow opening and grabbed the nuts; but then he could not get his hand out. He pulled frantically, but what he had seized held him prisoner. The negroes came back, tied up the poor animal, broke the calabash and freed its fist, full of nuts.

I have often thought about this film when trying to escape from the Gurdjieff teaching. I realized that I had to relax my hand, to loosen my grip; that I had to abandon, at least for the time being, this attempt to find the real ME, complete and static, if I wanted to regain health and freedom. But it was very difficult, and I, like most of the members of the group, was prisoner of my own ambition, dedicated thenceforward to dessication and, like the monkey, doomed to prison or death.

I knew, to be sure, that Gurdjieff's teaching was of very great importance and interest, but I guessed that it was presented in a way that could not but be harmful to me, or else that my nature and circumstances were such that I was tempted to use it in a way that impoverished rather than nourished me. I had to unclench my hand and run, which in the end I did, thanks to help and luck over which I am still wondering.

Today, I see that in Gurdjieff's teaching, or rather in the essentials of esotericism, there is something extremely valuable to someone really anxious to live the adventures of the present, but he must know how to release the traps set by so-called initiatory societies in the real world. There is no doubt that the Gurdjieff society was and still is the most lively and the most profoundly compelling. One must examine and finger the nuts in the bottom of the calabash and then withdraw gracefully.

It is this that I am asking you to do when you have finished reading.

Never mind the "Magician Gurdjieff" as Huxley says, the strange atmosphere of the groups, the spiritual and emotional terrorism of a society such as this, the magical promises made during the course of the enterprise. In a word, never mind the darkly fascinating underground world that I have tried to describe in this book. Once curiosity is satisfied — a genuine curiosity such as yours — we have to re-adapt our attention to this surface world, in order to regain our freedom and lucidity of mind and to find our way again on this earth, among our fellow-men where we belong.

After the Gurdjieff experience, or the study of it, the important thing is to see in what way the essentials of "traditional" thought are related to contemporary thought; to see that a certain regenerated and very powerful expression of esoteric knowledge can be integrated with the most far-reaching of modern researches. Gurdjieff was certainly one of the purveyors of this knowledge in the Western world of our day.

Philosophy in its latest phase, and notably phenomenology, physics, biology, mathematics and cybernetics, are recovering, at their furthest reach, the same knowledge that is given us in primeval tradition, and linking up with certain visions of the cosmos, of the relation between energy and matter, and of the freedom and unity of being, which are ancestral visions. The sciences today discourse with the last sages of Tibet, the last alchemists, the last "traditional" miracle-workers. A revolution is taking place before our eyes (if we open them wide); there is an unhoped-for re-discovery and re-marriage of reason (undervalued by itself at the height of its conquests) and of long-neglected religious intuition. For really attentive observers, the problems that present themselves to contemporary minds, whether of sociology or nuclear physics, are not problems of progress. Several years ago, the idea of progress died in the West. The real problems are those of radical changes of state, of transmutation. In this sense, the members of the family of minds that I was speaking of at the beginning of this book, together with the leading scientists and the poets, are the only men really *committed* to the adventure of modern life. Everything else is conformity, holding back and futility. Far from denying present reality, far from being what the " progressives " (that is to say, the dull, conventional spirits) call " reactionaries "—it is those with a leaning towards the reality of inner experience who are going in the direction of the future. They are in the company of philosophers, physicists, mathematicians and biologists, who are at this moment preparing the arrival of a very different world from the heavy transitional one in which we have to live for another few hours. They embody in unexpected, and as yet inexpressible, ways the ancient virtues of faith, hope and charity.

ACKNOWLEDGEMENTS

GOD IS MY ADVENTURE with the kind permission of the author Rom Landau and the publisher George Allen & Unwin Limited.

THE DEVILS OF LOUDUN with the kind permission of the author Aldous Huxley and the publisher Chatto & Windus Limited.

THE UNKNOWABLE GURDJIEFF (extracts from " The Fiery Fountain") with the kind permission of the author Margaret Anderson and the publisher Routledge & Kegan Paul Ltd.

LA MACHINE A COURAGE with the kind permission of Margaret Anderson on behalf of the estate of the late Georgette Leblanc.

A PERSONAL HISTORY with the kind permission of Margaret Anderson, on behalf of the estate of the late Dorothy Caruso, and the publisher Neville Spearman Limited.

VENTURE WITH IDEAS with the kind permission of the author Kenneth Walker and the publisher Jonathan Cape Limited.

GORHAM MUNSON with the kind permission of Tomorrow Publications Limited, publishers of *TOMORROW*, a magazine of parapsychology.

KATHERINE MANSFIELD with the kind permission of the Society of Authors, literary representatives of her estate.